AF539026

Islam :
Philosophy and Ethics

Islam : Philosophy and Ethics

Edited by

RATAN SINGH

GLOBAL PUBLICATIONS
NEW DELHI-110 002 (INDIA)

GLOBAL PUBLICATIONS
4378/4B, G-4 JMD House
Murari Lal Street, Ansari Road
Daryaganj, New Delhi - 110 002
Phone : 23278062 (Off.)
e-mail : omega_publications@yahoo.com

Head Office :
79/23, Laxmi Garden
Near Satya Jyoti School,
Gurgaon (Haryana)
Mob : 9213562438

Islam : Philosophy and Ethics

First Published : 2011

ISBN : 978-93-80833-24-8

PRINTED IN INDIA

Published by Ishwari Prasad Garg for Global Publications, New Delhi-110002
and Printed at Suman Printers, Delhi

Preface

Islam's fundamental theological concept is *tawhid*—the belief that there is only one god. The Arabic term for God is *Allah;* most scholars believe it was derived from a contraction of the words *al-* (the) and *ailah* (deity, masculine form), meaning "the god" (*al-ilah*), but others trace its origin to the Aramaic *Alaha*. The first of the Five Pillars of Islam, *tawhid* is expressed in the *shahadah* (testification), which declares that there is no god but God, and that Muhammad is God's messenger. In traditional Islamic theology, God is beyond all comprehension; Muslims are not expected to visualize God but to worship and adore him as a protector. Although Muslims believe that Jesus was a prophet, they reject the Christian doctrine of the Trinity and divinity of Jesus, comparing it to polytheism. In Islamic theology, Jesus was just a man and not the son of God; God is described in a chapter (*sura*) of the Qur'an as "...God, the One and Only; God, the Eternal, Absolute; He begetteth not, nor is He begotten; And there is none like unto Him."

Muslims regard their religion as the completed and universal version of a primordial, monotheistic faith revealed at many times and places before, including, notably, to the prophets Abraham, Moses and Jesus. Islamic tradition holds that previous messages and revelations have been changed and distorted over time. Religious practices include the Five Pillars of Islam, which are five obligatory acts of worship. Islamic law touches on virtually every aspect of life and society, encompassing everything from banking and warfare to welfare and the environment.

The majority of Muslims belong to one of two major denominations, the Sunni and Shi'a. Islam is the predominant religion in the Middle East, North Africa, and large parts of Asia and Sub-Saharan Africa. Sizable communities are also found in China and Russia, and parts of the Balkans. About 13% of Muslims live in Indonesia, the largest Muslim country, 31% in the Indian Subcontinent, and 20% in Arab countries. Converts and immigrant communities are found in almost every part of the world. With approximately 1.57 billion Muslims, Islam is the second-largest religion in the world and arguably the fastest growing religion in the world.

The major topics dealt in this book are : *Introduction to Islam; Early Social Changes under Islam; Contemporary Islamic Philosophy; History of the Qur'an; Islamic Eschatology; Islamic Ethics; Muhammad and Islam; Tawhid and Termagant; Ismailism; Reforms of Umar's Era; Druze Religious Community; etc.*

No doubt, these will serve the purpose of trainees and trainers, professional and policy planners in the field. Since the sources of information are all secondary, we express our gratitude to the scholars whose works are cited or substantially made use of. We are thankful to all those who rendered ready help and cooperation while working on this project.

We express our gratitude to various scholars, teachers and friends for their assistance and guidance. Finally, we thank our publishers for bringing out this book in very limited time.

—Editor

Contents

1

Introduction to Islam

Islam is the Abrahamic religion articulated by the Qur'an, a text considered by its adherents to be the verbatim word of the one, incomparable God (Allah), and by the Prophet of Islam Muhammad's demonstrations and real-life examples (called the Sunnah, collected through narration of his companions in collections of Hadith). *Islam* literally means "submission (to God)." *Muslim*, the word for an adherent of Islam, is the active participle of the same verb of which *Islam* is the infinitive).

Muslims regard their religion as the completed and universal version of a primordial, monotheistic faith revealed at many times and places before, including, notably, to the prophets Abraham, Moses and Jesus. Islamic tradition holds that previous messages and revelations have been changed and distorted over time. Religious practices include the Five Pillars of Islam, which are five obligatory acts of worship. Islamic law touches on virtually every aspect of life and society, encompassing everything from banking and warfare to welfare and the environment.

The majority of Muslims belong to one of two major denominations, the Sunni and Shi'a. Islam is the predominant religion in the Middle East, North Africa, and large parts of Asia and Sub-Saharan Africa. Sizable communities are also found in China and Russia, and parts of the Balkans. About 13% of Muslims live in Indonesia, the largest Muslim country, 31% in the Indian Subcontinent, and 20% in Arab countries.

Converts and immigrant communities are found in almost every part of the world. With approximately 1.57 billion Muslims, Islam is the second-largest religion in the world and arguably the fastest growing religion in the world.

The word *Islam* is a verbal noun originating from the triliteral root *s-l-m,* and is derived from the Arabic verb *Aslama,* which means "to accept, surrender or submit." Thus, Islam means acceptance of and submission to God, and believers must demonstrate this by worshiping him, following his commands, and avoiding polytheism. The word is given a number of meanings in the Qur'an. In some verses (*ayat*), the quality of Islam as an internal conviction is stressed: "Whomsoever God desires to guide, He expands his breast to Islam."

Other verses connect *islam* and *din* (usually translated as "religion"): "Today, I have perfected your religion (*din*) for you; I have completed My blessing upon you; I have approved Islam for your religion." Still others describe Islam as an action of returning to God—more than just a verbal affirmation of faith. Another technical meaning in Islamic thought is as one part of a triad of *islam, iman* (faith), and *ihsan* (excellence) where it represents acts of worship (*`ibadah*) and Islamic law (*sharia*).

Articles of Faith

The Qur'an states that all Muslims must believe in God, his revelations, his angels, his messengers, and in the "Day of Judgment". Also, there are other beliefs that differ between particular sects. The Sunni concept of predestination is called divine decree, while the Shi'a version is called divine justice. Unique to the Shi'a is the doctrine of *Imamah,* or the political and spiritual leadership of the Imams.

Muslims believe that God revealed his final message to humanity through the Islamic prophet Muhammad via the archangel Gabriel (*Jibril*). For them, Muhammad was God's final prophet and the Qur'an is the holy book of revelations he received over more than two decades. In Islam, prophets are men selected by God to be his messengers: Muslims believe that prophets are human and not divine, though some are able to perform miracles to prove their claim. Islamic prophets are considered to be the closest to perfection of all humans, and are uniquely the recipients of divine revelation—either directly from God or through angels. The Qur'an mentions the names of numerous figures considered prophets in Islam, including Adam, Noah, Abraham, Moses and Jesus, among others. Islamic theology says that all of God's messengers since Adam preached the message of Islam—submission to the will of God. According to the Qur'an the will of God is brought to the nations by the descendants of Abraham and Imran. Islam is described in the Qur'an as "the primordial nature upon which God created mankind", and the Qur'an states that the proper name *Muslim* was given by Abraham.

As a historical phenomenon, Islam originated in Arabia in the early 7th century. Islamic texts depict Judaism and Christianity as prophetic successor traditions to the teachings of Abraham. The Qur'an calls Jews and Christians "People of the Book" (*ahl al-kitab*), and distinguishes them from polytheists. Muslims believe that parts of the previously revealed scriptures, the *Tawrat* (Torah) and the *Injil* (Gospels), had become distorted—either in interpretation, in text, or both.

God

Islam's fundamental theological concept is *tawhid*—the belief that there is only one god. The Arabic term for God is *Allah*; most scholars believe it was derived from a contraction of the words *al-* (the) and *ailah* (deity, masculine form), meaning "the god" (*al-ilah*), but others trace its origin to the Aramaic *Alaha*. The first of the Five Pillars of Islam, *tawhid* is expressed in the *shahadah* (testification), which declares that there is no god but God, and that Muhammad is God's messenger. In traditional Islamic theology, God is beyond all comprehension; Muslims are not expected to visualize God but to worship and adore him as a protector. Although Muslims believe that Jesus was a prophet, they reject the Christian doctrine of the Trinity and divinity of Jesus, comparing it to polytheism. In Islamic theology, Jesus was just a man and not the son of God; God is described in a chapter (*sura*) of the Qur'an as "...God, the One and Only; God, the Eternal, Absolute; He begetteth not, nor is He begotten; And there is none like unto Him."

Qur'an

Muslims consider the Qur'an to be the literal word of God; it is the central religious text of Islam revealed in Arabic. Muslims believe that the verses of the Qur'an were revealed to Muhammad by God through the angel Gabriel on many occasions between 610 and his death on June 8, 632. The Qur'an was reportedly written down by Muhammad's companions (*sahabah*) while he was alive, although the prime method of transmission was orally. It was compiled in the time of Abu Bakr, the first caliph, and was standardized under the administration of Uthman, the third caliph. From textual evidence Islamic studies scholars find that the Qur'an of today has not changed significantly since it was standardized

The Qur'an is divided into 114 suras, or chapters, which combined, contain 6,236 *ayat*, or verses. The chronologically earlier suras, revealed at Mecca, are primarily concerned with ethical and spiritual topics. The later Medinan suras mostly discuss social and moral issues relevant to the Muslim community. The Qur'an is more concerned with moral guidance than legal instruction, and is considered the "sourcebook of Islamic principles and values". Muslim jurists consult the *hadith*, or the written record of Muhammad's life, to both supplement the Qur'an and assist with its interpretation. The science of Qur'anic commentary and exegesis is known as *tafsir*.

The word *Qur'an* means "recitation". When Muslims speak in the abstract about "the Qur'an", they usually mean the scripture as recited in Arabic rather than the printed work or any translation of it. To Muslims, the Qur'an is perfect only as revealed in the original Arabic; translations are necessarily deficient because of language differences, the fallibility of translators, and the impossibility of preserving the original's inspired style. Translations are therefore regarded only as commentaries on the Qur'an, or "interpretations of its meaning", not as the Qur'an itself.

Hadith

Hadith are narrations originating from the words and deeds of the Islamic prophet Mohammad. Hadith are regarded by traditional schools of jurisprudence as important tools for understanding the Qur'an and in matters of jurisprudence. Hadith were evaluated and gathered into large collections mostly during the reign of Umar bin Abdul Aziz during the 8th and 9th centuries. These works are referred to in matters of Islamic law and history to this day. The two main denominations of Islam, Shi'ism and Sunnism, have different sets of Hadith collections.

The Hadith enables Muslims to acquire the Sunnah (habits) or usual practices of Muhammad. The Muslim usage of this term refers to the sayings and living habits of Muhammad, the last prophet of Islam. Recording sunnah was an Arabic tradition, and once people converted to Islam, they brought the tradition to the religion. Among Sunni Muslims, Sahih al-Bukhari and Sahih Muslim collections are considered authentic.

Angels

Belief in angels is crucial to the faith of Islam. The Arabic word for angel (*malak*) means "messenger", like its counterparts in Hebrew (*malakh*) and Greek (*angelos*). According to the Qur'an, angels do not possess free will, and worship God in perfect obedience. Angels' duties include communicating revelations from God, glorifying God, recording every person's actions, and taking a person's soul at the time of death. They are also thought to intercede on man's behalf. The Qur'an describes angels as "messengers with wings—two, or three, or four (pairs): He adds to Creation as He pleases..."

Muhammad

Muhammad (c. 570 – June 8, 632) was a trader later becoming a religious, political, and military leader. Muslims view him not as the creator of a new religion, but as the restorer of the original, uncorrupted monotheistic faith of Adam, Abraham, Moses, Jesus and others. In Muslim tradition, Muhammad is viewed as the last and the greatest in a series of prophets—as the man closest to perfection, the possessor of all virtues. For the last 22 years of his life, in 610, beginning at age 40, Muhammad reported receiving revelations from God. The content of these revelations, known as the Qur'an, was memorized and recorded by his companions.

During this time, Muhammad preached to the people of Mecca, imploring them to abandon polytheism. Although some converted to Islam, Muhammad and his followers were persecuted by the leading Meccan authorities. After 12 years of preaching, Muhammad and the Muslims performed the *Hijra* ("emigration") to the city of Medina (formerly known as *Yathrib*) in 622. There, with the Medinan converts (*Ansar*) and the Meccan migrants (*Muhajirun*), Muhammad established his political and religious authority. Within years, two battles had been fought against Meccan forces: the Battle of Badr in

624, which was a Muslim victory, and the Battle of Uhud in 625, which ended inconclusively. Conflict with Medinan Jewish clans who opposed the Muslims led to their exile, enslavement or death, and the Jewish enclave of Khaybar was subdued. At the same time, Meccan trade routes were cut off as Muhammad brought surrounding desert tribes under his control. By 629 Muhammad was victorious in the nearly bloodless Conquest of Mecca, and by the time of his death in 632 (at the age of 62) he ruled over the Arabian peninsula.

In Islam, the "normative" example of Muhammad's life is called the *Sunnah* (literally "trodden path"). This example is preserved in traditions known as hadith ("reports"), which recount his words, his actions, and his personal characteristics. The classical Muslim jurist ash-Shafi'i (d. 820) emphasized the importance of the Sunnah in Islamic law, and Muslims are encouraged to emulate Muhammad's actions in their daily lives. The Sunnah is seen as crucial to guiding interpretation of the Qur'an.

Resurrection and Judgment

Belief in the "Day of Resurrection", *yawm al-Qiyamah* (also known as *yawm ad-din*, "Day of Judgment" and *as-sa`a*, "the Last Hour") is also crucial for Muslims. They believe that the time of *Qiyamah* is preordained by God but unknown to man. The trials and tribulations preceding and during the *Qiyamah* are described in the Qur'an and the hadith, and also in the commentaries of Islamic scholars. The Qur'an emphasizes bodily resurrection, a break from the pre-Islamic Arabian understanding of death. It states that resurrection will be followed by the gathering of mankind, culminating in their judgment by God.

The Qur'an lists several sins that can condemn a person to hell, such as disbelief, usury and dishonesty. Muslims view paradise (*jannah*) as a place of joy and bliss, with Qur'anic references describing its features and the physical pleasures to come. There are also references to a greater joy—acceptance by God (*ridwan*). Mystical traditions in Islam place these heavenly delights in the context of an ecstatic awareness of God.

Predestination

In accordance with the Islamic belief in predestination, or divine preordainment (*al-qada wa'l-qadar*), God has full knowledge and control over all that occurs. This is explained in Qur'anic verses such as "Say: 'Nothing will happen to us except what Allah has decreed for us: He is our protector'..." For Muslims, everything in the world that occurs, good or evil, has been preordained and nothing can happen unless permitted by God. According to Muslim theologians, although events are pre-ordained, man possesses free will in that he has the faculty to choose between right and wrong, and is thus responsible for his actions. According to Islamic tradition, all that has been decreed by God is written in *al-Lawh al-Mahfuz*, the "Preserved Tablet".

The Shi'a understanding of free will is called "divine justice" (*Adalah*). This doctrine, originally developed by the Mu'tazila, stresses the importance of man's responsibility for his own actions. In contrast, the Sunni deemphasize the role of individual free will in the context of God's creation and foreknowledge of all things.

Duties and Practices

Five Pillars

The Five Pillars of Islam are five practices essential to Sunni Islam. Shi'a Muslims subscribe to different sets of pillars which substantially overlap with the Five Pillars.

The Five Pillars of Islam are:

1. The ***shahadah,*** which is the basic creed or tenet of Islam that must be recited under an oath with the following specific statement: "'*ašhadu 'al-la ilaha illa-llahu wa 'ašhadu*

'anna mu'ammadan rasulu-llah", or "I testify that there is none worthy of worship except God and I testify that Muhammad is the Messenger of God." This testament is a foundation for all other beliefs and practices in Islam. Muslims must repeat the *shahadah* in prayer, and non-Muslims wishing to convert to Islam are required to recite the creed.

2. ***Salah,*** or ritual prayer, which must be performed five times a day. Each salah is done facing towards the Kaaba in Mecca. Salah is intended to focus the mind on God, and is seen as a personal communication with him that expresses gratitude and worship. Salah is compulsory but flexibility in the specifics is allowed depending on circumstances. In many Muslim countries, reminders called Adhan (call to prayer) are broadcast publicly from local mosques at the appropriate times. The prayers are recited in the Arabic language, and consist of verses from the Qur'an.

3. ***Zakat,*** or alms-giving. This is the practice of giving based on accumulated wealth, and is obligatory for all Muslims who can afford it. A fixed portion is spent to help the poor or needy, and also to assist the spread of Islam. The zakat is considered a religious obligation (as opposed to voluntary charity) that the well-off owe to the needy because their wealth is seen as a "trust from God's bounty". The Qur'an and the hadith also suggest a Muslim give even more as an act of voluntary alms-giving (*sadaqah*).

4. ***Sawm,*** or fasting during the month of Ramadan. Muslims must not eat or drink (among other things) from dawn to dusk during this month, and must be mindful of other sins. The fast is to encourage a feeling of nearness to God, and during it Muslims should express their gratitude for and dependence on him, atone for their past sins, and think of the needy. *Sawm* is not obligatory for several groups for whom it would constitute an undue burden. For others, flexibility is allowed depending on circumstances, but missed

fasts usually must be made up quickly. Some Muslim groups do not fast during Ramadan, and instead have fasts at different times of the year.

5. The ***Hajj***, which is the pilgrimage during the Islamic month of *Dhu al-Hijjah* in the city of Mecca. Every able-bodied Muslim who can afford it must make the pilgrimage to Mecca at least once in his or her lifetime. When the pilgrim is about ten kilometers from Mecca, he must dress in *Ihram* clothing, which consists of two white seamless sheets. Rituals of the Hajj include walking seven times around the Kaaba, touching the black stone if possible, walking or running seven times between Mount Safa and Mount Marwah, and symbolically stoning the Devil in Mina. The pilgrim, or the *hajji*, is honored in his or her community, although Islamic teachers say that the Hajj should be an expression of devotion to God instead of a means to gain social standing.

Law

The *Sharia* (literally: "the path leading to the watering place") is Islamic law formed by traditional Islamic scholarship, which most Muslim groups adhere to. In Islam, Sharia is the expression of the divine will, and "constitutes a system of duties that are incumbent upon a Muslim by virtue of his religious belief".

Islamic law covers all aspects of life, from matters of state, like governance and foreign relations, to issues of daily living. The Qur'an defines *hudud* as the punishments for five specific crimes: unlawful intercourse, false accusation of unlawful intercourse, consumption of alcohol, theft, and highway robbery. The Qur'an and Sunnah also contain laws of inheritance, marriage, and restitution for injuries and murder, as well as rules for fasting, charity, and prayer. However, these prescriptions and prohibitions may be broad, so their application in practice varies. Islamic scholars (known as *ulema*) have elaborated systems of law on the basis of these rules and their interpretations.

Fiqh, or "jurisprudence", is defined as the knowledge of the practical rules of the religion. The method Islamic jurists use to derive rulings is known as *usul al-fiqh* ("legal theory", or "principles of jurisprudence"). According to Islamic legal theory, law has four fundamental roots, which are given precedence in this order: the Qur'an, the Sunnah (actions and sayings of Muhammad), the consensus of the Muslim jurists (*ijma*), and analogical reasoning (*qiyas*). For early Islamic jurists, theory was less important than pragmatic application of the law. In the 9th century, the jurist ash-Shafi'i provided a theoretical basis for Islamic law by codifying the principles of jurisprudence (including the four fundamental roots) in his book *ar-Risalah*.

Religion and State

Mainstream Islamic law does not distinguish between "matters of church" and "matters of state"; the ulema function as both jurists and theologians. In practice, Islamic rulers frequently bypassed the Sharia courts with a parallel system of so-called "Grievance courts" over which they had sole control. As the Muslim world came into contact with Western secular ideals, Muslim societies responded in different ways. Turkey has been governed as a secular state ever since the reforms of Mustafa Kemal Atatürk. In contrast, the 1979 Iranian Revolution replaced a mostly secular regime with an Islamic republic led by the Ayatollah Khomeini.

Etiquette and Diet

Many practices fall in the category of *adab*, or Islamic etiquette. This includes greeting others with *"as-salamu `alaykum"* ("peace be unto you"), saying *bismillah* ("in the name of God") before meals, and using only the right hand for eating and drinking. Islamic hygienic practices mainly fall into the category of personal cleanliness and health, such as the circumcision of male offspring. Islamic burial rituals include saying the *Salat al-Janazah* ("funeral prayer") over the bathed and enshrouded dead body, and burying it in a grave. Muslims are restricted in their diet. Prohibited foods include pork products, blood, carrion, and alcohol. All meat must come from a herbivorous animal slaughtered in the name of God by a Muslim, Jew, or Christian, with the exception of game that one has hunted or fished for oneself. Food permissible for Muslims is known as halal food.

Jihad

Jihad means "to strive or struggle" (in the way of God) and is considered the "Sixth Pillar of Islam" by a minority of Sunni Muslim authorities. Jihad, in its broadest sense, is classically defined as "exerting one's utmost power, efforts, endeavors, or ability in contending with an object of disapprobation." Depending on the object being a visible enemy, the devil, and aspects of one's own self, different categories of Jihad are defined. Jihad, when used without any qualifier, is understood in its military aspect. Jihad also refers to one's striving to attain religious and moral perfection. Some Muslim authorities, especially among the Shi'a and Sufis, distinguish between the "greater jihad", which pertains to spiritual self-perfection, and the "lesser jihad", defined as warfare.

Within Islamic jurisprudence, jihad is usually taken to mean military exertion against non-Muslim combatants in the defense or expansion of the Ummah. The ultimate purpose of military jihad is debated, both within the Islamic community and without, with some claiming that it only serves to protect the Ummah, with no aspiration of offensive conflict, whereas others have argued that the goal of Jihad is global conquest. Jihad is the only form of warfare permissible in Islamic law and may be declared against apostates, rebels, highway robbers, violent groups, and leaders or states, Islamic or otherwise, who oppress Muslims or hamper proselytizing efforts. Most Muslims today interpret Jihad as only a defensive form of warfare: the external Jihad includes a struggle to make the Islamic societies conform to the Islamic norms of justice.

Under most circumstances and for most Muslims, jihad is a collective duty (*fard kifaya*): its performance by some individuals exempts the others. Only for those vested with authority, especially the sovereign (imam), does jihad become an individual duty. For the rest of the populace, this happens only in the case of a general mobilization. For most Shias, offensive jihad can only be declared by a divinely appointed leader of the Muslim community, and as such is suspended since Muhammad al-Mahdi's occultation in 868 AD.

History

Islam's historical development resulted in major political, economic, and military effects inside and outside the Islamic world. Within a century of Muhammad's first recitations of the Qur'an, an Islamic empire stretched from the Atlantic Ocean in the west to Central Asia in the east ; one of the best preserved architectural examples of Islamic spread, is the Great Mosque of Kairouan (in Tunisia) considered as the ancestor of all the mosques in the western Islamic world. This new polity soon broke into civil war, and successor states fought each other and outside forces. However, Islam continued to spread into regions like Africa, the Indian subcontinent, and Southeast Asia. The Islamic civilization was one of the most advanced in the world during the Middle Ages, but was surpassed by Europe with the economic and military growth of the West. During the 18th and 19th centuries, Islamic dynasties such as the Ottomans and Mughals fell under the sway of European imperial powers. In the 20th century new religious and political movements and newfound wealth in the Islamic world led to both rebirth and conflict.

Rise of the Caliphate and Civil War (632–750)

Muhammad began preaching Islam at Mecca before migrating to Medina, from where he united the tribes of Arabia into a singular Arab Muslim religious polity. He made his last farewell sermon at the age of 63 in the year 632 and died 72 days later. Right after his death disagreement broke out over who would succeed him as leader of the Muslim community. Umar ibn al-Khattab, a prominent companion of Muhammad, nominated Abu Bakr, who was Muhammad's intimate friend and collaborator. Others added their support and Abu Bakr was made the first caliph. Abu Bakr's immediate task was to avenge a recent defeat by Byzantine (or Eastern Roman Empire) forces, although he first had to put down a rebellion by Arab tribes in an episode known as the Ridda wars, or "Wars of Apostasy".

His death in 634 resulted in the succession of Umar as the caliph, followed by Uthman ibn al-Affan and Ali ibn Abi Talib. These four are known as *al-khulafa' ar-rashidun* ("Rightly Guided Caliphs"). Under them, the territory under Muslim rule expanded deeply into Persian and Byzantine territories.

When Umar was assassinated in 644, the election of Uthman as successor was met with increasing opposition. In 656, Uthman was also killed, and Ali assumed the position of caliph. After fighting off opposition in the first civil war (the "First Fitna"), Ali was assassinated by Kharijites in 661. Following this, Mu'awiyah, who was governor of the Levant, seized power and began the Umayyad dynasty. Although there was discord, the period until the death of Ali in 661 is remembered as a kind of golden age by some Muslims. It was the Age of the Rashidun or "rightly-guided ones," when Muhammad's close companions led the community of Muslims.

These disputes over religious and political leadership would give rise to schism in the Muslim community. The majority accepted the legitimacy of the three rulers prior to Ali, and became known as Sunnis. A minority disagreed, and believed that Ali was the only rightful successor; they became known as the Shi'a. After Mu'awiyah's death in 680, conflict over succession broke out again in a civil war known as the "Second Fitna". Afterward, the Umayyad dynasty prevailed for seventy years, and was able to conquer the Maghrib and Al-Andalus (the Iberian Peninsula, former Visigothic Hispania) and the Narbonnese Gaul in the west as well as expand Muslim territory into Sindh and the fringes of Central Asia. While the Muslim-Arab elite engaged in conquest, some devout Muslims began to question the piety of indulgence in a worldly life, emphasizing, rather, poverty, humility, and avoidance of sin based on renunciation of bodily desires. Devout Muslim ascetic exemplars such as Hasan al-Basri would inspire a movement that would evolve into Sufism.

For the Umayyad aristocracy, Islam was viewed as a religion for Arabs only; the economy of the Umayyad empire was based on the assumption that a majority of non-Muslims (Dhimmis) would pay taxes to the minority of Muslim Arabs. A non-Arab who wanted to convert to Islam was supposed to first become a client of an Arab tribe. Even after conversion, these new Muslims (*mawali*) did not achieve social and economic equality with the Arabs. The descendants of Muhammad's uncle Abbas ibn Abd al-Muttalib rallied discontented *mawali*, poor Arabs, and some Shi'a against the Umayyads and overthrew them with the help of their propagandist and general Abu Muslim, inaugurating the Abbasid dynasty in 750. Under the Abbasids, Islamic civilization flourished in the "Islamic Golden Age", with its capital at the cosmopolitan city of Baghdad.

Golden Age (750–1258)

The Golden Age saw new legal, philosophical, and religious developments. The major hadith collections were compiled and the four modern Sunni Madh'habs were established. Islamic law was advanced greatly by the efforts of the early 9th century jurist al-Shafi'i; he codified a method to establish the reliability of hadith, a topic which had been a locus of dispute among Islamic scholars. Philosophers Ibn Sina (Avicenna) and Al-Farabi sought to incorporate Greek principles into Islamic theology, while others like the 11th century theologian Abu Hamid al-Ghazzali argued against them and ultimately prevailed. Finally, Sufism and Shi'ism both underwent major changes in the 9th century. Sufism became a full-fledged movement that had moved towards mysticism and away from its ascetic roots, while Shi'ism split due to disagreements over the succession of Imams.

The spread of the Islamic dominion induced hostility among medieval ecclesiastical Christian authors who saw Islam as an adversary in the light of the large numbers of new Muslim converts. This opposition resulted in polemical treatises which depicted Islam as the religion of the antichrist and of Muslims as libidinous and subhuman. In the medieval period, a few Arab philosophers like the poet Al-Ma'arri adopted a critical approach to Islam, and the Jewish philosopher Maimonides contrasted Islamic views of morality to Jewish views that he himself elaborated.

Fragmentation and Invasions

By the late 9th century, the Abbasid caliphate began to fracture as various regions gained increasing levels of autonomy. Across North Africa, the Middle East and Central Asia, emirates formed as provinces broke away. The monolithic Arab empire gave way to a more religiously homogenized Muslim world where the Shia Fatimids contested even the religious authority of the caliphate. In the 10th century the powerful Ghaznavids conquered the Persian region and a large part of the Indian subcontinent in the name of Islam. They were replaced by the Ghurids in the 12th century. By

1055 the Seljuq Turks had eliminated the Abbasids as a military power, nevertheless they continued to respect the caliph's titular authority. During this time expansion of the Muslim world continued, by both conquest and peaceful proselytism even as both Islam and Muslim trade networks were extending into sub-Saharan West Africa, Central Asia, Volga Bulgaria and the Malay archipelago.

Starting in the 9th century, Muslim conquests in the West began to be reversed. The Reconquista was launched against Muslim principalities in Iberia, and Muslim Italian possessions were lost to the Normans. From the 11th century onwards alliances of European Christian kingdoms mobilized to launch a series of wars known as the Crusades, aimed at reversing Muslim military conquests within the eastern part of the former Roman Empire, especially in the Holy Land. Initially successful in this aim, and establishing the Crusader states, these gains were later reversed by subsequent Muslim generals such as Saladin, who recaptured Jerusalem in 1187.

In the east the Mongol Empire put an end to the Abbassid dynasty at the Battle of Baghdad in 1258, as they overran the Muslim lands in a series of invasions. Meanwhile in Egypt, the slave-soldier Mamluks took control in an uprising in 1250 and in alliance with the Golden Horde halted the Mongol armies at the Battle of Ain Jalut. Over the next century the Mongol Khanates converted to Islam and this religious and cultural absorption ushered in a new age of Mongol-Islamic synthesis that shaped the further spread of Islam in central Asia, eastern Europe and the Indian subcontinent. The Crimean Khanate was one of the strongest powers in Eastern Europe until the end of the 17th century.

The Black Death ravaged much of the Islamic world in the mid-14th century. It is probable that the Mongols and merchant caravans making use of the opportunities of free passage offered by the Pax Mongolica inadvertently brought the plague from Central Asia to the Middle East and Europe. Plague epidemics kept returning to the Islamic world up to the 19th century.

New Dynasties and Colonialism (1030–1918)

The Seljuk Turks conquered Abbassid lands, adopted Islam and become the *de facto* rulers of the caliphate. They captured Anatolia by defeating the Byzantines at the Battle of Manzikert, thereby precipitating the call for Crusades. They fell apart in the second half of the 12th century giving rise to various semi-autonomous Islamic dynasties such as the powerful Ayyubids who conquered Egypt and a Jerusalem in the name of Islam. In the 13th and 14th centuries the Ottoman Empire (named after Osman I) emerged from among these *"Ghazi emirates"* and established itself after a string of conquests that included the Balkans, parts of Greece, and western Anatolia. In 1453 under Mehmed II the Ottomans laid siege to Constantinople, the capital of Byzantium, which succumbed shortly thereafter, having been overwhelmed by a far greater number of Ottoman troops and to a lesser extent, cannonry.

Beginning in the 13th century, Sufism underwent a transformation, largely as a result of the efforts of al-Ghazzali to legitimize and reorganize the movement. He developed the model of the Sufi order—a community of spiritual teachers and students. Also of importance to Sufism was the creation of the Masnavi, a collection of mystical poetry by the 13th century Persian poet Rumi. The Masnavi had a profound influence on the development of Sufi religious thought; to many Sufis it is second in importance only to the Qur'an. From the 14th century to the 16th century much of the eastern Islamic world was experiencing another golden age under the Timurid dynasty. In the early 16th century, the Safavid dynasty assumed control in Persia and established Shi'a Islam as an official religion there, and despite periodic setbacks, the Safavids remained in power for two centuries until being usurped by the Hotaki dynasty in the early-18th century. Meanwhile, Mamluk Egypt fell to the Ottomans in 1517, who then launched a European campaign which reached as far as the gates of Vienna in 1529.

After the invasion of Persia and sack of Baghdad by the Mongols in the mid 13th century, Delhi became the most important cultural centre of the Muslim east. Many Islamic dynasties ruled parts of the Indian subcontinent starting with the Ghaznavids in the 10th century. The prominent ones included the Delhi Sultanate (1206–1526) and the Mughal Empire (1526–1857). These empires helped in the spread of Islam in South Asia, but by the early-18th century the Sikh Maratha Empire was becoming the pre-eminent power in northern India until they were weaken by the Durrani Empire in the mid-18th century.

Around the 18th century, despite attempts at modernization, the Ottoman empire had begun to feel threatened by European economic and military advantages. It was during the 18th century that the Wahhabi movement took hold in Saudi Arabia. Founded by the preacher Ibn Abd al-Wahhab, Wahhabism is a fundamentalist ideology that condemns practices like Sufism and the veneration of saints as un-Islamic.

By the 19th century the British Empire had formally ended the last Mughal dynasty, and overthrew the Muslim-ruled Kingdom of Mysore. In the 19th century, the rise of nationalism resulted in Greece declaring and winning independence in 1829, with several Balkan states following suit after the Ottomans suffered defeat in the Russo-Turkish War of 1877–1878. The Ottoman era came to a close at the end of World War I and the Caliphate was abolished in 1924.

In the 19th century, the Salafi, Deobandi and Barelwi movements were initiated.

Modern Times (1918–present)

By the early years of the 20th century, most of the Muslim world outside the Ottoman empire had been absorbed into the empires of non-Islamic European powers. After World War I losses, nearly all of the Ottoman empire was also parceled out as European protectorates or spheres of influence. In the course of the 20th century, most of these European-ruled territories became independent, and new issues such as oil wealth and relations with the State of Israel have assumed prominence.

During this time, many Muslims migrated, as indentured servants, from mostly India and Indonesia to the Caribbean, forming the largest Muslim populations by percentage in the Americas. Additionally, the resulting urbanization and increase in trade in Africa brought Muslims to settle in new areas and spread their faith. As a result, Islam in sub-Saharan Africa likely doubled between 1869 and 1914. The Organisation of the Islamic Conference (OIC), consisting of Muslim countries, was formally established in September 1969 after the burning of the Al-Aqsa Mosque in Jerusalem.

Islamic revival and Islamist Movements

The 20th century saw the Islamic world increasingly exposed to outside cultural influences, bringing potential changes to Muslim societies. In response, new Islamic "revivalist" movements were initiated as a counter movement to non-Islamic ideas. Groups such as Jamaat-e-Islami in Pakistan and the Muslim Brotherhood in Egypt advocate a totalistic and theocratic alternative to secular political ideologies. Sometimes called Islamist, they see Western cultural values as a threat, and promote Islam as a comprehensive solution to every public and private question of importance.

In countries like Iran revolutionary movement replaced secular regime with an Islamic state, while transnational groups like Osama bin Laden's al-Qaeda engage in terrorism to further their goals. In contrast, Liberal Islam is a movement that attempts to reconcile religious tradition with modern norms of secular governance and human rights. Its supporters say that there are multiple ways to read Islam's sacred texts, and stress the need to leave room for "independent thought on religious matters".

Modern criticism of Islam includes accusations that Islam is intolerant of criticism and that Islamic law is too hard on apostates from Islam. Critics like Ibn Warraq question the morality of the Qu'ran, saying that its contents justify the mistreatment of women and encourage antisemitic remarks by Muslim theologians. Such claims have been challenged by many Muslim scholars and writers including Fazlur Rahman Malik, Syed Ameer Ali, Ahmed Deedat, Yusuf Estes, as well as Zakir Naik and others of Peace TV, which is a global Islamic satellite channel intended to correct the misconceptions about Islam.

Others like Daniel Pipes and Martin Kramer focus more on criticizing the spread of Islamic fundamentalism, a danger they feel has been ignored. Montgomery Watt and Norman Daniel dismiss many of the criticisms as the product of old myths and polemics. The rise of Islamophobia, according to Carl Ernst, had contributed to the negative views about Islam and Muslims in the West. In contrast, Pascal Bruckner and Paul Berman have entered the "Islam in Europe" debate. Berman identifies a "reactionary turn in the intellectual world" represented by Western scholars who idealize Islam.

Community

Demographics

A comprehensive 2009 demographic study of 232 countries and territories reported that 23% of the global population or 1.57 billion people are Muslims. Of those, 87–

90% are Sunni and 10–13% are Shi'a, with a small minority belonging to other sects. Approximately 50 countries are Muslim-majority, and Arabs account for around 20% of all Muslims worldwide.

The majority of Muslims live in Asia and Africa. Approximately 62% of the world's Muslims live in Asia, with over 683 million adherents in Indonesia, Pakistan, India, and Bangladesh. In the Middle East, non-Arab countries such as Turkey and Iran are the largest Muslim-majority countries; in Africa, Egypt and Nigeria have the most populous Muslim communities. According to a recent study in the United States, the People's Republic of China has the eighth highest Muslim population with up to 65.3 million individuals but other figures show only 20 million. Islam is the second largest religion after Christianity in many European countries, and is slowly catching up to that status in the Americas and Australia.

Mosques

A mosque is a place of worship for Muslims, who often refer to it by its Arabic name, *masjid*. The word *mosque* in English refers to all types of buildings dedicated to Islamic worship, although there is a distinction in Arabic between the smaller, privately owned mosque and the larger, "collective" mosque (*masjid jami`*). Although the primary purpose of the mosque is to serve as a place of prayer, it is also important to the Muslim community as a place to meet and study. Modern mosques have evolved greatly from the early designs of the 7th century, and contain a variety of architectural elements such as minarets.

Family Life

The basic unit of Islamic society is the family, and Islam defines the obligations and legal rights of family members. The father is seen as financially responsible for his family, and is obliged to cater for their well-being. The division of inheritance is specified in the Qur'an, which states that most of it is to pass to the immediate family, while a portion is set aside for the payment of debts and the making of bequests. The woman's share of inheritance is generally half of that of a man with the same rights of succession. Marriage in Islam is a civil contract which consists of an offer and acceptance between two qualified parties in the presence of two witnesses. The groom is required to pay a bridal gift (*mahr*) to the bride, as stipulated in the contract.

A man may have up to four wives if he believes he can treat them equally, while a woman may have only one husband. In most Muslim countries, the process of divorce in Islam is known as *talaq*, which the husband initiates by pronouncing the word "divorce". Scholars disagree whether Islamic holy texts justify traditional Islamic practices such as veiling and seclusion (purdah).

Starting in the 20th century, Muslim social reformers argued against these and other practices such as polygamy in Islam, with varying success. At the same time, many Muslim women have attempted to reconcile tradition with modernity by combining an active life with outward modesty. Certain Islamist groups like the Taliban have sought to continue traditional law as applied to women.

Calendar

The formal beginning of the Muslim era was chosen to be the Hijra in 622 CE, which was an important turning point in Muhammad's fortunes. The assignment of this year as the year 1 AH (*Anno Hegirae*) in the Islamic calendar was reportedly made by Caliph Umar. It is a lunar calendar, with nineteen ordinary years of 354 days and eleven leap years of 355 days in a thirty-year cycle. Islamic dates cannot be converted to CE/AD dates simply by adding 622 years: allowance must also be made for the fact that each Hijri century corresponds to only 97 years in the Christian calendar.

The year 1428 AH coincides almost completely with 2007 CE.

Islamic holy days fall on fixed dates of the lunar calendar, which means that they occur in different seasons in different years in the Gregorian calendar. The most important Islamic festivals are *Eid al-Fitr* on the 1 of *Shawwal,* marking the end of the fasting month *Ramadan,* and *Eid al-Adha* on the 10 of *Dhu al-Hijjah,* coinciding with the pilgrimage to Mecca. Similar to the Jewish calendar, days in the Islamic calendar last from sunset to sunset.

Other Religions

According to Islamic doctrine, Islam was the primordial religion of mankind, professed by Adam. At some point, a religious split occurred, and God began sending prophets to bring his revelations to the people. In this view, Abraham, Moses, Hebrew prophets, and Jesus were all Prophets in Islam, but their message and the texts of the Torah and the Gospels were corrupted by Jews and Christians. Similarly, every child is born in the domain of Islam, but is converted to some other faith if the parents/guardians are not Muslims.

Islamic law divides non-Muslims into several categories, depending on their relation with the Islamic state. Christians and Jews who live under Islamic rule are known as *dhimmis* ("protected peoples"). According to this regulation, the personal safety and security of property of the dhimmis is guaranteed in return for paying tribute (*jizya*) to the Islamic state. The status was extended to other groups like Zoroastrians and Hindus, but not to atheists or agnostics.

Those who live in non-Muslim lands (*dar al-harb*) are known as *harbis,* and upon entering into an alliance with the Muslim state become known as *ahl al-ahd*. Those who receive a guarantee of safety while residing temporarily in Muslim lands are known as *ahl al-aman*. Their legal position is similar to that of the dhimmi except that they are not required to pay the jizya. The people of armistice (*ahl al-hudna*) are those who live outside of Muslim territory and agree to refrain from attacking the Muslims. Apostasy from Islam is prohibited, and is punishable by death.

The Alevi, Yazidi, Druze, Bábí, Bahá'í, Berghouata and Ha-Mim movements either emerged out of Islam or came to share certain beliefs with Islam. Some consider themselves separate while others still sects of Islam though controversial in certain beliefs with mainstream Muslims. Ahmadiyyat, a reformatory sect in Islam is considered to be non-Muslim by many mainstream Muslims. For this reason the government of Pakistan has declared them to be non-Muslim, although international organisations such as Amnesty International have viewed such a move is against international human rights. Sikhism, founded by Guru Nanak in late 15th century Punjab, incorporates aspects of both Islam and Hinduism.

Denominations

Islam consists of a number of religious denominations that are essentially similar in belief but which have significant theological and legal differences. The primary division is between the Sunni and the Shi'a, with Sufism generally considered to be a mystical inflection of Islam rather than a distinct school. According to most sources, 70% of the world's Muslims are Sunni, 20% are Shi'a with the 10% being other various small minorities and Islamic sects.

Sunni

Sunni Muslims are the largest group in Islam, comprising 70% of the world's 1.5 billion Muslims, hence the title 'Ahl as-Sunnah wa'l-Jama'ah' (people of the principle and majority). In Arabic, *as-Sunnah* literally means "principle" or "path".

The Sunnah (the example of Muhammad's life) as recorded in the Qur'an and the hadith is the main pillar of Sunni doctrine. Sunnis believe that the first four caliphs were the rightful successors to Muhammad; since God did not specify any particular leaders to succeed him, those leaders had to be elected. There are four recognised madh'habs (schools of thought): Hanafi, Maliki, Shafi'i, and Hanbali. All four accept the validity of the others and a Muslim may choose any one that he or she finds agreeable.

There are other Islamic sects that may be considered as being Sunni yet are believed to have departed from the majority by introducing *bidah* (innovations) and extreme political views which are divorced from Islam.

Shi'a

The Shi'a constitute about 15% of Islam, coming as the second-largest branch. They believe in the political and religious leadership of Imams from the progeny of Ali ibn Abi Talib, who according to most Shi'a are in a state of *ismah,* meaning infallibility. They believe that Ali ibn Abi Talib, as the cousin and son-in-law of Muhammad, was his rightful successor, and they call him the first *Imam* (leader), rejecting the legitimacy of the previous Muslim caliphs. To most Shi'a, an Imam rules by right of divine appointment and holds "absolute spiritual authority" among Muslims, having final say in matters of doctrine and revelation.

Approximately 40% of worldwide Shi'a adherents are concentrated in Iran, with other significant population in Iraq, Pakistan, and India. Shi'a make up the majority of the Muslim population in several countries, including Iran (90–95%), Iraq (65–70%), Azerbaijan, Bahrain, and Lebanon.

Shi'a Islam has several branches, the largest of which is the Twelvers (*ionasašariyya*) which the label Shi'a generally refers to. Although the Twelver Shi'a share many core practices with the Sunni, the two branches disagree over the proper importance and validity of specific collections of hadith. The Twelver Shi'a follow a legal tradition called Ja'fari jurisprudence. Other smaller groups include the Ismaili and Zaidi, who differ from Twelvers in both their line of successors and theological beliefs.

Sufism

Sufism is a mystical-ascetic form of Islam. By focusing on the more spiritual aspects of religion, Sufis strive to obtain direct experience of God by making use of "intuitive and emotional faculties" that one must be trained to use. Sufism and Islamic law are usually considered to be complementary, although Sufism has been criticised by some Muslims for being an unjustified religious innovation. Many Sufi orders, or *tariqas*, can be classified as either Sunni or Shi'a, but others classify themselves simply as 'Sufi'. Some Sufi groups can be described as non-Islamic when their teachings are very distinct from Islam.

Others

Ahmadiyya

Ahmadiyya is a religious movement founded towards the end of the 19th century and originating with the life and teachings of Mirza Ghulam Ahmad (1835–1908). Ghulam Ahmad was an important religious figure who claimed to have fulfilled the prophecies about the world reformer of the end times, who was to herald the Eschaton as predicted in the traditions of various world religions and bring about the final triumph of Islam as per Islamic prophecy. He claimed that he was the Mujaddid (divine reformer) of the 14th Islamic century, the promised Messiah ("Second Coming of Christ") and Mahdi awaited by Muslims. Ahmadi emphasis lay in the belief that Islam is the final law for humanity as revealed to Muhammad and the necessity of restoring to it its true essence and pristine form, which had been lost through the centuries. Thus, Ahmadis view themselves as leading the revival and peaceful propagation of Islam. The Ahmadis were among the earliest Muslim communities to arrive in Britain and other Western countries. Ahmadis are considered to be non-Muslims by many mainstream Muslims. They have been formally declared as non-Muslims by Pakistan.

Ibadi

The Kharijites are a sect that dates back to the early days of Islam. The only surviving branch of the Kharijites is Ibadism. Unlike most Kharijite groups, Ibadism does not regard sinful Muslims as unbelievers. The Imamate is an important topic in Ibadi legal literature, which stipulates that the leader should be chosen solely on the basis of his knowledge and piety, and is to be deposed if he acts unjustly. Most Ibadi Muslims live in Oman. There are communities of Ibadis that took refuge in the Mzab oases in southern Algeria, the Nafusa Mountains in western Libya, and in Djerba Island (Tunisia), in order to avoid persecution in certain periods of history.

Ijtihad

Liberal and progressive movements have in common a religious outlook which depends mainly on Ijtihad or personal interpretations of scriptures.

Salafi

The recent Salafi movement, also known as Wahhabi, which sees itself as restorationist and claims to derive its teachings from the original sources of Islam by refuting the established schools of thought of Sunni Islam.

Quranist

Quranist is a term used to refer to Muslims who reject hadith, or reported traditions of the Islamic prophet

Muhammad, and follow the Qur'an, a sacred text of Islam, exclusively.

Cultural Muslim

Generally, a Muslim is defined by faith in the religion of Islam; however, in the modern world there are religiously unobservant, agnostic or atheist individuals who still identify with the Muslim culture due to family background, personal experiences or fear of retribution for apostasy, an approach discussed by Malise Ruthven.

●●

2
Early Social Changes under Islam

Many **social changes took place under Islam** between 610 and 661, including the period of Muhammad's mission and the rule of his four immediate successors who established the Rashidun Caliphate.

According to William Montgomery Watt, for Muhammad, religion was not a private and individual matter but rather "the total response of his personality to the total situation in which he found himself. He was responding [not only]... to the religious and intellectual aspects of the situation but also the economic, social, and political pressures to which contemporary Mecca was subject."

Bernard Lewis says that there are two important political traditions in Islam - one that views Muhammad as a statesman in Medina, and another that views him as a rebel in Mecca. He sees Islam itself as a type of revolution that greatly changed the societies into which the new religion was brought.

Historians generally agree that Islamic social reforms in areas such as social security, family structure, slavery and the rights of women and ethnic minorities improved on what was present in existing Arab society. For example, according to Lewis, Islam "from the first denounced aristocratic privilege, rejected hierarchy, and adopted a formula of the career open to the talents."

Advent of Islam

Bernard Lewis believes that the advent of Islam was a revolution which only partially succeeded due to tensions between the new religion and very old societies that the Muslims conquered. He thinks that one such area of tension was a consequence of what he sees as the egalitarian nature of Islamic doctrine. Islam from the first denounced aristocratic privilege, rejected hierarchy, and adopted a formula of the career open to the talents. Lewis however notes that the equality in Islam was restricted to free adult male Muslims, but even that "represented a very considerable advance on the practice of both the Greco-Roman and the ancient Iranian world."

Bernard Lewis writes about the significance of Muhammad's achievements:

> "He had achieved a great deal. To the pagan peoples of western Arabia he had brought a new religion which, with its monotheism and its ethical doctrines, stood on an incomparably higher level than the paganism it replaced. He had provided that religion with a revelation which was to become in the centuries to follow the guide to thought and count of countless millions of Believers. But he had done more than that; he had established a community and a well organised and armed state, the power and prestige of which made it a dominant factor in Arabia"

Constitution of Medina

The Constitution of Medina, also known as the *Charter of Medina,* was drafted by Muhammad in 622. It constituted a formal agreement between Muhammad and all of the significant tribes and families of Yathrib (later known as Medina), including Muslims, Jews, and pagans. The document was drawn up with the explicit concern of bringing to an end the bitter inter tribal fighting between the clans of the Aws (Banu Aus) and Banu Khazraj within Medina. To this effect it instituted a number of rights and responsibilities for the Muslim, Jewish, and pagan communities of Medina bringing them within the fold of one community-the *Ummah*.

The precise dating of the Constitution of Medina remains debated but generally scholars agree it was written shortly after the *hijra* (622). It effectively established the first Islamic state. The Constitution established: the security of the community, religious freedoms, the role of Medina as a *haram* or sacred place (barring all violence and weapons), the security of women, stable tribal relations within Medina, a tax system for supporting the community in time of conflict, parameters for exogenous political alliances, a system for granting protection of individuals, a judicial system for resolving disputes, and also regulated the paying of blood-wite (the payment between families or tribes for the slaying of an individual in lieu of *lex talionis*).

Social Reforms

Muhammad preached against what he saw as the social evils of his day, *Encyclopedia of World History* states.

Practices

John Esposito sees Muhammad as a reformer who condemned practices of the pagan Arabs such as female infanticide, exploitation of the poor, usury, murder, false contracts, fornication, adultery, and theft. He states that Muhammad's "insistence that each person was personally accountable not to tribal customary law but to an overriding divine law shook the very foundations of Arabian society... Muhammad proclaimed a sweeping programme of religious and social reform that affected religious belief and practices, business contracts and practices, male-female and family relations". Esposito holds that the Qur'an's reforms consist of "regulations or moral guidance that limit or redefine rather than prohibit or replace existing practices." He cites slavery and women's status as two examples.

According to some scholars, Muhammad's condemnation of infanticide was the key aspect of his attempts to raise the status of women. Regarding the prevalence of this practice, we know it was "common enough among the pre-Islamic Arabs to be assigned a specific term, *waad*" A much cited verse the Qur'an that addresses this practice is: "When the sun shall be darkened, when the stars shall be thrown down, when the mountains shall be set moving, when the pregnant camels shall be neglected, when the savage beasts shall be mustered, when the seas shall be set boiling, when the souls shall be coupled, *when the buried infant shall be asked for what sin she was slain*, when the scrolls shall be unrolled..."

Social Security

William Montgomery Watt states that Muhammad was both a social and moral reformer. He asserts that Muhammad created a "new system of social security and a new family structure, both of which were a vast improvement on what went before. By taking what was best in the morality of the nomad and adapting it for settled communities, he established a religious and social framework for the life of many races of men."

In pre-Islamic Arabia, upon capture, those captives not executed, were maode to beg for their subsistence. During his life, Muhammad changed this custom and made it the responsibility of the Islamic government to provide food and clothing, on a reasonable basis, to captives, regardless of their religion. If the prisoners were in the custody of a person, then the responsibility was on the individual.

Slavery

The Qur'an makes numerous references to slavery, regulating but thereby also implicitly accepting this already existing institution. Lewis states that Islam brought two major changes to ancient slavery which were to have far-reaching consequences. "One of these was the presumption of freedom; the other, the ban on the enslavement of free persons except in strictly defined circumstances," Lewis continues. The position of the Arabian slave was "enormously improved": the Arabian slave "was now no longer merely a chattel but was also a human being with a certain religious and hence a social status and with certain quasi-legal rights."

Lewis states that in Muslim lands slaves had a certain legal status and had obligations as well as rights to the slave owner, an improvement over slavery in the ancient world. Due to these reforms the practice of slavery in the Islamic empire represented a "vast improvement on that inherited from antiquity, from Rome, and from Byzantium."

Although there are many common features between the institution of slavery in the Qur'an and that of neighboring cultures, however the Qur'anic institution had some unique new features. According to Jonathan Brockopp, professor of History and Religious Studies, the idea of using alms for the manumission of slaves appears to be unique to the Qur'an (assuming the traditional interpretation of verses and). Similarly, the practice of freeing slaves in atonement for certain sins appears to be introduced by the Qur'an. Brockopp adds that: "Other cultures limit a master's right to harm a slave but few exhort masters to treat their slaves kindly, and the placement of slaves in the same category as other weak members of society who deserve protection is unknown outside the Qur'an. The unique contribution of the Qur'an, then, is to be found in its emphasis on the place of slaves in society and society's responsibility toward the slave, perhaps the most progressive legislation on slavery in its time."

Muhammad highly recommended the freeing of slaves as a charitable act. The freeing of slaves was recommended both for the expiation of sins and as an act of simple benevolence. It exhorted masters to either free their slaves or allow slaves to earn or purchase their own freedom through *Mukataba* (manumission contracts).

Women's Rights

To evaluate the effect of Islam on the status of women, many writers have discussed the status of women in pre-Islamic Arabia, and their findings have been mixed. Some writers have argued that women before Islam were more liberated drawing most often on the first marriage of Muhammad and that of Muhammad's parents, but also on other points such as worship of female idols at Mecca. Other writers, on the contrary, have argued that women's status in pre-Islamic Arabia was poor, citing practices of female infanticide, unlimited polygyny, patrilineal marriage and others.

Valentine Moghadam analyzes the situation of women from a Marxist theoretical framework and argues that the position of women are mostly influenced by the extent of urbanization, industrialization, poletarization and political ploys of the state managers rather than culture or intrinsic properties of Islam; Islam, Moghadam argues, is neither more nor less patriarchal than other world religions especially Hinduism, Christianity and Judaism.

Majid Khadduri writes that under the Arabian pre-Islamic law of status, women had virtually no rights. Sharia (Islamic law), however, provided women with a number of rights. John Esposito states that the reforms affected marriage, divorce, and inheritance. Women were not accorded with such legal status in other cultures, including the West, until centuries later. *The Oxford Dictionary of Islam* states that the general improvement of the status of Arab women included prohibition of female infanticide, and recognizing women's full personhood. Gerhard Endress states: "The social system ... build up a new system of marriage, family and inheritance; this system treated women as an individual too and guaranteed social security to her as well as to her children. Legally controlled polygamy was an important advance on the various loosely defined arrangements which had previously been both possible and current; it was only by this provision (backed up by severe punishment for adultery), that the family, the core of any sedentary society could be placed on a firm footing."

Marriage

Under the Arabian pre-Islamic law, no limitations were set on men's rights to marry or to obtain a divorce. Islamic law, however, restricted polygamy () The institution of marriage, characterized by unquestioned male superiority in the pre-Islamic law of status, was redefined and changed into one in which the woman was somewhat of an interested partner. 'For example, the dowry, previously regarded as a bride-price paid to the father, became a nuptial gift retained by the wife as part of her personal property' Under Islamic law, marriage was no longer viewed as a "status" but rather as a "contract". The essential elements of the marriage contract were now an offer by the man, an acceptance by the woman, and the performance of such conditions as the payment of dowry. The woman's consent was imperative. Furthermore, the offer and acceptance had to be made in the presence of at least two witnesses. A man was not allowed to leave his wife and marry some one else just because the other women pleased him more.(quran).

Inheritance and Wealth

'Women were given inheritance rights in a patriarchal society that had previously restricted inheritance to male relatives.' Annemarie Schimmel states that "Compared to the pre-Islamic position of women, Islamic legislation meant an enormous progress; the woman has the right, at least according to the letter of the law, to administer the wealth she has brought into the family or has earned by her own work" According to *The Oxford Dictionary of Islam*, women were also granted the right to live in the matrimonial home and receive financial maintenance during marriage and a waiting period following the death and divorce.

The Status of Women

Watt states that Islam is still, in many ways, a man's religion. However, he states that Muhammad, in the historical context of his time, can be seen as a figure who testified on behalf of women's rights and improved things considerably. Watt explains the historical context surrounding women's rights at the time of Muhammad: "It appears that in some parts of Arabia, notably in Mecca, a matrilineal system was in the process of being replaced by a patrilineal one at the time of Muhammad. Growing prosperity caused by a shifting of trade routes was accompanied by a growth in individualism. Men were amassing considerable personal wealth and wanted to be sure that this would be inherited by their own actual sons, and not simply by an extended family of their sisters' sons. This led to a deterioration in the rights of women. At the time Islam began, the conditions of women were terrible - they had no right to own property, were supposed to be the property of the man, and if the man died everything went to his sons." Muhammad, however, by "instituting rights of property ownership, inheritance, education and divorce, gave women certain basic safeguards."

> "In the earliest centuries of Islam, the position of women was not bad at all. Only over the course of centuries was she increasingly confined to the house and was forced to veil herself." The Quran and Muhammad's example were more favorable to the security and status of women than

history and later Muslim practice might suggest. For example, the Qur'an does not require women to wear veils; rather, it was a social habit picked up with the expansion of Islam. In fact, since it was impractical for working women to wear veils, "A veiled woman silently announced that her husband was rich enough to keep her idle."

Haddad and Esposito state that 'although Islam is often criticised for the low status it has ascribed to women, many scholars believe that it was primarily the interpretation of jurists, local traditions, and social trends which brought about a decline in the status of Muslim women. In this view Muhammad granted women rights and privileges in the sphere of family life, marriage, education, and economic endeavors, rights that help improve women's status in society.' However, 'the Arab Bedouins were dedicated to custom and tradition and resisted changes brought by the new religion.' Haddad and Esposito state that in this view 'the inequality of Muslim women happened because of the preexisting habits of the people among whom Islam took root. The economics of these early Muslim societies were not favorable to comfortable life for women. More important, during Islam's second and third centuries the interpretation of the Qur'an was in the hands of deeply conservative scholars, whose decisions are not easy to challenge today. The Qur'an is more favorable to women than is generally realized. In principle, except for a verse or two, the Qur'an grants women equality. For example, Eve was not the delayed product of Adam's rib (as in the tradition for Christians and Jews); the two were born from a single soul. It was Adam, not Eve, who let the devil convince them to eat the forbidden fruit. Muslim women are instructed to be modest in their dress, but only in general terms. Men are also told to be modest. Many Muslims believe the veiling and seclusion are later male inventions, social habits picked up with the conquest of the Byzantine and Persian Empires.'

Children

The Qur'an rejected the pre-Islamic idea of children as their fathers' property and abolished the pre-Islamic custom of adoption.

A. Giladi holds that Quran's rejection of the idea of children as their fathers' property was a Judeo-Christian influence and was a response to the challenge of structural changes in tribal society.

The Quran also replaced the pre-Islamic custom of adoption (assimilation of an adopted child into another family in a legal sense) by the recommendation that "believers treat children of unknown origin as their brothers in the faith and clients. Adoption was viewed "as a lie, as an artificial tie between adults and children, devoid of any real emotional relationship, as a cause of confusion where lineage was concerned and thus a possible source of problems regarding marriage between members of the same family and regarding inheritance.But a child that was not born into a family can still be raised by a foster family but the child must retain his identity, such as his last name and lineage. In a modern perspective this may seem cruel but in fact if you reflect on this issue you will realize that if both parents were deceased that what they would wish their son would be raised with their identity rather than a strangers personality. The prophet has stated that a person who assists and aids an orphan, is on the same footing in heaven to the prophet himself."

Sociological Reforms

Sociologist Robert N. Bellah (*Beyond Belief*) argues that Islam in its 7th century origins was, for its time and place, "remarkably modern...in the high degree of commitment, involvement, and participation expected from the rank-and-file members of the community." This because, he argues, that Islam emphasized on the equality of all Muslims. Leadership positions were open to all. However, there were restraints on the early Muslim community that kept it from exemplifying these principles, primarily from the "stagnant localisms" of tribe and kinship. Dale Eickelman writes that Bellah suggests "the early Islamic community placed a particular value on individuals, as opposed to collective or group responsibility."

The Islamic idea of community (that of *ummah*), established by Muhammad, is flexible in social, religious, and political terms and includes a diversity of Muslims who share a general sense of common cause and consensus concerning beliefs and individual and communal actions.

Moral Reforms

Muslims believe that Muhammad, like other prophets in Islam, was sent by God to remind human beings of their moral responsibility, and challenge those ideas in society which opposed submission to God. According to Kelsay, this challenge was directed against five main characteristics of pre-Islamic Arabia:

1. The division of Arabs into varying tribes (based upon blood and kinship). This categorization was confronted by the ideal of a unified community based upon *taqwa* (Islamic piety), an "*ummah;*"

2. The acceptance of the worship of a multitude of deities besides Allah - a view challenged by strict *Tawhid* (Islamic monotheism), which dictates that Allah has no partner in worship nor any equal;

3. The trait of *muruwwa* (manliness), which Islam discouraged, instead emphasizing on the traits of humility and piety;

4. The focus on achieving fame or establishing a legacy, which was replaced by the concept that mankind would be called to account before God on the *Qiyamah;*

5. The reverence of and compliance with ancestral traditions, a practice challenged by Islam — which instead assigned primacy to submitting to God and following revelation.

These changes lay in the reorientation of society as regards to identity, world view, and the hierarchy of values. From the viewpoint of subsequent generations, this caused a great transformation in the society and moral order of life in the Arabian Peninsula. For Muhammad, although pre-Islamic Arabia exemplified "heedlessness," it was not entirely without merit. Muhammad approved and exhorted certain aspects of the Arab pre-Islamic tradition, such as the care for one's near kin, for widows, orphans, and others in need and for the establishment of justice. However, these values would be re-ordered in importance and placed in the context of strict monotheism.

Although Muhammad's preaching produced a "radical change in moral values based on the sanctions of the new religion, and fear of God and of the Last Judgment", the pre-Islamic tribal practices of the Arabs by no means completely died out.

Economic Reforms

Michael Bonner writes on poverty and economics in the Qur'an that the Qur'an provided a blueprint for a new order in society, in which the poor would be treated more fairly than before. This "economy of poverty" prevailed in Islamic theory and practice up until the 13th and 14th centuries. At its heart was a notion of property circulated and purified, in part, through charity, which illustrates a distinctively Islamic way of conceptualizing charity, generosity, and poverty markedly different from "the Christian notion of perennial reciprocity between rich and poor and the ideal of charity as an expression of community love." The Qur'an prohibits bad kind of circulation (*riba,* often understood as usury or interest) and asks for good circulation (*zakat* [legal alms giving]). Some of the recipients of charity appear only once in the Qur'an, and others—such as orphans, parents, and beggars—reappear constantly. Most common is the triad of kinsfolk, poor, and travelers.

Unlike pre-Islamic Arabian society, the Qur'anic idea of economic circulation as a return of goods and obligations was for everyone, whether donors and recipients know each other or not, in which goods move, and society does what it is supposed to do. The Qur'an's distinctive set of economic and social arrangements, in which poverty and the poor have important roles, show signs of newness. The Qur'an told that the guidance comes to a community that regulates its flow of money and goods in the right direction (from top down) and practices generosity as reciprocation for God's bounty. In a broad sense, the narrative underlying the Qur'an is that of a tribal society becoming urbanized. Many scholars have characterized both the Qur'an and Islam as highly favorable to commerce and to the highly mobile type of society that emerged in the medieval] Near East. Muslim tradition (both *hadith* and historiography) maintains that Muhammad did not permit the construction of any buildings in the market of Medina other than mere tents; nor did he permit any tax or rent to be taken there. This expression of a "free market"—involving the circulation of goods within a single space without payment of fees, taxes, or rent, without the construction of permanent buildings, and without any profiting on the part of the caliphal authority (indeed, of the Caliph himself)—was rooted in the term *sadaqa*, "voluntary alms." This coherent and highly appealing view of the economic universe had much to do with Islam's early and lasting success. Since the poor were at the heart of this economic universe, the teachings of the Qur'an on poverty had a considerable, even a transforming effect in Arabia, the Near East, and beyond.

Civil Reforms

Social welfare in Islam started in the form of the construction and purchase of wells. Upon his hijra to Medina, Muhammad found only one well to be used. The Muslims bought that well, and consequently it was used by the general public. After Muhammad's declaration that "water" was a better form of *sadaqah* (charity), many of his companions sponsored the digging of new wells. During the Caliphate, the Muslims repaired many of the aging wells in the lands they conquered.

In addition to wells, the Muslims built many tanks and canals. Many canals were purchased, and new ones constructed. While some canals were excluded for the use of monks (such as a spring purchased by Talhah), and the needy, most canals were open to general public use. Some canals were constructed between settlements, such as the Saad canal that provided water to Anbar, and the Abi Musa Canal to providing water to Basra.

During a famine, Umar (Umar ibn al-Khattab) ordered the construction of a canal in Egypt to connect the Nile with the Red Sea. The purpose of the canal was to facilitate the transport of grain to Arabia through a sea-route, hitherto transported only by land. The canal was constructed within a year by 'Amr ibn al-'As, and Abdus Salam Nadiv writes, Arabia was rid of famine for all the times to come."

Ecological Responsibility

Perhaps due to resource scarcity in most Islamic nations, there was an emphasis on limited (and some claim also sustainable) use of natural capital, i.e. producing land. Traditions of *haram* and *hima* and early urban planning were expressions of strong social obligations to stay within carrying capacity and to preserve the natural environment as an obligation of *khalifa* or "stewardship". Muhammad is considered a pioneer in environmentalism for his teachings on environmental preservation. His *ahadith* on agriculture and environmental philosophy were compiled in the "Book of Agriculture" of the *Sahih al-Bukhari*.

Welfare State

The concepts of welfare and pension were introduced in early Islamic law as forms of *Zakat* (charity), one of the Five Pillars of Islam, under the Rashidun caliph Umar in the 7th century. This practiced continued well into the Abbasid era, as seen under Al-Ma'mun's rule in the 8th century, for example. The taxes (including *Zakat* and *Jizya*) collected in the treasury of an Islamic government were used to provide income for the needy, including the poor, elderly, orphans, widows, and the disabled. According to the Islamic jurist Al-Ghazali (Algazel, 1058-1111), the government was also expected to stockpile food supplies in every region in case a disaster or famine occurred. The Caliphate can thus be considered the world's first major welfare state.

Political Changes

Arabia

Islam began in Arabia in the 7th century under the leadership of Muhammad, who eventually united many of the independent nomadic tribes of Arabia under Islamic law. There were also some Jewish and Christian tribes in Arabia. Some tension between Muhammad and the Jews of Medina soon arose and intensified. Muhammad accused the Jews of Medina of treason and expelled some of them from Medina and wiped out some others who he deemed to be traitors.

Middle East

The pre-Islamic Middle East was dominated by the Byzantine and Sassanian empires. The Roman–Persian Wars between the two had devastated the inhabitants, making the empires unpopular amongst the local tribes. The Byzantines persecuted Jews as well as Christians they deemed "heretic".

During the early Islamic conquests, the Rashidun army, mostly led by Khalid ibn al-Walid and 'Amr ibn al-'As, defeated both empires, making the Islamic state the dominant power in the region. Within only a decade, Muslims conquered Mesopotamia and Persia during the Muslim conquest of Persia and Roman Syria and Roman Egypt during the early Byzantine–Arab Wars.

According to Francis Edwards Peters:

> The conquests destroyed little: what they did suppress were imperial rivalries and sectarian bloodletting among the newly subjected population. The Muslims tolerated Christianity, but they disestablished it; henceforward Christian life and liturgy, its endowments, politics and theology, would be a private and not a public affair. By an exquisite irony, Islam reduced the status of Christians to that which the Christians had earlier thrust upon the Jews, with one difference. The reduction in Christian status was merely judicial; it was unaccompanied by either systematic persecution or a blood lust, and generally, though not elsewhere and at all times, unmarred by vexatious behaviour.

The Islamic conquest lowered taxes, and provided greater local autonomy and religious freedom for Jews and as well as most of the Christian Churches in the conquered areas (such as Nestorians, Monophysites, Jacobites and Copts who were deemed heretic by Christian Orthodoxy). Bernard Lewis wrote:

> Some even among the Christians of Syria and Egypt preferred the rule of Islam to that of Byzantines... The people of the conquered provinces did not confine themselves to simply accepting the new regime, but in some cases actively assisted in its establishment. In

Palestine the Samaritans, according to tradition, gave such effective aid to the Arab invaders that they were for some time exempted from certain taxes, and there are many other reports in the early chronicles of local Jewish and Christian assistance.

Other Reforms

Islam reduced the devastating effect of blood feuds, which was common among Arabs, by encouraging compensation in money rather than blood. In case the aggrieved party insisted on blood, unlike the pre-Islamic Arab tradition in which any male relative could be slain, only the culprit himself could be executed.

The Cambridge History of Islam states that the nomadic structure of pre-Islamic Arabia had the serious moral problem of the care of the poor and the unfortunate. "Not merely did the Qur'an urge men to show care and concern for the needy, but in its teaching about the Last day it asserted the existence of a sanction applicable to men as individuals in matters where their selfishness was no longer restrained by nomadic ideas of dishonour."

Islam teaches support for the poor and the oppressed. In an effort to protect and help the poor and orphans, regular almsgiving — *zakat* — was made obligatory for Muslims. This regular alms-giving developed into a form of income tax to be used exclusively for welfare.

●●

3
Contemporary Islamic Philosophy

Contemporary Islamic philosophy refers to Islamic philosophy in the 20th century. New movements have emerged during this time due to encounters with modernity and Western philosophy.

On one hand, some scholars such as Al-Afghani and Muhammad Abduh sought to find rational principles which would establish a form of thought which is both distinctively Islamic and also appropriate for life in modern scientific societies, a debate which is continuing within Islamic philosophy today. Muhammad Iqbal is one of the prominent figure of this group who provided a rather eclectic mixture of Islamic and European philosophy. On the other hand, some thinkers reacted to the phenomenon of modernity by developing Islamic fundamentalism. This resuscitated the earlier antagonism to philosophy by arguing for a return to the original principles of Islam and rejected modernity as a Western imperialist intrusion. The other group, who are more loyal to traditional Islamic philosophy, have tried to keep alive this school and use it to deal with Modernism.

Also contemporary Islamic philosophy revives some of the trends of medieval Islamic philosophy, notably the tension between Mutazilite and Asharite views of ethics in science and law, and the duty of Muslims and role of Islam in the sociology of knowledge and in forming ethical codes and legal codes, especially the fiqh (or "jurisprudence") and rules of jihad (or "just war").

Key Figures of Modern Islamic Philosophy

Key figures representing important trends include:

- **Fazlur Rahman** was professor of Islamic thought at the University of Chicago and McGill University, and an expert in Islamic philosophy. Not as widely known as his scholar-activist contemporary Ismail Raji al-Faruqi, he is nonetheless considered an important figure for Islam in the 20th century. He argued that the basis of Islamic revival was the return to the intellectual dynamism that was the hallmark of the Islamic scholarly tradition (these ideas are outlined in *Revival and Reform in Islam: A Study of Islamic Fundamentalism* and his magnum opus, *Islam*). He sought to give philosophy free rein, and was keen on Muslims appreciating how the modern nation-state understood law, as opposed to ethics; his view being that the shari'ah was a mixture of both ethics and law. He was critical of historical Muslim theologies and philosophies for failing to create a moral and ethical worldview based on the values derived from the Qur'an: 'moral values', unlike socioeconomic values, 'are not exhausted at any point in history' but require constant interpretation. Rahman was driven to exile from his homeland, Pakistan, where he was part of a committee which sought to interpret Islam for the fledging modern state. Some of his ideas from English (which he claimed were from the Islamic tradition) were reprinted in Urdu and caused outrage among conservative Muslim scholars in Pakistan. These were quickly exploited by opponents of his political paymaster, General Ayyub Khan, and led to his eventual exile in the United States.

- **Muhammad Iqbal** sought an Islamic revival based on social justice ideals and emphasized traditional rules, e.g. against usury. He argued strongly that dogma, territorial nationalism and outright racism, all of which were profoundly rejected in early Islam and especially by Muhammad himself, were splitting Muslims into warring factions, encouraging materialism and nihilism. His thought was influential in the emergence of a movement for independence of Pakistan, where he was revered as the national poet. Indirectly this strain of Islam also influenced Malcolm X and other figures who sought a global ethic through the Five Pillars of Islam. Iqbal can be credited with at least trying to reconstruct Islamic thought from the base, though some of his philosophical and scientific ideas would appear dated to us now. His basic ideas concentrated on free-will, which would allow Muslims to become active agents in their own history. His interest in Nietzsche (who he called 'the Wise Man of Europe') has led later Muslim scholars to criticise him for advocating dangerous ideals that, according to them, have eventually formed in certain strains of pan-Islamism. Some claim that the Four Pillars of the Green Party honor Iqbal and Islamic traditions.

- **Muhammad Hamidullah** (9 February, 1908 - 17 December, 2002) belonged to a family of scholars, jurists, writers and sufis. He was a world-renowned scholar of Islam and International Law from India, who was known for contributions to the research of the history of Hadith, translations of the Qur'an, the advancement of Islamic learning, and to the dissemination of Islamic teachings in the Western world.

- **Morteza Motahhari** was a lecturer at Tehran University. Motahhari is considered important for developing the ideologies of the Islamic Republic. He wrote on exegesis of the Qur'an, philosophy, ethics, sociology, history and many other subjects. In all his writings the real object he had in view was to give replies to the objections raised by others against Islam, to prove the shortcomings of other schools of thought and to manifest the greatness of Islam. He believed that in order to prove the falsity of Marxism and other ideologies like it, it was necessary not only to comment on them in a scholarly manner but also to present the real image of Islam.

- **Ali Shariati** was a sociologist and a professor of Mashhad University. He was one of the most influential figures in the Islamic world in the 20th century. He attempted to explain and provide solutions for the problems faced by Muslim societies through traditional Islamic principles interwoven with and understood from the point of view of modern sociology and philosophy. Shariati was also deeply influenced by Mowlana and Muhammad Iqbal.
- **Musa al-Sadr** was a prominent Muslim intellectual and one of the most influential Muslim philosophers of 20th century. He is most famous for his political role, but he was also a philosopher who had been trained by Allameh Tabatabaei. As Professor Seyyed Hossein Nasr said: "his great political influence and fame was enough for people to not consider his philosophical attitude, although he was a well-trained follower of long living intellectual tradition of Islamic Philosophy". One of his famous writings is a long introduction for the Arabic translation of Henry Corbin's *History of Islamic Philosophy*.
- Syed Zafarul Hasan was a prominent twentieth-century Muslim philosopher. From 1924 to 1945 he was professor of philosophy at the Muslim University,

Aligarh - where he also served as Chairman of the Department of Philosophy and Dean of the Faculty of Arts. There, in 1939, he put forward the 'Aligarh Scheme'. From 1945 until the partition of the sub-continent, Dr Hasan was Emeritus Professor at Aligarh. Dr. Zafarul Hasan was born on February 14, 1885. He died on June 19, 1949.

- Ismail al-Faruqi looked more closely at the ethics and sociology of knowledge, concluding that no scientific method or philosophy could exist that was wholly ignorant of a *theory of conduct* or the consequences a given path of inquiry and technology. His "Islamization of knowledge" programme sought to converge early Muslim philosophy with modern sciences, resulting in, for example, Islamic economics and Islamic sociology.
- Seyyed Hossein Nasr, a political ecologist, argues that khalifa in Islam is fundamentally compatible with ideals of the ecology movement and peace movement, more so than conventional interpretations of Islam. He argues for an ecology-based ecumenism that would seek unity among the faiths by concentrating on their common respect for life as a Creation, i.e. the Earth's biosphere, Gaia, or whatever name. Pope John Paul II has made similar suggestions that "mankind must be reconciled to the Creation", and there is a *Parliament of World Religions* seeking a "global ethic" on similar grounds.
- Akbar S. Ahmed is an anthropologist, filmmaker and an outstanding scholar on Islam, International Relations/Politics and Contemporary Islamic philosophy from Pakistan. He is Ibn Khaldun Chair of Islamic Studies at the American University in Washington DC and was the High Commissioner of Pakistan to UK. He has advised Prince Charles and

met with President George W. Bush on Islam. His numerous books, films and documentaries have won awards. His books have been translated into many languages including Chinese and Indonesian. Ahmed is "the world's leading authority on contemporary Islam" according to the BBC.

- **Javed Ahmad Ghamidi** is a well-known Pakistani Islamic scholar, exegete, and educator. A former member of the Jamaat-e-Islami, who extended the work of his tutor, Amin Ahsan Islahi. He is frequently labeled a modernist for his insistence on the historical contextualization of Muhammad's revelation in order to grasp its true moral import.

- Imam Feisal Abdul Rauf is a well-known proponent of cultural reconciliation between the Muslim World and the West, basing his views on Classical Islamic governance's similarity to Western governance models in terms of religious freedoms and democratic inclination. Abdul Rauf is a highly-visible American-Egyptian Imam at New York's Masjid al-Farah in addition to being Founder and Chairman of Cordoba Initiative, a non-profit organisation seeking to bridge the divide between the Muslim world and the West.

- Mohammad Azadpur is an associate professor of philosophy at San Francisco State University. He teaches courses on Islamic philosophy, mysticism, and political philosophy. His research focuses on Alfarabi and Avicenna, and he does comparative work between Islamic and Heideggerian thought as well.

ALLAH

Allah is the standard Arabic word for **God**. While the term is best known in the West for its use by Muslims as a reference to God, it is used by Arabic-speakers of all Abrahamic faiths, including Jews and Christians, in reference to "God". The term was also used by pagan Meccans as a reference to the creator-god, possibly the supreme deity in pre-Islamic Arabia.

The concepts associated with the term *Allah* (as a deity) differ among the traditions. In pre-Islamic Arabia amongst pagan Arabs, *Allah* was not considered the sole divinity, having associates and companions, sons and daughters - a concept which Islam thoroughly and resolutely abrogated. In Islam, the name Allah is the supreme and all-comprehensive divine name. All other divine names are believed to refer back to Allah. *Allah* is unique, the only Deity, creator of the universe and omnipotent. Arab Christians today use terms such as *Allah al-Ab* ("God the Father") to distinguish their usage from Muslim usage. There are both similarities and differences between the concept of God as portrayed in the Qur'an and the Hebrew Bible.

Usage in Arabic

Pre-Islamic Arabia

In pre-Islamic Arabia, Allah was used by Meccans as a reference to the creator-god, possibly the supreme deity.

Allah was not considered the sole divinity; however, Allah was considered the creator of the world and the giver of rain. The notion of the term may have been vague in the Meccan religion. Allah was associated with companions, whom pre-Islamic Arabs considered as subordinate deities. Meccans held that a kind of kinship existed between Allah and the jinn. Allah was thought to have had sons and that the local deities of al-»Uzzá, Manat and al-Lat were His daughters. The Meccans possibly associated angels with Allah. Allah was invoked in times of distress. Muhammad's father's name was 'Abdallah meaning the "servant of Allah." or "the slave of Allah"

Islam

According to Islamic belief, Allah is the proper name of God, and humble submission to His Will, Divine Ordinances and Commandments is the pivot of the Muslim faith. "He is the only God, creator of the universe, and the judge of humankind." "He is unique (*wahid*) and inherently one (*ahad*), all-merciful and omnipotent." The Qur'an declares "the reality of Allah, His inaccessible mystery, His various names, and His actions on behalf of His creatures."

In Islamic tradition, there are 99 Names of God (*al-asma al-husna* lit. meaning: "The best names") each of which evoke a distinct characteristic of Allah. All these names refer to Allah, the supreme and all-comprehensive divine name. Among the 99 names of God, the most famous and most frequent of these names are "the Merciful" (*al-rahman*) and "the Compassionate" (*al-rahim*).

Most Muslims use the untranslated Arabic phrase "insha' Allah" (meaning "God willing") after references to future events. Muslim discursive piety encourages beginning things with the invocation of "bismillah"(meaning "In the name of God").

There are certain phrases in praise of God that are favored by Muslims, including "Subhan-Allah" (Holiness be to God), "Alhamdulillah" (Praise be to God), "La-il-la-ha-illa-Allah" (There is no deity but God) and "Allahu Akbar" (God is great) as a devotional exercise of remembering God (zikr). In a Sufi practice known as *zikr Allah* (lit. remembrance of God), the Sufi repeats and contemplates on the name *Allah* or other divine names while controlling his or her breath.

Some scholars have suggested that Muhammad used the term Allah in addressing both pagan Arabs and Jews or Christians in order to establish a common ground for the understanding of the name for God, a claim Gerhard Böwering says is doubtful. According to Böwering, in contrast with Pre-Islamic Arabian polytheism, God in Islam does not have associates and companions nor is there any kinship between God and jinn. Pre-Islamic pagan Arabs believed in a blind, powerful, inexorable and insensible fate over which man had no control. This was replaced with the Islamic notion of a powerful but provident and merciful God.

According to Francis Edwards Peters, "The Qur'an insists, Muslims believe, and historians affirm that Muhammad and his followers worship the same God as the Jews (29:46). The Quran's Allah is the same Creator God who covenanted with Abraham". Peters states that the Qur'an portrays Allah as both more powerful and more remote than Yahweh, and as a universal deity, unlike Yahweh who closely follows Israelites.

Christianity

Arabic-speakers of all Abrahamic faiths, including Christians and Jews, use the word "Allah" to mean "God". The Christian Arabs of today have no other word for 'God' than 'Allah'. (Even the Arabic-descended Maltese language of Malta, whose population is almost entirely Roman Catholic, uses *Alla* for 'God'.) Arab Christians for example use terms *Allah al-ab* meaning God the Father, *Allah al-ibn* mean God the Son, and *Allah al-ruh al-quds* meaning God the Holy Spirit.

Arab Christians have used two forms of invocations that were affixed to the beginning of their written works. They adopted the Muslim *basm-Allah,* and also created their own Trinitized *basm-Allah* as early as the eight century CE. The Muslim *basm-Allah* reads: "In the name of God, the Compassionate, the Merciful." The Trinitized *basm-Allah* reads: "In the name of Father and the Son and the Holy Spirit, One God." The Syriac, Latin and Greek invocations do not have the words "One God" at the end. This addition was made to emphasize the monotheistic aspect of Trinitian belief and also to make it more palatable to Muslims.

According to Marshall Hodgson, it seems that in the pre-Islamic times, some Arab Christians made pilgrimage to the Kaaba, a pagan temple at that time, honoring Allah there as God the Creator.

As a Loanword

English and Other European Languages

The history of the word "Allah" in English was probably influenced by the study of comparative religion in 19th century; for example, Thomas Carlyle (1840) sometimes used the term Allah but without any implication that Allah was anything different from God. However, in his biography of Muhammad (1934), Tor Andrae always used the term Allah, though he allows that this 'conception of God' seems to imply that it is different from that of the Jewish and Christian theologies. By this time Christians were also becoming accustomed to retaining the Hebrew term "Yahweh" untranslated (it was previously translated as 'the Lord').

Languages which may not commonly use the term *Allah* to denote a deity may still contain popular expressions which use the word. For example, because of the centuries long Muslim presence in the Iberian Peninsula, the word ojalá in the Spanish language and oxalá in the Portuguese language exist today, borrowed from Arabic. This word literally means "God willing" (in the sense of "I hope so").

Some Muslims leave the name "Allah" untranslated in English. Sometimes this comes from a zeal for the Arabic text of the Qur'an and sometimes with a more or less conscious implication that the Jewish and Christian concept of God is not completely true in its details. Conversely, the usage of the term Allah by English speaking non-Muslims in reference to the God in Islam, Marshall G. S. Hodgson says, can imply that Muslims are worshiping a mythical god named 'Allah' rather than God, the creator. This usage is therefore appropriate, Hodgson says, only for those who are prepared to accept its theological implications.

Malay and Indonesian Language

Christians in Indonesia and Malaysia also use *Allah* to refer to God in the Malay language and Indonesian Language (both language although different referred to as *Bahasa*). Mainstream Bible translations in Bahasa use *Allah* as the translation of Hebrew Elohim (translated in English Bibles as "God"). This goes back to early Bahasa translation work by Francis Xavier in the 16th century.

The government of Malaysia in 2007 outlawed usage of the term *Allah* in any other but Muslim contexts, but the High Court in 2009 revoked the law, ruling that it was unconstitutional. While *Allah* had been used for the Christian God in Malay for more than four centuries, the contemporary controversy was triggered by usage of *Allah* by the Roman Catholic newspaper *The Herald*. The government has in turn appealed the court ruling, and the High Court has suspended implementation of its verdict until the appeal is heard.

NAMES OF GOD

Various monotheist religions have different **names of God**. The **Name of God**, or *Holy Name* is a form of addressing God present in a majority of world religions as used in liturgy or prayer. Prayer with the Holy Name or the Name of God has been established as a most common spiritual practice in Western and Eastern spiritual practices. A number of traditions have lists of many Names of God which enumerate various qualities. The Qur'an contains the Ninety-nine Most Beautiful Names of Allah, Judaism refers to 72 Divine Names and Mahabharata text contains a thousand names of Vishnu.

In English the word *God* is used to refer to the deity by multiple religions.

Eastern and Western correlation and intercultural interpretations of the philosophy of the Name of God have been a subject of study for thinkers in the east and west. In Christian theology the Logos must be a personal and a proper name of God; hence it is asserted that it cannot be dismissed as mere metaphor. On the other hand, the Names of God in a different tradition are sometimes referred as symbols. The question whether divine names used by different religions are equivalent has been raised and analyzed.

The exchange of symbols of religion between different traditions is limited; symbols of religious core are shared (for example Om and Gayatri by members of the Indian Christian community) but the usage of the names themselves mostly remain in the domain of a particular religion, such as in the case of recitation of the names of God (japa). *The Divine Names,* the classic treatise by Pseudo-Dionysius defines the scope of traditional understandings of the Names of God in Western traditions such as Hellenic, Christian, Jewish and Islamic, with further historical interfaith lists such as *The 72 Names of the Lord* showing parallels in history and interpretation of the lists of the Names of God in Kabbalah, Christianity, Hebrew and Slavic, Palestine, Balkans and Provence etc.

Some suggest that the "name of God represents the nature of God". The attitude as to the transmission of the Name in many cultures was surrounded by secrecy. The pronunciation of the Name of God, in Judaism, has always been guarded with great care. It is believed that in ancient times the sages communicated the pronunciation only once every seven years.. This system was challenged by more recent movements. The nature of the name can be described as personal and attributive. In many cultures it is often difficult to distinguish between the personal and the attributive names of God, the two divisions necessarily shading into each other.

Indian Religions

Hinduism

Within Hinduism, there are a number of names of God which are generally in Sanskrit, each supported by a different tradition within the religion. Brahman, Bhagavan, Ishvara, and Paramatma are among the most commonly used terms for God in the scriptures of Hinduism.

- **Bhagwan** (Bhagwan) means "God".
- **Ishvara** (iœvara) means "Cosmic Controller" or "Lord".
- **Maheshvara** (maha-iœvara) means "Great Lord", used as an attribute of god **Shiva** within Shaivism traditions.
- **Parameshvara** (parama-iœvara) means "Supreme Lord".
- **Paramatman** (parama-atman) means "Supreme Soul".
- **Para Brahman** (para-brahma), an ineffable entity, best translated as "The Absoute Truth", Supreme Brahman, or Supreme Cosmic Spirit.
- **Adi Purusha** (adi-puruca) means "Timeless Being", "Primordial Lord", "First Person".
- **Vishnu** is seen as Para Brahman within Vaishnava traditions, and the Vishnu Sahasranama enumerates 1000 names of Vishnu, each name eulogizing one of His countless great attributes. The names of Vishnu's Dasavatara in particular are considered divine names.
- **Krishna** is associated with Vishnu and certain Vaishnava traditions also regard Him as Para

Brahman and *Svayam Bhagavan* (svayambhagavan) or the Lord Himself. In Krishna-centered schools of Vaishnavism, which includes the Nimbarka, Vallabha and Caitanya schools Krishna is held as the Supreme Personality of Godhead based on the descriptions of Him within the Bhagavata Purana and Mahabharata, with particular reference to the Bhagavad-Gita.

- **Rama** (Rama) is associated with Vishnu and is especially venerated in *bhakti* literature, such as that of Kabir and Ravidas, and more recently in the writings of Mohandas Gandhi.

Sikhism

There are multiple names for God in Sikhism. Some of the popular names for God in Sikhism are:

- **Waheguru**, meaning *Wonderful Teacher bringing light to remove darkness,* this name is considered the greatest among Sikhs, and it is known as "Gurmantar", the Guru's Word.
- **Ek Onkar**, *ek* meaning "one", emphasizes the singularity of God. It is the beginning of the Sikh Mool Mantra.
- **Satnam** meaning *True Name,* some are of the opinion that this is a name for God in itself, others believe that this is an adjective used to describe the "Gurmantar", Waheguru
- **Nirankar**, meaning formless One

God according to Guru Nanak is beyond full comprehension by humans; has endless number of virtues; takes on innumerable forms; and can be called by an infinite number of names thus *"Your Names are so many, and Your Forms are endless. No one can tell how many Glorious Virtues You have."*

Semitic Religions

Judaism

In the Hebrew scriptures the Jewish name of God is considered sacred and, out of deep respect for the name, Jews do not say the name of God and do not erase it if it is written. The tetragrammaton is the name for the group of four Hebrew letters which represent the name of God. The Tetragrammaton occurs 6,828 times in the Hebrew text in the Biblia Hebraica and the Biblia Hebraica Stuttgartensia. Neither vowels nor vowel points were used in ancient Hebrew writings.

Some claim the pronunciation of YHWH has been lost, other authorities say it has not and that it is pronounced *Yahweh*. References, such as *The New Encyclopædia Britannica,* validate the above by offering additional specifics:

Early Christian writers, such as Clement of Alexandria in the 2nd century, had used a form like Yahweh, and claim that this pronunciation of the tetragrammaton was never really lost. Other Greek transcriptions also indicated that YHWH should be pronounced Yahweh.

Clement of Alexandria transliterated the tetragrammaton as Éáïõ. The above claims were founded upon the understanding that Clement of Alexandria had transliterated YHWH as Éáïõå in Greek, which is pronounced "Yahweh" in English. However, the final -e in the latter form has been shown as having been a later addition. For a more in-depth discussion of this, see the article Yahweh.

Instead of pronouncing YHWH during prayer, Jews say *Adonai* ("Lord"). Halakha requires that secondary rules be placed around the primary law, to reduce the chance that the main law will be broken. As such, it is common Jewish practice to restrict the use of the word *Adonai* to prayer only. In conversation, many Jewish people, even when not speaking

Hebrew, will call God "*Hashem*", which is Hebrew for "the Name" (this appears in Leviticus 24:11).

A common title of God in the Hebrew Bible is *Elohim;* as opposed to other titles of God in Judaism, this name also describes gods of other religions, angels, or even humans of great importance (John 10:34-36).

Christianity

English translations of the New Testament render *ho theos* as God and *ho kurios* as "the Lord".

Regarding the Old Testament, the Israelite theonyms Elohim and Yahweh are mostly rendered as "God" and "the Lord" respectively, although in the Protestant tradition, the personal names Yahweh and Jehovah, based on the tetragrammaton, are also used. *Jehovah* appears in Tyndale's Bible, the King James Version, and other translations from that time period and later. Many translations of the Bible translate the tetragrammaton as *LORD*, following the Jewish practice of substituting the spoken Hebrew word 'Adonai' (translated as 'Lord') for YHWH when read aloud. Many avoid using either Yahweh or Jehovah altogether on the basis that the actual pronunciation of the 'tetragrammaton has been lost in antiquity. They use *God* or *The Lord* instead. Similarly, the original Hebrew pronunciation of "Jesus" is unknown. Many agree that the 'new word translation of the holy scriptures' is the most acurate and most easily understood bible translation than any other.

Jesus (Iesus, Yeshua, Joshua, or Yehoshûa) is a Hebraic personal name meaning "Yahweh saves/helps/is salvation",. *Christ* means "the anointed" in Greek. *Khristos* is the Greek equivalent of the Hebrew word Messiah; while in English the old Anglo-Saxon Messiah-rendering *hæland* 'healer' was practically annihilated by the Latin Christ, some cognates such as *heiland* in Dutch and Afrikaans survive.

In Messianic Judaism, generally regarded as a form of Christianity, YHWH (pre-incarnate) and Yeshua (incarnate) are one and the same, the second Person, with the Father and Ruach haQodesh (the Holy Spirit) being the first and third Persons, respectively, of ha'Elohiym (the Godhead). YHWH is expressed as "haShem," which means 'the Name.'

The less evangelical branch of the Quakers often refers to God as The Light. Another term used is 'King of Kings' or 'Lord of Lords' and Lord of the Hosts. Other names used by Christians include Ancient of Days, Father/Abba, 'Most High' and the Hebrew names Elohim, El-Shaddai, and Adonai. The name, "Abba/Father" is the most common term used for the creator within Christianity, because it was the name Jesus Christ (Yeshua Messiah) himself used to refer to God.

In the movement Imiaslavie ("Name glorification") opposed by the Russian Orthodox Church, the name of God is *God Himself* and can be used to evoke miracles.

The Assemblies of Yahweh is currently the only Christian group to use the name Yahweh exclusively and consistently.

Shangdi (Hanyu Pinyin: shàng dì) (literally *King Above*) is also used to refer to the Christian god in the Standard Mandarin Union Version of the Bible. Likewise, Korean Christians and Vietnamese Christians also use cognates of this name, to refer to the Biblical god.

Shen (lit. *God, spirit,* or *deity*) was adopted by Protestant missionaries in China to refer to the Christian god. In this context it is usually rendered with a space, to demonstrate reverence. (An alternate explanation for adding a space is that doing so simplified typesetting with two versions carrying or made parallel.)

Zhu, Tian Zhu (lit. *Lord* or *Lord in Heaven*) is translated from the English word, "Lord", which is a formal title of the Christian god in Mainland China's Christian churches.

Islam

Allah is the most frequently used name of God in Islam. It is an Arabic word meaning "The God" .The word Allah is a cognate of the Hebrew word Eloah.

A well established Islamic tradition enumerates 99 names of God, each representing certain attributes or descriptions of God; in which God is seen as being the source and maximum extent of each name's meaning. The names Ar-Rahman and Ar-Raheem are the most frequently mentioned in the Qur'an, both meaning the "Most Merciful", but with different emphasis of meaning, either of which are also often translated as the "Most Compassionate" or the "Most Beneficent".

Besides these Arabic names, Muslims of non-Arab origins may also sometimes use other names in their own languages to God, such as the Ottoman anachronism Tanrý (originally the pagan Turks' celestial chief god, corresponding to the Ancient Turkish Tengri), or Khoda in Persian language. The use of the word "God" in English is also seen as acceptable to Muslims.

Bahá'í Faith

The Bahá'í scriptures often refer to God by various titles and attributes, such as Almighty, All-Powerful, All-Wise, Incomparable, Gracious, Helper, All-Glorious, and Omniscient. Baha'is believe the greatest of all the names of God is "All-Glorious" or *Bahá* in Arabic. *Bahá* is the root word of the following names and phrases: the greeting *Alláh-u-Abhá* (God is the All-Glorious), the invocation *Yá Bahá'u'l-Abhá* (O Thou Glory of the Most Glorious), *Bahá'u'lláh* (The Glory of God), and *Bahá'i* (Follower of the All-Glorious). These are expressed in Arabic regardless of the language in use. Bahá'ís believe Bahá'u'lláh, the founder of the Bahá'í Faith, is the "complete incarnation of the names and attributes of God".

Chief Gods in Polytheistic Religions

The distinction between a chief deity presiding over a pantheon, worship of a single god in the sense of monolatry, and genuine monotheism is gradual. A number of polytheistic religions have chief deities with some aspects of monotheism.

- in Chinese folk religion (see also Chinese terms for God):
    - o **Shangdi** (Hanyu Pinyin: shàng dì) (literally *King Above*) was a supreme deity worshipped in ancient China.
    - o **Shen** (lit. *God, spirit,* or *deity*) is commonly used to refer to various spirits, including gods.
    - o **Tian** (lit. *sky* or *heaven*) is used to refer to the sky, but is not a personification of the sky. Whether it possesses sentience in the embodiment of an omnipotent, omniscient being is a debated by linguists and philosophers: in the Analects of Confucius, it apparently did, but less often in later Confucian texts.
- **Odin** is considered the chief god in Norse mythology
- **Tengri**, also used to refer to the sky, is the one God of many Turkic ethnic groups during the Middle Ages, a tradition now called Tengriism.

Taboos

Several religions have taboos related to names of their gods. In some cases, the name may never be spoken, only spoken by inner-circle initiates, or only spoken at prescribed moments during certain rituals. In other cases, the name may be never freely spoken, but when written, more limited taboos apply. To avoid saying names of God, they are often modified, such as by clipping and substitution of phonetically similar words. It is common to regard the written name of one's god as deserving of respect; it ought not, for instance, be stepped upon or dirtied, or made common slang in such a way as to show disrespect. It may be permissible to burn the written name when there is no longer a use for it.

Judaism

Most observant Jews forbid discarding holy objects, including any document with a name of God written on it. Once written, the name must be preserved indefinitely. This leads to several noteworthy practices:

- Commonplace materials are written with an intentionally abbreviated form of the name. For instance, a Jewish letter-writer may substitute "G-d" for the name *God*. Thus, the letter may be discarded along with ordinary trash. (Note that not all Jews agree that non-Hebrew words like *God* are covered under the prohibition.)
- Since the Divine presence (or possibly an appearance of God) can supposedly be called simply by pronouncing His true name correctly, substitute names are used.
- Copies of the Torah are, like most scriptures, heavily used during worship services, and will eventually become worn out. Since they may not be disposed of in any way, including by burning, they are removed, traditionally to the synagogue attic. *See* genizah. There they remain until they are buried.
- All religious texts that include the name of God are buried.

Zoroastrianism

Most Zoroastrians believe that once a product bears the name or image of Zoroaster or Ahura Mazda it cannot be thrown away in the garbage. Yet, it does not have to be kept indefinitely. There are several ways to dispose of the item:

They can be thrown away if they mix back with the seven creations :

- Placed in a river, lake or other body of water
- Buried in the ground (earth)

Islam

- In Islam, the name (or any names) of God is generally treated with the utmost respect. It is referred to in many verses of the Qur'an that the real believers respect the name of God very deeply. (e.g. stated in 33/35, 57/16, 59/21, 7/180, 17/107, 17/109, 2/45, 21/90, 23/2) On the other hand the condition is openly stressed by prohibiting people from unnecessary swearing using the name of Allah. (e.g. stated in 24/53, 68/, 63/2, 58/14, 58/16, 2/224) Thus the mention of the name of God is expected to be done so reverently. In Islam there are 100 different names of Allah.Allah is the name use in majority of arab countries.whereas in iran,indian subcontinent and through out central asia the word, Khuda is widely used instead of allah.

Christianity

- In Christianity, God's name may not "be used in vain" (see the Ten Commandments), which is commonly interpreted to mean that it is wrong to curse while making reference to God (ex. "Oh my God!" as an expression of frustration or anger). Another natural interpretation of this passage is in relation to oath taking, where the command is to hold true to those commands made 'in God's name'. (The idea that Christians should hold to their word is reinforced by certain statements by Jesus in the Gospels - cf

Matthew 5:37) God's name being used in vain can also be interpreted as trying to invoke the power of God, as a means to impress, intimidate, punish, condemn, and/or control others. This can also be used to refer to the idea of saying that one acts "in God's behalf" when doing things that are clearly personal actions.

- Different Christian cultures have different views on the appropriateness of naming people after God. English speaking Christians generally would not name a son "Jesus", but "*Jesús*" is a common Spanish first name. This taboo does not apply to more indirect names and titles like Emmanuel or Salvador. The word "Christian" is sometimes used as a first name, and is currently the name of about 1 out of every 1500 males in the United States.

- Perhaps because of taboos on the use of the name of God and religious figures like Mary, mother of Jesus, these names are used in profanity (a clear case is Quebec French profanity, based mostly on Catholic concepts). More pious swearers try to substitute the blasphemy against holy names with minced oaths like *Jeez!* instead of *Jesus!*, or *Judas Priest!* instead of *Jesus Christ!*.

●●

4
History of the Qur'an

The study of the **origins and development of the Qur'an** can be said to fall into two major schools of thought, the first being a traditionalist view and the later being a non-traditionalist view.

The traditionalist view, which relies on the early Islamic literature as authentic or reliable, ascribes to the view that the Qur'an began with Muhammad's claims of divine revelations in 610. Most of these revelations were either memorised or obscurely written down during the lifetime of Muhammad. These revelations were subsequently collected and were standardised in today's version by the caliph Uthman c. 653/654. The text was later given vowel pointing and punctuation in the seventh and eighth centuries.

The non-traditionalist view covers a variety of schools of thought generally anathematised by Muslim academia. Their view generally treats the early Muslim traditions, which arose over a century post-hoc, with scepticism and evaluates the claim of the Qur'an as a text on the basis of higher critical analysis, independent evidence and source hypotheses.

The Traditionalist View

According to the traditional Muslim view, the origin and development of the Qur'an began with Muhammad receiving divine revelations in 610. According to traditional Muslim history the verses of the Qur'an were written on palm trees and fiber and memorized during the life of

Muhammad and collected shortly after his death. During the caliphate of Uthman the Qur'an was standardized in 653. Slight developments in dotting and other punctuation happened during the seventh and eighth centuries.

Muhammad

The Qur'anic revelation started one night during the month of Ramadan in 610 AD, when Muhammad believed that the angel Gabriel visited him, and considered himself responsible for inscribing these messages from God.

Muslim scholars believe that prophet Muhammad was an illiterate, as mentioned in the Qur'an itself,

> "Those who follow the messenger, the Prophet who can neither read nor write, whom they will find described in the Torah and the Gospel (which are) with them......"Qur'an 7:157.

However, the Arabic word translated here as 'illiterate' also means 'gentile'.

He would memorize the Qur'an by ear, and later recite it to his companions, who also memorized it. Before the Qur'an was written down, speaking it from memory prevailed as the mode of teaching it to others. This fact, taken in the context of seventh century Arabia, was not at all an extraordinary feat. People of that time had a penchant for recited poetry and had developed their skills in memorization to a remarkable degree. Events and competitions that featured the recitation of elaborate poetry were of great interest. Some scholars, like William Montgomery Watt and Maxime Rodinson believe that Muhammad was literate and educated.

Written Text

The initial revelations were written on different sorts of parchments, tablets of stone, branches of date trees, other wood, leaves, leather and even bones.

Sahaba began recording Suras in writing before Muhammad died in 632. Allusions to written portions of the Qur'an can be found in many events. Immediately before his conversion in 615, Umar ibn al-Khattab caught his sister reading the Qur'anic text (Ta-Ha) from parchment. Muhammad said that reading the Qur'anic text earns a believer twice as much reward as reciting it from memory yet he prohibited carrying written copies of it into battle. He sent some copies of the Qur'an to different tribes and cities in order to teach people the religion of Islam.

At Medina, about forty companions are believed to have acted as scribes for the Qur'an. Twenty-two such persons are mentioned by name in the Hadith. Among them were well known persons, such as Abu Bakr, Umar, Uthman, Ali, Ibn Masud, Abu Huraira, Abdullah bin Abbas, Abdullah bin Amr bin al-As, Aisha, Hafsa and Umm Salama.

Narrated Qatada: *I asked Anas bin Malik: 'Who collected the Qur'an at the time of the prophet?' He replied, "Four, all of whom were from the Ansar: Ubai bin Ka'b, Muadh bin Jabal, Zaid bin Thabit and Abu Zaid".*

Also, after the fall of Mekkah, Muawiyah ibn Abu Sufyan also became a scribe of the Prophet after he accepted Islam.

The Sahaba wrote down the revelations under Muhammad's guidance:

> Narrated al Bara: *There was revealed 'Not equal are those believers who sit and those who strive and fight in the cause of Allah' . The prophet said: 'Call Zaid for me and let him bring the board, the ink pot and the scapula bone.' Then he said: 'Write: Not equal are those believers..."*

Muslim scribes believed that they would receive heavenly reward by writing down the Qur'an.

Abu Bakr

During the life of Muhammad, parts of the Qur'an, though written, were scattered amongst his companions, much of it as private possession. After Muhammad's death, Abu Bakr initially exercised a policy of laissez faire as well. This policy was reversed after the Battle of Yamama in 633. During the battle, 700 Muslims who had memorized the Qur'an were killed. The death of Salim, however, was most significant, as he was one of the very few who had been entrusted by Muhammad to teach the Qur'an. Consequently, upon Umar's insistence, Abu Bakr ordered the collection of the hitherto scattered pieces of the Qur'an into one copy.

Zaid ibn Thabit, Muhammad's primary scribe, was assigned the duty of collecting all of the Qur'anic text. This was his reaction:

> *"...By Allah, if he (Abu Bakr) had ordered me to shift one of the mountains it would not have been harder for me than what he had ordered me concerning the collection of the Qur'an... So I started locating the Qur'anic material and collecting it from parchments, scapula, leafstalks of date palms and from the memories of men.]*

He also said:

> *"So I started looking for the quran and collected it from (what was written on) palm-leaf stalks, thin white stones, and also from men who knew it by heart, till I found the last verse of Surat at-Tauba (repentance) with Abi Khuzaima al-Ansari, and I did not find it with anybody other than him. (Sahih al-Bukhari, Vol.6, p.478).*

The task required ibn Thabit to collect written copies of the Qur'an, with each verse having validated with the oral testimony of at least two companions. Usually the written copies were verified by himself and Umar - both of whom had memorized portions of the Qur'an. Thus, eventually the entire Qur'an was collected into a single copy, but it still wasn't given any particular order.

This compilation was kept by the Caliph Abu Bakr, after his death by his successor, Caliph Umar, who on his deathbed gave them to Hafsa bint Umar, his daughter and one of Muhammad's widows.

Ali ibn Abu Talib

According to Shia as well as some Sunni scholars Ali compiled a *mushaf*, a complete version of Qur'an, within six months after the death of the Prophet. When the volume was completed it was brought to Medina, where it was shown. The order of chapters of Ali's volume were rejected by some and Ali.

Compilation

By the time of the caliphate of Uthman ibn Affan, there was a perceived need for the compilation of the Qur'an. The Caliphate had grown considerably, bringing into Islam's fold many new converts from various cultures with varying degrees of isolation. These converts spoke a variety of languages but were not well learned in Arabic and so a complete written text of the Qur'an had to be compiled. Another reason for compiling the Qur'an was that many of the Muslims who had memorised portions of the Qur'an were dying, especially in battle.

Uthman is said to have begun a committee (including Zayd and several prominent members of Quraysh) to produce a standard copy of the text. Some accounts say that this compilation was based on the text kept by Hafsa. Other stories say that Uthman made his compilation independently, Hafsa's text was brought forward, and the two texts were found to coincide perfectly.

Until this time there was reportedly only one written text of the Qur'an. According to Islamic accounts, this text was faithful to its original version. Non-Muslim scholars believe that, while this is entirely possible, there must at least have been slight variations produced from some corruptions.

Thus, this became known as *al-mushaf al-Uthmani* or the "Uthmanic codex".

Uthman's reaction in 653 is recorded in the following:

> *"So 'Uthman sent a message to Hafsa saying, "Send us the manuscripts of the Qur'an so that we may compile the Qur'anic materials in perfect copies and return the manuscripts to you." Hafsa sent it to 'Uthman. 'Uthman then ordered Zaid bin Thabit, 'Abdullah bin AzZubair, Said bin Al-As and 'AbdurRahman bin Harith bin Hisham to rewrite the manuscripts in perfect copies. 'Uthman said to the three Quraishi men, "In case you disagree with Zaid bin Thabit on any point in the Qur'an, then write it in the dialect of Quraish, the Qur'an was revealed in their tongue." They did so, and when they had written many copies, 'Uthman returned the original manuscripts to Hafsa. 'Uthman sent to every Muslim province one copy of what they had copied, and ordered that all the other Qur'anic materials, whether written in fragmentary manuscripts or whole copies, be burnt. Said bin Thabit added, "A Verse from Surat Ahzab was missed by me when we copied the Qur'an and I used to hear Allah's Apostle reciting it. So we searched for it and found it with Khuzaima bin Thabit Al-Ansari. (That Verse was): 'Among the Believers are men who have been true in their covenant with Allah.' ()"*

Although the order of his earlier script differed from the Uthmanic codex, Ali accepted this standardized version.

Some scholars suggest that the early Uthmanic texts of the Qur'an differed in terms of punctuation from the version traditionally read today. It is believed that early versions of the text did not contain diacritics, markers for short vowels, and dots that are used to distinguish. One claim is that dots were introduced into the writing system sometime about half a century after the standardization of the Uthmanic text around 700 A.D.

When the compilation was finished, sometime between 650 and 656, Uthman sent copies of it to the different centers of the expanding Islamic empire. From then on, thousands of Muslim scribes began copying the Qur'an.

Canonization

It is a point of contention among Muslims that the entire Qu'ran was preserved by Uthman, but some hadith attest that some verses could not be found, that variant copies were burnt, and that a saying of Muhammad was misremembered as a Qu'ranic verse. A contemporary essay from John of Damascus describes a surah called the "Camel of God" which is no longer extant, although the story of the camel is preserved somewhat in other surat. For these reasons and others, Western scholars believe that Uthman performed a recension of the Qu'ran.

Oldest Copy known Today

Fragments from a large number of Qur'an codices were discovered in Yemen in 1972. They are now lodged in the House of Manuscript in Sana'a. Carbon-14 tests date some of the parchments to 645-690 CE. However, the text itself is somewhat younger, since Carbon-14 estimates the year of the death of an organism, and the process from that to the final writing on the parchment involves an unknown amount of time. Calligraphic datings have pointed to 710-715 CE.

Several manuscripts, including the Samarkand manuscript, Topkapi manuscript, and others claim to have been distributed by Uthman.

There have also been large numbers of manuscripts alleged to be the Damascus manuscript — or even one of the other perished manuscripts. However, there is no sufficient evidence to prove such a link.

Having studied early Qur'an manuscripts, John Gilchrist states: "The oldest manuscripts of the Quran still in existence date from not earlier than about one hundred years after Muhammad's death." He comes to this conclusion by analysing the state of development of the script used in the two of the oldest manuscripts available at the time he is writing, the Samarkand and Topkapi codices. The codices are both written in the Kufic script. It "can generally be dated from the late eight century depending on the extent of development in the character of the script in each case." This technique has been criticised by some Muslim scholars, who have cited many instances of early Kufic and pre-Kufic inscriptions. The most important of these is 240m of Qur'anic inscriptions in Kufic script from the founding of the Dome of the Rock in Jerusalem (692CE/70AH). Inscriptions on rock Hijaaze and early Kufic script may date as early as (646CE/24AH). Clearly early Kufic scripts existed in the seventh century. The debate between the scholars has moved from one over the date origin of the script to one over state of development of the Kufic script in the early manuscripts and in datable 7th Century inscriptions.

As for the copies that were destroyed, Islamic traditions say that Abdallah Ibn Masud, Ubay Ibn Ka'b, and Ali, Muhammad's cousin and son-in-law, had preserved versions that differed in some ways from the Uthmanic text. Muslim scholars record certain of the differences between the versions; those recorded consist almost entirely of orthographical and lexical variants, or different verse counts. All three (Ibn Masud, Ubay Ibn Ka'b, and Ali) are recorded as having accepted the Uthmanic text as final.

Uthman's version was written in an older Arabic script that left out most vowel markings; thus the script could be interpreted and read in various ways. This basic Uthmanic script is called the rasm; it is the basis of several traditions of oral recitation, differing in minor points. The Qur'an is always written in the Uthmanic Rasm (Rasm al Uthman). In order to fix these oral recitations and prevent any mistakes, scribes and scholars began annotating the Uthmanic rasm with various diacritical marks indicating how the word was to be pronounced. It is believed that this process of annotation began around 700 CE, soon after Uthman's compilation, and finished by approximately 900 CE. The Qur'an text most widely used today is based on the Rasm Uthmani(Uthmanic way of writing the Qur'an) and in the Hafs tradition of recitation, as approved by Al-Azhar University in Cairo in 1922.

Traditionalists

Some secular scholars accept something like the traditional Islamic version; they say that Muhammad put forth verses and laws that he claimed to be of divine origin; that his followers memorized or wrote down his revelations; that numerous versions of these revelations circulated after his death in 632 CE, and that Uthman ordered the collection and ordering of this mass of material in the time period (650-656). These scholars point to many characteristics of the *Qur'an* – the repetitions, the scientific mentions, the arbitrary order, the mixture of styles and genres – as indicative of a human collection process that was extremely respectful of a miscellaneous collection of original texts. Examples of traditionalists would be Richard Bell, Montgomery Watt, and Andrew Rippin.

Sceptical Scholars

Other secular scholars, such as John Wansbrough, Michael Cook and Patricia Crone, were less willing to attribute the entire Qur'an to Muhammad (or Uthman), arguing that there "is no hard evidence for the existence of the Koran in any form before the last decade of the seventh century...[and that]...the tradition which places this rather opaque revelation in its historical context is not attested before the middle of the eighth." "There is no proof that the text of the Qur'an was collected under Uthman, since the earliest surviving copies of the complete Qur'an are centuries later than Uthman. They contend that Islam was formed gradually over a number of centuries after the Muslim conquests, as the Islamic conquerors elaborated their beliefs in response to Jewish and Christian challenges.

Wansbrough wrote in a dense, complex, almost hermetic style, and has had much more influence on Islamic studies through his students than he has through his own writings. His students Crone and Cook co-authored a book called *Hagarism: The Making of the Islamic World* (1977), which was extremely controversial at the time, as it challenged not only Muslim orthodoxy, but the prevailing attitudes among secular Islamic scholars.

Crone, Wansbrough and Nevo argue that all the primary sources which exist are from 150–300 years after the events which they describe, and thus are chronologically far removed from those events

The absence of contemporaneous corroborating material from the very first century of Islam has raised numerous questions as to the authenticity of the account provided by later traditionalist sources. All that is preserved from this time period are a few commemorative building inscriptions and assorted coins. Secular scholars point out that the earliest account of Muhammad's life by Ibn Ishaq was written about a century after Muhammad died and all later narratives by Islamic biographers contain far more details and embellishments about events which are entirely lacking in Ibn Ishaq's text.

Another school of secular study of the origins of the Qur'an has focused on the examination of the vast body of the Greek, Armenian, Hebrew, Aramaic, Syriac and Coptic accounts of non-Muslim neighbors of the 7th and 8th centuries which in many cases contradict the traditional Islamic narratives. Historian Patricia Crone for instances argues that the consistency of the non-Muslim sources spread over a large geographic area would tend to rule out a non-Muslim anti-Islamic motive to these sources.

The untraditionalist approach has been further expanded by Christoph Luxenberg, who supports claims for a late composition of the Qur'an, and traces much of it to sources other than Muhammad. Luxenberg is known for his thesis that the Qur'an is merely a re-working of an earlier Christian text, a Syriac lectionary.

Fred Donner has argued for an early date for the collection of the Qur'an, based on his reading of the text itself. He points out that if the Qur'an had been collected over the tumultuous early centuries of Islam, with their vast conquests and expansion and bloody incidents between rivals for the caliphate, there would have been some evidence of this history in the text. However, there is nothing in the Qur'an that does not reflect what is known of the earliest Muslim community.

In 1972, during the restoration of the Great Mosque of San'a, in Yemen, laborers stumbled upon a "paper grave" containing tens of thousands of fragments of parchment on which verses of the Qur'an were written. Some of these fragments were believed to be the oldest Qur'anic texts yet found.

In well known Professor G.R. Hawting's academic review and in partial support of Puin's book, *Hidden Origins of Islam: New Research into Its Early History,* Hawting says Puin refers "to some puzzling evidence that must be taken into account by anyone concerned by a period that is, indeed, in many ways obscure."

The variations from the received text that he found seemed to match minor variations in sequence reported by some Islamic scholars, in their descriptions of the variant Qur'ans once held by Abdallah Ibn Masud, Ubay Ibn Ka'b, and Ali, and suppressed by Uthman's order.

Similarities to the Bible

Skeptical scholars account for the many similarities between the Qur'an and the Jewish and Hebrew Scriptures by saying that Muhammad was teaching what he believed a universal history, as he had heard it from the Jews and Christians he had encountered in Arabia and on his travels. These scholars also disagree with the Islamic belief that the whole of the Qur'an is addressed by God to humankind. They note that there are numerous passages where God is directly addressed, or mentioned in the third person, or where the narrator swears by various entities, including God.

Completeness

There are three arguments which suggest that the Qur'an is not complete. Some Muslims, Sunni and Shia alike, believe that the Qur'an itself was never abrogated, but instead that the Qur'anic verse is referring to Muhammad's recitations being abrogations of the Torah and the Injil. However, the consensus of the early and most authoritative Tafsir writers hold to the perspective that the verse in fact refers to abrogation of the Qur'an.

According to both Shia and Sunni authentic traditions, there are a number of authentic hadith that make reference to disputes over the Uthmanic edition of the Qur'an. These disputes include variant readings of individual ayats, missing ayats, missing surahs and surahs of substantially different lengths.

The two arguments presented for the incompleteness of the Qur'an are:

- Muhammad had revelations before he revealed those currently attributed to him and that it is possible that Muhammad being human and imperfect did not fully comprehend the significance of the first revelations. Muslims respond to this by saying that this view is of a speculative nature and not based on any grounds, and that the same logic could be applied to any revelation received, prior to Muhammad, by any human. Usually either Surah 96 or 74 is accepted as the first Surah to be revealed to Muhammad.

- The Qur'an itself allows for there to be revelations which might have been forgotten (87:6-7), replaced (,), divinely changed (). But here too Muslims cite the Bible and torah as examples to elucidate these verses, and not the Quran itself.

ISLAMIC VIEW OF ANGELS

Angels in Islam are light-based creatures, created from light by God to serve and worship Him.

Believing in angels is one of the six Articles of Faith in Islam, without which there is no faith. The six articles are belief in: God, His angels, His Books, His Messengers, the Last Day, and that predestination, both good and evil, comes from God.

Qu'ran, Chapter 17. Al-Isra verse 95.

"Say, 'If there were settled, on earth, angels walking about in peace and quiet, We should certainly have sent them down from the heavens an angel for a messenger. (Al-Isra: 95)"

Angel Hierarchy

There is no standard hierarchical organisation in Islam that parallels the division into different "choirs" or spheres, as hypothesised and drafted by early medieval Christian theologians. Most Islamic scholars agree that this is an unimportant topic in Islam, especially since such a topic has never been directly mentioned or addressed in the Qur'an. However, it is clear that there is a set order or hierarchy that exists between Angels, defined by the assigned jobs and various tasks to which angels are commanded by God. The Angel Jibreel is the most recognised angel, as in Islam this angel delivers the message of Allah (Quran) to the prophets.

Some scholars suggest that Islamic angels can be grouped into fourteen categories. Numbers 2-5 are considered archangels.

- **Hamalat al-'Arsh**, Those who carry the 'Arsh (throne of God) (40:7)
- **Jibraaiyl/Jibril** (Judeo-Christian Gabriel), the angel of revelation, who is said to be the greatest of the angels.
- **Israfil/Israafiyl** (Judeo-Christian Raphael), who will blow the trumpet twice at the end of time. At the first blow, everyone in heaven and earth will die including all angels (e.g., Azrael, Gabriel and Raphael himself) and at the second blow, all will be brought forth to meet their Lord.
- **Mikaaiyl** (Judeo-Christian Michael) (2:98), who provides nourishments for bodies and souls.
- **Malik al-maut** (Judeo-Christian Azrael), the angel of death.
- The **angels of the seven heavens**.
- **Hafaza** (The Guardian Angel):
    - **Kiraman Katibin** (Honourable Recorders) (Al Infithaar 82:11), two of whom are charged with each human being; one writes down good deeds, and the other writes down evil deeds.

- **Mu'aqqibat** (The Protectors) (Ar-Raad 13:10-11), who keep people from death until its decreed time and who bring down blessings.

- **Nakir and Munkar,** who question the dead in their graves.

- **Darda'il** (The Journeyers), who travel in the earth searching out assemblies where people remember God's name.

- **Harut and Marut** are believed to be two angels who came down to Babylon. The knowledge gained from these angels was misused by the evil ones in teaching sorcery to the inhabitants there.(2:102).

- The angels charged with each existent thing, maintaining order and warding off corruption. Their number is known only to God.

  (Due to varied methods of translation from Arabic and the fact that these Angels also exist in Christian contexts and the Bible, several of their Christian and phonetic transliteral names are listed.)

- **Jibraaiyl/Jibril** (Judeo-Christian Gabriel) Jibraaiyl is the archangel responsible for revealing the Qur'an to Muhammad, verse by verse. Jibrayil is known as the angel who communicates with (all of) the prophets.

- **Mikaaiyl** (Judeo-Christian Michael) Mikaaiyl is often depicted as the Archangel of mercy who is responsible for bringing rain and thunder to Earth. He is also responsible for the rewards doled out to good persons in this life.

- **Israfil/Israafiyl** (Judeo-Christian Raphael) According to the Hadith, Israafiyl is the Angel responsible for signaling the coming of Qiyamah (Judgment Day) by blowing a horn and sending out a Blast of Truth. The blowing of the trumpet is described in many places in Qur'an. It is said that the first blow will destroy everything , while the second blow will bring all human beings back to life again .

- **Malik al-maut** (Judeo-Christian Azrael) who is responsible for parting the soul from the body. His name means the angel of death in the Qur'an (Surah al-Sajdah 32:11).

Other Angels

- **Maalik** is the chief of the angels who governs Hell.
- **Zabaniah** are 19 angels who torment sinful persons in hell.
- **Ridwan** is the angel who is responsible for Heaven (Paradise).

The Qur'an also mentions angels who Allah has chosen to punish the sinful in hell, these angels take no pity on punishing them as they do what the Lord has commanded them to precisely and perfectly. A verse stipulates this:

"O you who believe! Save yourselves and your families from a Fire (Jahannam) whose fuel is Men and Stones, over which are (appointed) angels stern and severe, who flinch not (from executing) the Commands they receive from God, but do (precisely) what they are commanded." At-Tahrim 66:6

Also the number of Angels of Fire mentioned as Nineteen:

"Over it (The Great Fire) are nineteen (Angels) And We have not made the wardens of the Fire others than angels and We have not made their number but as a trial for those who disbelieve, that those who have been given the book) Tawrat and Bible [may be certain and those who believe may increase in faith and those who have been given the book and the believers may

not doubt and that those in whose hearts is a disease and the unbelievers may say: What does Allah mean by this parable? Thus does Allah make err whom He pleases, and He guides whom He pleases" Qur'an 74:30,31

The Qur'an also mentions that angels have qualities that may be typified by the word wings. Another ayah (verse) stipulates this:

"Praise be to God, Who created (out of nothing) the heavens and the earth, Who made the angel messengers with wings - two, or three, or four (pairs) and adds to Creation as He pleases: for God has power over all things." Fatir 35:1

The preceding sentence does not imply that all angels have two to four wings. Most notably, archangels (namely Gabriel and Michael) are described as having thousands of wings. The angels also accompanied Muhammad up to Jannah (Heaven) when he received commands from Allah. Instead of riding on an angel, Muhammad rode a creature called a Buraq whose stride spans from horizon to horizon.

Verses in the Qur'an that Directly Name Angels

Gabriel (Jibreel) and Michael (Mikaa'eel) are mentioned early on the Qur'an in Sura Al-Baqarah:

"Say: Whoever is an enemy to Gabriel - for he brings down the (revelation) to your heart by God's will, a confirmation of what went before, and guidance and glad tidings to those who believe - Whoever is an enemy to God, and His angels and prophets, to Gabriel and Michael - Lo! God is an enemy to those who reject Faith." (Al-Baqarah 2:97-98)

Another Angel, Malik is defined in the Qur'an as a being who is the warden of Hell. However Malik is not an evil angel, nor a fallen one, a notion Islam rejects, rather Malik is merely doing what he is commanded to do by God.

"They [the people in Hell] will cry: 'O Malik! Would that your Lord put an end to us!'..." (Az-Zukhruf 43:77)

Two other Angels are also mentioned directly in the Qur'an: Haaroot and Maaroot (OR Harut and Marut).

> *". . . and such things as came down at Babylon to the angels Haaroot and Maaroot . . ." (al-Baqarah 2:102)*

Several Angels, Angel of death Izra'il, Israfil and Munkar and Nakir are not mentioned directly in the Qur'an but are explained further in the Hadiths of Muhammad. They are also mentioned in traditional myths, however, they seldom retain complete originality from the Hadith.

ISLAMIC VIEW OF THE LAST JUDGMENT

In Islam, **Yawm al-Qiyamah** "the Day of Resurrection" or **Yawm ad-Din** "the Day of Judgement" is God's final assessment of humanity. al-Qiyamah is also the name of the 75th surah of the Qur'an.

The sequence of events according to the most common understanding is the annihilation of all creatures, resurrection of the body, and the judgment of all sentient creatures. The time of the Hour is not known, however there are Major and Minor Signs which, according to Islam, are to occur near the time of Qiyamah (Doomsday). Final judgment forms one of the main themes of the Qur'an. Many Qur'anic verses, especially the earliest ones, are dominated by the idea of the nearing Day of Resurrection.

Importance and Terminology

Belief in al-Qiyamah is considered a fundamental tenet of faith by all Muslims. The trials and tribulations associated with it are detailed in both the Qur'an and the hadith, as well as in the commentaries of the Islamic expositors and scholarly authorities such as al-Ghazali, Ibn Kathir, Ibn Majah, Muhammad al-Bukhari, and Ibn Khuzaimah who explain them in detail. Every human, Muslim and non-Muslim alike, is held accountable for his or her deeds and are judged by God accordingly.

The importance of the Last Judgement is underlined by the many references to it in the Qur'an and its many names. For example, it is also called "the Day of Reckoning", "the Hour", "Day of the Account", "Day of the Gathering", "Day of the Reckoning", and the "Great Announcement".

Overview

The Qur'an states that even the smallest acts of the believers will not be wasted.

Anyone who has an atom's worth of goodness will see it and anyone who has done an atom's worth of evil will also see it.

Those whose belief in God shaped their correct perception on life, and who did good deeds and are faithful will be tested in this world but will be rewarded in the hereafter if their deeds are deemed acceptable by Allah and vice versa.

There are some translations of the Qur'an in which we read statements like these:

> Surely Allah does not do injustice to the weight of an atom, and if it is a good deed He multiplies it and gives from Himself a great reward. S. 4:40 Shakir

And you are not (engaged) in any affair, nor do you recite concerning it any portion of the Quran, nor do you do any work but We are witnesses over you when you enter into it, and there does not lie concealed from your Lord the weight of an atom in the earth or in the heaven, nor any thing less than that nor greater, but it is in a clear book. S. 10:61 Shakir

The Unbelievers say, "Never to us will come the Hour": Say, "Nay! but most surely, by my Lord, it will come upon you; - by Him Who knows the unseen, - from Whom is not hidden the least little atom in the heavens or on earth: Nor is there anything less than that, or greater, but is in the Record Perspicuous: S. 34:3 Yusuf Ali

Barzakh

Barzakh is a sequence that happens after death, in which the soul separates from the body and then rests in a cold sleep state.

Judgment

During judgment, a man's or a woman's own book of deeds will be opened, and will be apprised of every action one did and every word one spoke (Qur'an 54.52-53). Actions taken during childhood are not judged. The account of deeds is so detailed that the man or woman will be in awe at how comprehensive the account is, such that even lesser and trivial deeds are included. Throughout judgment, however, the underlying principle is that of a complete and perfect justice administered by Allah. The accounts of judgment are also replete with the emphasis that Allah is merciful and forgiving, and that mercy and forgiveness will be granted on that day insofar as it is merited.

While appearing similar to certain parts of the Bible (Ezekiel 18:27, James 2:14-17, 1 Peter 1:17, Revelation 2:23), this is dissimilar to some protestant branches of Christianity, where salvation is by the faith in Yahweh alone. Catholics, however cite James 2:24 that judgement is not based on faith alone. Islam, emphasizes that grace does not conflict with perfect justice.

The age of the hereafter or rest of eternity is the final stage commencing after the Day of Judgment and all of humanity has received their judgment from Allah. If they were righteous and did good deeds based on their own circumstances, then if Allah wills, by His mercy they go to Jannat (heaven) a state of bliss and if they have attained little in life, and were unrighteous in their actions—or were despite all evidence shown to them bent on denying the truth of life once it was presented to them—based on their own circumstances they shall go to Jahannam (a spiritual state of suffering). This stage of life commences officially after the embodiment of Death is brought up and is slain, thus Death dies literally, and no one will ever experience or behold the concept of Death everafter. Based on the verdict received which is brought upon by each person's individual deeds actions and circumstances in life the Day of Judgment which everyone is judged with the utmost sense of justice, each human will spend this stage of life in Heaven or Hell (which will be a place for purification of the soul so that one realizes the wrongs each has committed in life) . However, those in hell are eligible to go to the state heaven after being purified by the state described as hell at a later time if they "had an atom's worth of faith in them" and the soul is repentful. It is believed by many Muslims that a Muslim will end up in Jannah once their sins have been punished.

Minor Signs

According to some aspects of Muslim belief, there are signs which will possibly indicate the coming of the day of judgment. These signs are categorized into major and minor signs.

> *What are they waiting for but for the hour to come upon them suddenly? Its signs have already come. What good will their reminder be to them when it does arrive?*

Hazart Abu Musa Al Ashari narrates that The Holy Prophet said: "Qiyamah will come....

- When it will be regarded as a shame to act upon Quranic injunctions.
- When untrustworthy people will be regarded as trustworthy and the trustworthy will be regarded as untrustworthy.
- When the liars will be regarded as truthful and the truthful will be regarded as liars.

- When women with children become displeased and barren women remain happy (on account of having no responsibility of off-spring).
- When decisions will be given on mere conjecture.
- When legislation in matters pertaining to my right (religion) is handed over to the worst elements in my Ummah, and if people accept them and are satisfied with their findings, then such persons will not smell the fragrance of Jannah.
- When the off-spring become a cause of grief and anger (for their parents).
- When Islam will become a stranger (unwanted religion).
- When Malice and Hate will become common among people.
- When Islamic Knowledge (Ilm) is lifted.
- When people will boast upon their palatial mansions.
- When oppression, jealousy and greed become the order of the day.
- When lies prevail over the truth.
- When people dispute over petty issues.
- When people blatantly follow their passions and whims.
- When immorality overtakes shamelessness and is perpetrated publicly.

The Major Signs

The major signs are those that will occur closer to the Day of Judgment, and they are said to be very extraordinary.These are the seven major signs of this day.

1. The appearance of Al-Maseeh-ud-Dajjal, the False Messiah. Ad-Dajjal is said to be a beast who will come

claiming to be God holding heaven and hell. His sole purpose is to deceive people and lead them away from the remembrance of Allah, and the unbelievers will follow him. He will have only one good eye and he will be blind in the other eye. On his forehead there will be a sign saying "Kafir," or disbeliever. He will perform some miracles which will serve to deceive some people.

The prophet Muhammed warned,

Whoever hears about the coming of Ad-Dajjal should stay away from him because by Allah, a man could come to him thinking of himself a strong believer but then he will follow Ad-Dajjal because of the doubts he will spread

There are many deceiving miracles Ad-Dajjal will perform to mislead the people on earth. He will appear between the cities of Iraq and Syria and will create disaster left and right. He will command the sky to rain and it will rain. He will command the earth, and it will produce crops. After grazing on these crops, their animals will return with their udders full of milk and their flanks stretched. When he will call people to come to a false region with him and they reject his call, he will leave them and they will suffer famine and will possess no form of wealth. Then lastly he will call a young man brimming with youth; he will strike him with a sword and cut him in two, then place the two pieces at a distance between an archer and his target. Then he will call to him, and the young man will come to him running and laughing. At that point, Allah will send Isa, Jesus. He will search for the Ad-Dajjal and will find him at the Gate of Ludd (a city in Israel). They will engage in fierce battle and Isa will win. Then the Ad-Dajjal will be no more.

2. The appearance of Ya'jooj and Ma'jooj: Ya'jooj and Ma'jooj are two hidden tribes of people.These tribes were disbelieving descendants of prophet Adam. They

will come in enormous numbers and will outnumber all the believers of the world. They will break through a barrier that Allah created to hold them back and ravage the earth. There will be multiple killings throughout the world, but Prophet Isa will take the believers to Mount Tur for protection. They will drink all the water, destroy plants and animals and kill people. This will occur roughly around the time of the second coming of Prophet Isa, Jesus. Finally, Allah will send a type of worm or insect that will wipe them out.

3. The appearance of the Dabbat al-ard (the strange beast): The Dabbah is a strange beast who will have the Rod of Moses and the seal of Solomon. He will call people back to Islam. Some will heed to the call while others will reject it. The believers will then have a sign that says: "Believer" while the disbelievers will have a "Disbeliever" sign. The exact description of the animal is unknown.

4. Three huge earthquakes: Three major earthquakes will occur on the day of judgment and they will damage a great deal of the earth. One earthquake will occur in the east, another in the west, and the third will be in the Arabian Peninsula.

5. The smoke: Smoke will appear all over the earth that will cause believers to catch something similar to the common cold, whereas disbelivers will be hit harder by it. Finally, a cool wind will cause all the believers to die. This leaves all the unbelievers left on earth to experience the last hour of the day of judgment.

6. The sun will rise from the west: This will be a major sign indicating that the world has reached its end. Allah has created the sun and He always made it rise

in the East, however, at the end of time He will reverse this process by making it rise from the West. Once this happens, Allah will not accept the repentance of the disbelievers, it will be too late for them. "The rising of the sun to half of the sky after continuous darkness (in Arabian Peninsula) equal to the time of three days. The sun will set again in its direction after reaching the sky's middle" as stated by the prophet goes parallel to the phenomenon of the polar shift.

7. The return of Prophet 'Isa (Jesus): Authentic narrations indicate that one of the major signs is that Prophet Is'a (Jesus) will descend from the heavens in Damascus. Prophet Jesus will be the one to lead the believers in battle against the forces of The Dajjal. It is said that he will "break the cross" (disassociate himself from the Christianity) and "kill the pigs" (return to the eating habits of the Jews), thus establishing The True Religion of God i.e. submitting to His Divine Will.

●●

5
Islamic Eschatology

Islamic eschatology is concerned with the al-Qiyamah "Last Judgement". Eschatology relates to one of the six (five according to Shi'a traditions) articles of faith (aqidah) of Islam according to the Sunni traditions. Like the other Abrahamic religions, Islam teaches the bodily resurrection of the dead, the fulfillment of a divine plan for creation, and the immortality of the human soul; the righteous are rewarded with the pleasures of Jannah "Heaven" while the unrighteous are punished in Jahannam "Hell"). A significant portion (about one third) of the Qur'an deals with these beliefs, with many hadith elaborating on the themes and details. It also emphasizes the inevitability of resurrection, judgment, and the eternal division of the righteous and the wicked. Islamic apocalyptic literature describing the Armageddon is often known as fitna "a test" or *malahim* (or *ghayba* to the Shi'a).

Signs of the Judgement Day

Among many hadith related to signs of day of judgement, one of the most famous hadith is *Hadith of Gabriel.*

A narration attributed to Abu Hurairah reports:

"One day while the Prophet was sitting in the company of some people, (The angel) Gabriel came and asked, "What is faith?" Allah's Apostle replied, 'Faith is to believe in Allah, His angels, (the) meeting with Him, His Apostles, and to believe in Resurrection." Then he further asked, "What is Islam?" Allah's Apostle replied, "To worship Allah Alone and none else, to offer prayers perfectly to pay the compulsory charity (Zakat) and to observe fasts during the month of Ramadan." Then he further asked, "What is Ihsan (perfection)?" Allah's Apostle replied, "To worship Allah as if you see Him, and if you cannot achieve this state of devotion then you must consider that He is looking at you." Then he further asked, "When will the Hour be established?" Allah's Apostle replied, "The answerer has no better knowledge than the questioner. But I will inform you about its portents.

1. When a slave (lady) gives birth to her master.
2. When the shepherds of black camels start boasting and competing with others in the construction of higher buildings. And the Hour is one of five things which nobody knows except Allah.

The Prophet then recited: "Verily, with Allah (Alone) is the knowledge of the Hour—." (31. 34) Then that angel (Gabriel) left and the Prophet asked his companions to call him back, but they could not see him. Then the Prophet said, "That was Gabriel who came to teach the people their religion." Abu 'Abdullah said: He (the Prophet) considered all that as a part of faith. Sahih al-Bukhari 1:2:47"

Jesus and the Dajjal

According to Islamic view, Isa (Jesus) is not the "Son of God", but was a prophet. It is believed that Jesus was not crucified; instead he was raised bodily. According to many hadith and believed by most Muslims, He will return to Earth. At the time appointed by Allah, Jesus will physically return to this world with the Mehdi (according to some sects of Shia Islam). He will break the cross, kill the swine, slaughter the Dajjal and end all wars, ushering in an era of peace. The messianic era comes after Jesus kills ad-Dajjal, the antichrist figure in Islam, and defeats his followers. The Ya'jooj and Ma'jooj

During the reign of Hadhrat Isa people will live an extremely peaceful life filled with prosperity and abundance. Then the wall which imprisons Ya'jooj and Ma'jooj will break and they will surge forth in large numbers.

But when Ya'jooj and Ma'jooj are let loose and they rush headlong down every hill" (Quran 21:97)

Who are the Ya'jooj and Majooj?

Zul Qarnain who was a pious and just Ruler travelled to many lands and conquered them, establishing justice and the Law of Allah therein. Allah Ta'ala provided him with all forms and material strength through which he was able to carry out his conquests and missions.

He once carried out a mission in three directions, the far west, the far east, and then in a northerly direction. It was here that he came across a tribe of people who complained to him about the tribes of Ya'jooj and Majooj which inhabited the land behind two huge mountains and often emerged from behind these mountains to perpetrate acts of anarchy and plunder among them. They requested Zul Qarnain to erect a barrier between themselves and the tribes of Ya'jooj and Ma'jooj so that they could be saved from their atrocities. With the material strength at his disposal, Zul Qarnain enlisted their physical labour and set about erecting a high wall between the two mountains. The height of the wall or its exact length is unknown. What is known is that the height of this wall reaches that of the summit of both mountains. It is made with blocks or sheets of iron, which is further strengthened by molten lead. In this manner Ya'jooj and Majooj are unable to scale the wall, or cross it, except when it is the will of Allah.

And when the promise of my Rabb approaces, He will level it to dust" (Quran 18:98)

They are situated in a land of ice which is hidden from our gazes and the exact location of which is unknown. Though many interpretations do exist in this respect, none of these can be said to absolute.

Ya'jooj and Majooj are human beings and according to a narration they are from the progeny of Yafith ibn Nooh.

Some Ahadith...

In a lengthy hadith by Hadhrat Nawwas ibn Sam'aan Rasulullah is reported to have said:

> ...Allah will send revelation upon Eesa that 'Such a creation of mine is now going to emerge that no power will be able to stop them. Therefore take my servants and ascend the Mount of Toor.' Then Ya'jooj and Majooj will emerge and surge forth in all their fury. When those from among them who constitute the former part of their army pass the lake of Tiberias (which is in northern Palestine), they will drink up all the water of that lake and by the time those that constitute the latter part of that same army pass the lake, they will say, "There used to be water here (long ago). When they reach the Mount of Khamr in Jerusalem, they will arrogantly proclaim: 'We have conquered the people of the earth, now we will annihilate those in the sky.' So saying they will fire their arrows towards the sky. When the arrows return to the ground they will be blood stained.

In the meantime, Eesa will be on the Mount of Toor with his followers. At that time the head of and ox will be as valuable as is a hundred dinars to you in this day. [This indicates the scarcity of provisions]. Faced with these hardships, Eesa and his followers will make dua unto Allah (to remove this calamity). As a result, Allah will cause sores to appear on the necks of each and every individual of these people which will cause their death suddenly. When Eesa and his followers descend from the Mount of Toor there will not be a single space on the land where the dead rotting bodies of these people is not littered, giving off a horrendous odour. Eesa and his followers will once more supplicate unto Allah as a result of which Allah will send down huge birds whose necks will be as thick as that of the necks of camels, and they will dump these bodies in a place where Allah wills. (According to a narration by Tirmidhi, they will be dumped at a place called Nahbal). Allah Ta'ala will then send down a heavy rain, the waters of which will flow in every part of the earth cleansing it thoroughly. It will rain for a period of forty days.

The Muslims will then burn the bows and arrows of the Ya'jooj and Ma'jooj for a period of seven years.

Allah will order the earth to yield forth its crops in abundance and there will be such blessing and prosperity that one pomegranate will be sufficient for a whole group while the peel thereof will suffice to cast a shadow over them. The milk of one camel will be sufficient for many groups while one milk giving cow will be sufficient for a whole tribe. One milk giving goat will be sufficent for a whole family...

Muslim

Hadhrat Abu Saeed Khudri narrates that Rasulullah said:

> On the day of Qiyamah Allah will say to Adam to pick out the Jahannamis from his entire progeny. Adam will ask: 'O Rabb, who are they?'

Allah will say: 'Nine hundred and ninety nine of a thousand are Jahannami while the one is a Jannati.' On hearing this the Sahaba were overtaken by fear and they asked "O Rasulullah who will that one Janniti be?'

Rasulullah said: 'Do not grieve, the nine hundred and ninety nine will be Ya'jooj and Ma'jooj while you will be the Jannati."' (i.e. your numbers in relation to them will be one in a thousand).

Bukhari and Muslim

Hadhrat Abdullah ibn Umar says that Rasulullah said:

Allah Ta'ala divided mankind into ten parts. Nine tenths constitute Ya'jooj and Ma'jooj while the remaining tenths constitutues the rest of mankind.

Hadhrat Zainab bint Jahsh says:

> ...once Rasulullah awoke from such a sleep that his face was red and these words were on his tongue: 'There is none worthy of worship except Allah. Destruction is upon the Arabs on account of the evil which has come close to them. Today a hole as big as this has opened up in the wall of Ya'jooj and Ma'jooj.' ..and Rasulullah indicated the size of the hole forming a ring with his index finger and thumb.

Bukhari and Muslim

Hadhrat Abu Hurairah narrates that every day Ya'jooj and Ma'jooj break (dig) through the wall erected by Zul Qarnain until they reach the end of it to that extent that they can actually see the light on the other side. They then return (home) saying that 'We will break through tomorrow.' But Allah Ta'ala causes the wall to revert to its original thickness and the next day they start digging through the wall all over again, and this process continues each day until as long as Allah wills them to remain imprisoned. When Allah wishes them to be released, then at the end of the day they will say, "If Allah wills, tomorrow we will break through." The following day they will find the wall as they had left it the previous day (i.e. it will not have returned to its original state) and after breaking the remaining part of it they will emerge."

Ahmad, Tirmidhi

Commenting on the above hadith, Allamah Ibn Arabi says, Three miracles are evident in this Hadith:

1. It never occurs to these tribes that they must continue work during the night. After all, they are in such large numbers that they can easily delegate the work among themselves and work in shifts. But Allah does not allow this thought to occur to them.

2. It never occurs to them that they can merely cross the mountains or scale the wall, which they can do through the aid of equipment and implements which they possess in large numbers. According to a narration by Wahab ibn Munabbah it is known that these tribes are agriculturists and artisians possessing various types of equipment.

3. The thought of saying "If Allah wills" never enters their minds and it will only occur to them to say it when Allah wills that they be released.

Afterlife

A fundamental tenet of Islam is belief in the day of resurrection, Qiyamah. The trials and tribulations of Qiyamah are explained in both the Qur'an and the Hadith, as well as in the commentaries of Islamic scholars such as al-Ghazali, Ibn Kathir, and Muhammad al-Bukhari.

Muslims believe that God will hold every human, Muslim and non-Muslim, accountable for his or her deeds at a preordained time unknown to man. The archangel Israfil, will sound a horn sending out a "blast of truth". Traditions say Muhammad will be the first to be brought back to life.

Bodily resurrection is much insisted upon in the Qur'an, which challenges the Pre-Islamic Arabian concept of death. Resurrection is followed by judgement of all souls. According to the Qur'an, sins that can consign someone to hell include lying, dishonesty, corruption, ignoring God or God's revelations, denying the resurrection, refusing to feed the poor, indulgence in opulence and ostentation, the economic exploitation of others, and social oppression.

The punishments in hell includes *adhab*, "pain or torment inflicted by way of chastiment; punishment", a very painful punishment (see ,); *khizy*, "shame, disgrace, ignominy" (,). The descriptions in the Qur'an of hell are very descriptive.

The punishments in the Qur'an are contrasted not with release but with mercy (, , , etc.). Islam views paradise as a place of joy and bliss. Islamic descriptions of heaven are described as physical pleasures, sometimes interpreted literally, sometimes allegorically. Heaven is most often described as a cool garden with running streams of unlimited food and drink. Some interpretations also promise enormous palaces staffed with multitudes of servants, and perfect, perpetually-virginal spouses. Despite the graphical descriptions of the physical pleasures, there are clear references to a greater joy that exceeds the pleasures of flesh: The acceptance from God, or good pleasure of God.

Salvation

According to all the traditional schools of jurisprudence, faith (*Iman*) ensures salvation. There are however differing views concerning the formal constituents of the act of faith. "For the Asharis it is centred on internal tacdi3[internal judgment of veracity], for the Maturidi-$anafis on the expressed profession of faith and the adherence of the heart, for the Mustazilis on the performance of the 'prescribed duties', for the $anbalis and the Wahhabis on the profession of faith and the performance of the basic duties." The common denominator of these various opinions is summed up in bearing witness that God is the Lord, L. Gardet states.

There are traditions in which Muhammad stated that "No one shall enter hell who has an atom of faith in his heart" or that "Hell will not welcome anyone who has in his heart an atom of faith" however these passages are interpreted in different ways. Those who consider performance as an integral part of faith such as 4h2arid2j2is, consider anyone who does a grave sin to be out of faith, while the majority of Sunnis who view works as merely the perfecting the faith, hold that a believing sinner will be punished with a temporary stay in hell. Still there is disagreement over the possibility of a believing sinner being forgiven immediately (e.g. As2h2saris) and in full rather than undergoing temporary punishment. (e.g. Maturidis)

Rationalization

Ibn al-Nafis dealt with Islamic eschatology in some depth in his *Theologus Autodidactus,* where he rationalized the Islamic view of eschatology using reason, science, and philosophy to explain the events that would occur according to Islamic eschatology. He presented his rational and scientific arguments in the form of Arabic fiction, hence his *Theologus Autodidactus* may be considered the earliest science fiction work.

Various signs of day of judgment.

The Minor Signs:

1. The disappearance of knowledge and the appearance of ignorance (Bukhari, Muslim, Ibn Majah, & Ahmad)
2. Books/writing will be widespread and (religious) knowledge will be low (Ahmad)
3. Adultery and fornication will be prevalent (The Prophet said that this has never happened without new diseases befalling the people, which their

ancestors had not known.) (Bukhari, Muslim, Ibn Majah, & Al-Haythami)

4. When fornication becomes widespread among your leaders (The Prophet said that this will happen when the people stop forbidding evil) (Ibn Majah)
5. Adultery and fornication will be performed in the open
6. The consumption of intoxicants will be widespread (Bukhari & Muslim)
7. Women will outnumber men......eventually 50:1 (Bukhari, Muslim, & Ahmad)
8. Killing, killing, killing (Bukhari, Muslim, Ibn Majah, & Ahmad)
9. The nations of the earth will gather against the Muslims like hungry people going to sit down to a table full of food. This will occur when the Muslims are large in number, but "like the foam of the sea".
10. People will beat others with whips like the tails of oxen (Muslim) ?The Slave Trade
11. The children will be filled with rage (at-Tabarani, al-Hakim)
12. Children will be foul (at-Tabarani, al-Hakim)
13. Women will conspire (at-Tabarani, al-Hakim)
14. Rain will be acidic or burning (at-Tabarani, al-Hakim)
15. Children of fornication will become widespread or prevalent (at-Tabarani, al-Hakim)
16. When a trust becomes a means of making a profit (at-Tirmidhi, Al-Haythami)

17. Gains will be shared out only among the rich, with no benefit to the poor (at-Tirmidhi)

18. Paying zakat becomes a burden and miserliness becomes widespread; charity is given reluctantly (at-Tirmidhi & Al-Haythami)

19. Miserliness will be thrown into the hearts of people (Bukhari)

20. Episodes of sudden death will become widespread (Ahmad)

21. There will be people who will be brethren in public but enemies in secret (He was asked how that would come about and replied, "Because they will have ulterior motives in their mutual dealings and at the same time will fear one another.") (at-Tirmidhi)

22. When a man obeys his wife and disobeys his mother; and treats his friend kindly while shunning his father (at-Tirmidhi)

23. When voices are raised in the mosques (at-Tirmidhi)

24. People will walk in the marketplace with their thighs exposed

25. Great distances will be traversed in short spans of time

26. The people of Iraq will receive no food and no money due to oppression by the Romans (Europeans) (Muslim)

27. People will hop between the clouds and the earth

28. A tribulation will enter everyones home (Ahmad)

29. The leader of a people will be the worst of them (at-Tirmidhi)

30. Leaders of people will be oppressors (Al-Haythami)
31. People will treat a man with respect out of fear for some evil he might do (at-Tirmidhi)
32. Men will begin to wear silk (at-Tirmidhi)
33. Female singers and musical instruments will become popular (at-Tirmidhi)
34. When singers become common (Al-Haythami)
35. People will dance late into the night
36. When the last ones of the Ummah begin to curse the first ones (at-Tirmidhi)
37. People will claim to follow the Qur'an but will reject hadith & sunnah (Abu Dawood)
38. People will believe in the stars (Al-Haythami)
39. People will reject al-Qadr (the Divine Decree of Destiny) (Al-Haythami)
40. Time will pass rapidly (Bukhari, Muslim, & Ahmad)
41. Good deeds will decrease (Bukhari)
42. Smog will appear over cities because of the evil that they are doing
43. People will be carrying on with their trade, but their will only be a few trustworthy persons
44. Wealth will increase so much so that if a man were given 10,000, he would not be content with it (Ahmad & Bukhari)
45. A man will pass by a grave and wish that he was in their place (Bukhari)
46. Earthquakes will increase (Bukhari & Muslim)

47. There will be attempts to make the deserts green

48. The appearance of false messengers (30 dajjals) (Bukhari)

49. Women will be naked in spite of being dressed, these women will be led astray & will lead others astray (Muslim)

50. The conquest of Constantinople by the Muslims (Ahmad)

51. The conquest of India by the Muslims, just prior to the return of Jesus, son of Mary (Ahmad, an-Nisa'i, at-Tabarani, al-Hakim)

52. When people begin to compete with others in the construction of taller buildings (Bukhari)

53. There will be a special greeting for the people of distinction (Ahmad)

54. The Euphrates will disclose a treasure (The Prophet said that whoever is present should not take anything from it) (Bukhari & Muslim)

55. Two large groups, adhering to the same religious teaching will fight each other with large numbers of casualties (Bukhari & Muslim)

56. Wild animals will be able to talk to humans (Ahmad)

57. A man will leave his home and his thigh or hip will tell him what is happening back at his home (Ahmad)

58. Years of deceit in which the truthful person will not be believed and the liar will be believed (Ahmad)

59. Bearing false witness will become widespread (Al-Haythami & Ahmad)

60. When men lie with men and women lie with women (Al-Haythami)

61. Trade will become so widespread that a woman will be forced to help her husband in business (Ahmad)

62. A woman will enter the workforce out of love for this world (Ahmad)

63. Arrogance will increase in the earth (at-Tabarani, al-Hakim)

64. Family ties will be cut (Ahmad)

65. There will be many women of child-bearing age who will no longer give birth.

66. There will be an abundance of food, much of which has no blessing in it.

67. People will refuse when offered food.

68. Men will begin to look like women and women will begin to look like men

The Major Signs:

Although they appear here in no particular order, it is important to point out that the Prophet said that these last, major signs will follow each other like pearls falling off of a necklace...

1. Masih ad-Dajjal (The AntiChrist)

2. The Mahdi

3. The appearance of Masih al-Isa (Jesus Christ)

4. Yajuj and Majuj (Gog and Magog)

5. The destruction of the Kabah and the recovery of its treasure

6. Emergence of the Beast

7. The smoke

8. Three major landslides (one in the East, one in the West, and one on the Arabian peninsula)
9. The wind will take the souls of the believers
10. The rising of the sun from the west
11. The fire will drive the people to their final gathering place
12. Three blasts of the trumpet (fear & terror, death, resurrection)

JESUS IN ISLAM

In Islam, Jesus is considered a prophet Messenger of God who had been sent to guide the People of Israel (*bani isra'il*) with a new scripture, the *Injil* (gospel). The Qur'an, believed by Muslims to be God's final revelation, mentions Jesus 25 times. It states that Jesus was born to Mary (Arabic: Maryam) as the result of virginal conception, a miraculous event which occurred by the decree of God (Arabic: Allah). To aid him in his quest, Jesus was given the ability to perform miracles, all by the permission of God. According to Islamic texts, Jesus was neither killed nor crucified, but rather he was raised alive up to heaven. The Qur'an narrates that he will return to Earth near the day of judgment to restore justice and defeat *al-Masih ad-Dajjal* (*lit.* "the false messiah", also known as the Antichrist). Like all prophets in Islam, Jesus is considered to have been a Muslim, as he preached for people to adopt the straight path in submission to God's will. Islam rejects that Jesus was God incarnate or the son of God, stating that he was a mortal man who, like other prophets, had been divinely chosen to spread God's message. Islamic texts forbid the association of partners with God (*shirk*), emphasizing the notion of God's divine oneness (*tawhid*). Numerous titles are given to Jesus in the Qur'an, such as *al-Masih* ("the messiah; the anointed one" i.e. by means of blessings), although it does not correspond with the meaning accrued in Christian belief.

Jesus is seen in Islam as a precursor to Muhammad, and is believed by Muslims to have foretold the latter's coming.

Life

Birth

The Qur'an describes virginal conception of Jesus by Mary, which is recounted throughout several passages in the Qur'an. According to the Qur'anic narrations, Mary had withdrawn into a temple and was visited by angel Gabriel (Arabic: *Jibreel*) to give the glad tidings of a holy son. The Qur'an states that God (Allah) sent the message through the angel Gabriel to Mary that God had honoured Mary among the women of all nations as she will give birth to a holy son, named Isa' (Jesus), the Messiah (translated Christ) and he (Jesus) will be a great prophet, to whom God will give the Injil (the original Gospel) and he (Jesus) will speak in infancy and maturity and will be a companion to the most righteous. When this good news was given to Mary, she asked the angel how she can have a baby when no man has touched (sexually) her. This same question of Mary is confirmed in the Bible. But, in the answer of this question, the Qur'an differs from the Christian faith; the Christians believe that the Holy Spirit impregnated Mary, but the Qur'an denies it and states that the reply of the angel to Mary was "Even though when God wants to create a matter, he merely wills (Kun-fa-yakun) it and the things come into being". So, the Qur'anic version is, Jesus was created from the act of God's will. The Qur'an compares this miraculous creation of Jesus with the creation of Adam where God created Adam by His act of will (kun-fa-yakun). According to the Qur'an, the same answer was given to the question of Zechariah (in Qur'an Zakariyah), when he asked how could his wife conceive a baby while she was old.

After delivering Jesus, Mary was overtaken by the pangs of childbirth, resting near the trunk of a palm tree. Jesus then addressed her from the cradle, to instruct her to shake the tree and obtain its fruits and also to allay Mary's fears of a scandal surrounding his conception. She then showed the new-born to her family, and in silencing immodest rumors he declared: "Lo, I am God's servant; God has given me the Book, and made me a Prophet. Blessed he has made me, wherever I may be; and He has enjoined me to pray, and to give alms, so long as I live and likewise to cherish my mother."

Other references in hadith are:

> "When any human being is born. Satan touches him at both sides of the body with his two fingers, except Jesus, the son of Mary, whom Satan tried to touch but failed, for he touched the placenta-cover instead."

> According to al-Tabari, this was due to the prayer of Mary's mother: "I seek refuge in you for her and her progeny from the accursed Satan."

Mission

According to Islamic texts, Jesus was divinely chosen to preach the message of monotheism and submission to the will of God to the Children of Israel (*bani isra'il*). Muslims believe that God revealed to Jesus a new scripture, the *Injil* (gospel), while also declaring the truth of the previous revelations – the Tawrat (Torah) and the Zabur (Psalms). It is unclear or unknown whether Jesus declared the truth of the other holy book of Islam at that time, the Suhuf Ibrahim. Descended 600 years after Jesus' life on earth, the Qur'an speaks favorably of the *Injil,* which it describes as a scripture that fills the hearts of its followers with meekness and pity. Some scholars such as Bart D. Ehrman unintentionally support the assertion made in the Qur'an that the original Biblical message has been distorted or corrupted (tahrif) over time since the New Testament Bible that exists today is not composed of the original writings and is highly unlikely to represent the original teachings of Jesus.

The Qur'an states that Jesus was aided by a group of disciples (*hawariyun*) who believed in Jesus' message, and termed themselves the *ansar* ("helpers") of God. Jesus is also depicted in Islam as having been given miracles as evidence of his prophetic mission. Such miracles, all performed by the leave of God, include: speaking while still in the cradle; breathing life into clay models of birds; curing a leper and a life-long blind man; raising the dead; and requesting the descent of a table from heaven upon which was a feast, upon petition of his disciples. Some Muslim accounts also relate that the Islamic prophet Yahya ibn Zakariyya (known otherwise as John the Baptist) traveled to Palestine and met Jesus at the Jordan river.

Ascension

Islamic texts categorically deny the crucifixion and death of Jesus at the hands of the Jews. The Qur'an states that the Jews sought to kill Jesus, but they did not kill or crucify him, although a likeness of it was shown to them. Tradionalists believe that Jesus was not crucified but instead, he was raised alive unto the heavens. This raising is understood by them to mean bodily ascension.

> "That they said (in boast), "We killed Christ Jesus the son of Mary, the Messenger of God";- but they killed him not, nor crucified him, but so it was made to appear to them, and those who differ therein are full of doubts, with no (certain) knowledge, but only conjecture to follow, for of a surety they killed him not:- Nay, God raised him up unto the himself; and God is Exalted in Power, Wise."

According to most Muslim traditions, Jesus was replaced by a double, one of the people that was about to crucify him; others suggest it was Simon of Cyrene, or one of the disciples such as Judas Iscariot. The crucifixion interpretation was rejected, and according to the *Encyclopedia of Islam*, there was unanimous agreement amongst the scholars in denying the crucifixion. Modern commentators such as M. Hayek interpret the verse to say that the crucifixion "seemed thus to them" [i.e. the Jews].

Second Coming

Traditional Muslims believe that Jesus will return at a time close to the end of the world. The Qur'anic verse they allude to as an indicator to Jesus' future return is as follows:

> "And (Jesus) shall be a Sign (for the coming of) the Hour (of Judgment): therefore have no doubt about the (Hour), but follow ye Me: this is a Straight Way."

According to Islamic tradition which describes this graphically, Jesus' descent will be in the midst of wars fought by the Mahdi (*lit.* "the rightly guided one"), known in Islamic eschatology as the redeemer of Islam, against the Antichrist (*al-Masikh ad-Dajjal,* "false messiah") and his followers. Jesus will descend at the point of a white arcade, east of Damascus, dressed in yellow robes – his head anointed. He will then join the Mahdi in his war against the Dajjal. Jesus, considered in Islam as a Muslim, will abide by the Islamic teachings. Eventually, Jesus will slay the Dajjal, and then everyone from the people of the book (*ahl al-kitab,* referring to Jews and Christians) will believe in him. Thus, there will be one community, that of Islam.

Sahih Bukhari Volume 3, Book 43, Number 656: Narrated Abu Huraira: Allah's Apostle said, "The Hour will not be established until the son of Mary (i.e. Jesus) descends amongst you as a just ruler, he will break the cross, kill the pigs, and abolish the Jizya tax. Money will be in abundance so that nobody will accept it (as charitable gifts).

After the death of the Mahdi, Jesus will assume leadership. This is a time associated in Islamic narrative with universal peace and justice. Islamic texts also allude to the appearance of Ya'juj and Ma'juj (known also as Gog and Magog), ancient tribes which will disperse and cause disturbance on earth. God, in response to Jesus' prayers, will kill them by sending a type of worm in the napes of their necks. Jesus' rule is said to be around forty years, after which he will die. Muslims will then perform the funeral prayer for him and then bury him in the city of Medina in a grave left vacant beside Muhammad, Abu Bakr, and Umar.

In Islamic Thought

Jesus is described by various means in the Qur'an. The most common reference to Jesus occurs in the form of "Ibn Maryam" (son of Mary), sometimes preceded with another title. Jesus is also recognised as a prophet (*nabi*) and messenger (*rasul*) of God. The terms *wadjih* ("worthy of esteem in this world and the next"), *mubarak* ("blessed", or "a source of benefit for others"), *`abd-Allah* (servant of God) are all used in the Qur'an in reference to Jesus.

Another title frequently mentioned is *al-Masih,* which translates to "the Messiah". This does not correspond to the Christian concept of Messiah, as Islam regards all prophets, including Jesus, to be mortal and without any share in divinity. Muslim exegetes explain the use of the word *masih* in the Qur'an as referring to Jesus' status as the one anointed by means of blessings and honors; or as the one who helped cure the sick, by anointing the eyes of the blind, for example. Qur'anic verses also employ the term "*kalimat allah*" (meaning the "word of God") as a descriptor of Jesus, which is interpreted as a reference to the creating word of God, uttered at the moment of Jesus' conception; or as recognition of Jesus' status as a messenger of God, speaking on God's behalf.

Theology

Islamic texts regard Jesus as a righteous messenger of God, and reject him as being God or the begotten Son of God.

This belief, that Jesus is God or Son of God according to Islam, is tantamount to *shirk,* or the association of partners with God; and thereby a rejection of God's divine oneness (*tawhid*). A verse from the Qur'an reads:

> "In blasphemy indeed are those that say that God is Christ the son of Mary. Say: "Who then hath the least power against God, if His will were to destroy Christ the son of Mary, his mother, and all every – one that is on the earth? For to God belongeth the dominion of the heavens and the earth, and all that is between. He createth what He pleaseth. For God hath power over all things."

The Christian doctrine of the Trinity is similarly rejected in Islam. Such notions of the divinity of Jesus, Muslims state, resulted from human interpolations of God's revelation. The Muslims give the evidence of this interpolations as they say even the Chrsitian scholars nowadays have discovered that the doctrine of trinity was an interpolation, so thus, the verse on trinity (I John, Chapter 5, Verse:7) in all modern versions of bible except KJV has been removed. Islam views Jesus as an ordinary human like all other prophets, who preached that salvation came through submission to God's will and worshiping God alone. Thus, Jesus is considered in Islam to have been a Muslim, as with all prophets in Islam.

Precursor to Muhammad

Muslims believe that Jesus was a precursor to Muhammad, and that he announced the latter's coming. They base this on a verse of the Qur'an wherein Jesus speaks of a messenger to appear after him named Ahmad. Islam associates Ahmad with Muhammad, both words deriving from the *h-m-d* triconsonantal root which refers to praiseworthiness. Muslims also assert that evidence of Jesus' pronouncement is present in the New Testament, citing the mention of the Paraclete whose coming is foretold in the

Gospel of John. Muslim commentators claim that the original Greek word used was *periklutos*, meaning famed, illustrious, or praiseworthy – rendered in Arabic as Ahmad; and that this was substituted by Christians with *parakletos*.

Ascetic Literature

Jesus is widely venerated in Muslim ascetic and mystic literature, such as in Muslim mystic Al-Ghazzali's *Ihya 'ulum ad-Din* ("The revival of the religious sciences"). These works lay stress upon Jesus' poverty, his preoccupation with worship, his detachment from worldly life and his miracles. Such depictions also include advice and sermons which are attributed to him. Later Sufic commentaries adapted material from Christian gospels which were consistent with their ascetic portrayal. Sufi philosopher Ibn Arabi described Jesus as "the seal of universal holiness" due to the quality of his faith and "because he holds in his hands the keys of living breath and because he is at present in a state of deprivation and journeying."

Ahmadiyya Views

Similar to mainstream Islamic views, the Ahmadiyya Movement consider Jesus was a mortal man, but go a step further to describe Jesus as a mortal man who died a natural death in India – as opposed to having been raised up alive to Heaven.

Although the view of Jesus having migrated to India had also been researched in the literature of independent historians predating the foundation of the movement, the Ahmadiyya Movement are the only religious organisation to adopt these views as a characteristic of their faith, although in independence to the early historians. The general notion of Jesus in India has also been discussed at length by modern western historians Grönbold and Klatt and publicized in several documentaries.

●●

6
Islamic Ethics

Islamic ethics, defined as "good character," historically took shape gradually from the 7th century and was finally established by the 11th century. It was eventually shaped as a successful amalgamation of the Qur'anic teachings, the teachings of the Sunnah of Muhammad, the precedents of Islamic jurists (see Sharia and Fiqh), the pre-Islamic Arabian tradition, and non-Arabic elements (including Persian and Greek ideas) embedded in or integrated with a generally Islamic structure. Although Muhammad's preaching produced a "radical change in moral values based on the sanctions of the new religion and the present religion, and fear of God and of the Last Judgment", the tribal practice of Arabs did not completely die out. Later Muslim scholars expanded the religious ethic of the Qur'an and Hadith in immense detail.

The foundational source in the gradual codification of Islamic ethics was the Muslim understanding and interpretations of the Qur'an and practices of Muhammad. Its meaning has always been in context of active submission to God (Arabic: Allah), performed by the community in unison. The motive force in Islamic ethics is the notion that every human being is called to "command the good and forbid the evil" in all spheres of life. Muslims understand the role of Muhammad as attempting to facilitate this submission. Another key factor in the field of Islamic ethics is the belief that mankind has been granted the faculty to discern God's will and to abide by it. This faculty most crucially involves reflecting over the meaning of existence, which, as John

Kelsay in the *Encyclopedia of Ethics* phrases, "ultimately points to the reality of God." Therefore, regardless of their environment, humans are believed to have a moral responsibility to submit to God's will and to follow Islam.

This natural inclination is, according to the Qur'an, subverted by mankind's focus on material success: such focus first presents itself as a need for basic survival or security, but then tends to manifest into a desire to become distinguished amongst one's peers. Ultimately, the focus on materialism, according to the Islamic texts, hampers with the innate reflection as described above, resulting in a state of *jahiliyya* or "heedlessness."

Muslims believe that Muhammad, like other prophets in Islam, was sent by God to remind human beings of their moral responsibility, and challenge those ideas in society which opposed submission to God. According to Kelsay, this challenge was directed against five main characteristics of pre-Islamic Arabia:

1. The division of Arabs into varying tribes (based upon blood and kinship). This categorization was confronted by the ideal of a unified community based upon Islamic piety, an "*ummah;*"

2. The acceptance of the worship of a multitude of deities besides Allah - a view challenged by strict Islamic monotheism, which dictates that Allah has no partner in worship nor any equal;

3. The trait of *muruwwa* (manliness), which Islam discouraged, instead emphasizing on the traits of humility and piety;

4. The focus on achieving fame or establishing a legacy, which was replaced by the concept that mankind would be called to account before God on the day of resurrection;

5. The reverence of and compliance with ancestral traditions, a practice challenged by Islam — which instead assigned primacy to submitting to God and following revelation.

These changes lay in the reorientation of society as regards to identityand life of the Muslim belief, world view, and the hierarchy of values. From the viewpoint of subsequent generations, this caused a great transformation in the society and moral order of life in the Arabian Peninsula. For Muhammad, although pre-Islamic Arabia exemplified "heedlessness," it was not entirely without merit. Muhammad approved and exhorted certain aspects of the Arab pre-Islamic tradition, such as the care for one's near kin, for widows, orphans, and others in need and for the establishment of justice. However, these values would be re-ordered in importance and placed in the context of strict monotheism.

Moral Commandments

The Qur'an defines and sets the standards of social and moral values for Muslims. S. A. Nigosian, Professor of religious studies at the University of Toronto, states that a lengthy passage in the Qur'an "represents the fullest statement of the code of behaviour every Muslim must follow". Nigosian and Ghamidi hold that these resemble the Ten Commandments in the Bible.

Early Reforms under Islam

Many reforms in human rights took place under Islam between 610 and 661, including the period of Muhammad's mission and the rule of the four immediate successors who established the Rashidun Caliphate. Historians generally agree that Muhammad preached against what he saw as the social evils of his day, and that Islamic social reforms in areas such as social security, family structure, slavery, and the rights of women and ethnic minorities improved on what was present in existing Arab society at the time. For example, according to Bernard Lewis, Islam "from the first denounced aristocratic privilege, rejected hierarchy, and adopted a formula of the career open to the talents." John Esposito sees Muhammad as a reformer who condemned practices of the pagan Arabs such as female infanticide, exploitation of the poor, usury, murder, false contracts, and theft. Bernard Lewis believes that the egalitarian nature of Islam "represented a very considerable advance on the practice of both the Greco-Roman and the ancient Persian world."

The Constitution of Medina, also known as the *Charter of Medina*, was drafted by Muhammad in 622. It constituted a formal agreement between Muhammad and all of the significant tribes and families of Yathrib (later known as Medina), including Muslims, Jews, and pagans. The document was drawn up with the explicit concern of bringing to an end the bitter inter tribal fighting between the clans of the Aws (Aus) and Khazraj within Medina. To this effect it instituted a number of rights and responsibilities for the Muslim, Jewish and pagan communities of Medina bringing them within the fold of one community-the Ummah. The Constitution established the security of the community, freedom of religion, the role of Medina as a haram or sacred place (barring all violence and weapons), the security of women, stable tribal relations within Medina, a tax system for supporting the community in time of conflict, parameters for exogenous political alliances, a system for granting protection of individuals, a judicial system for resolving disputes, and also regulated the paying of blood-wite (the payment between families or tribes for the slaying of an individual in lieu of lex talionis).

Muhammad made it the responsibility of the Islamic government to provide food and clothing, on a reasonable basis, to captives, regardless of their religion. If the prisoners were in the custody of a person, then the responsibility was on the individual. Lewis states that Islam brought two major changes to ancient slavery which were to have far-reaching consequences. "One of these was the presumption of freedom; the other, the ban on the enslavement of free persons except in strictly defined circumstances," Lewis continues. The position of the Arabian slave was "enormously improved": the Arabian slave "was now no longer merely a chattel but was also a human being with a certain religious and hence a social status and with certain quasi-legal rights."

Esposito states that reforms in women's rights affected marriage, divorce, and inheritance. Women were not accorded with such legal status in other cultures, including the West, until centuries later. *The Oxford Dictionary of Islam* states that the general improvement of the status of Arab women included prohibition of female infanticide and recognizing women's full personhood. "The dowry, previously regarded as a bride-price paid to the father, became a nuptial gift retained by the wife as part of her personal property." Under Islamic law, marriage was no longer viewed as a "status" but rather as a "contract", in which the woman's consent was imperative. "Women were given inheritance rights in a patriarchal society that had previously restricted inheritance to male relatives." Annemarie Schimmel states that "compared to the pre-Islamic position of women, Islamic legislation meant an enormous progress; the woman has the right, at least according to the letter of the law, to administer the wealth she has brought into the family or has earned by her own work." William Montgomery Watt states that Muhammad, in the historical context of his time, can be seen as a figure who testified on behalf of women's rights and improved things considerably. Watt explains: "At the time Islam began, the conditions of women were terrible - they had no right to own property, were supposed to be the property of the man, and if the man died everything went to his sons." Muhammad, however, by "instituting rights of property ownership, inheritance, education and divorce, gave women certain basic safeguards." Haddad and Esposito state that "Muhammad granted women rights and privileges in the sphere of family life, marriage, education, and economic endeavors, rights that help improve women's status in society."

Sociologist Robert Bellah (*Beyond belief*) argues that Islam in its seventh-century origins was, for its time and place, "remarkably modern...in the high degree of commitment, involvement, and participation expected from the rank-and-file members of the community." This because, he argues, that Islam emphasized on the equality of all Muslims, where leadership positions were open to all. Dale Eickelman writes that Bellah suggests "the early Islamic community placed a particular value on individuals, as opposed to collective or group responsibility."

Environmentalism

Perhaps due to resource scarcity in most Islamic nations, there was an emphasis on limited (and some claim also sustainable) use of natural capital, i.e. producing land. Traditions of haram and hima and early urban planning were expressions of strong social obligations to stay within carrying capacity and to preserve the natural environment as an obligation of khalifa or "stewardship".

Muhammad is considered a pioneer of environmentalism for his teachings on environmental preservation. His hadiths on agriculture and environmental philosophy were compiled in the "Book of Agriculture" of the *Sahih Bukhari*, which included the following saying:

> "There is none amongst the believers who plants a tree, or sows a seed, and then a bird, or a person, or an animal eats thereof, but it is regarded as having given a charitable gift [for which there is great recompense]."

Several such statements concerning the environment are also found in the Qur'an, such as the following:

> "And there is no animal in the earth nor bird that flies with its two wings, but that they are communities like yourselves."

The earliest known treatises dealing with environmentalism and environmental science, especially pollution, were Arabic medical treatises written by al-Kindi, Qusta ibn Luqa, al-Razi, Ibn Al-Jazzar, al-Tamimi, al-Masihi, Avicenna, Ali ibn Ridwan, Ibn Jumay, Isaac Israeli ben Solomon, Abd-el-latif, Ibn al-Quff, and Ibn al-Nafis. Their works covered a number of subjects related to pollution such as air pollution, water pollution, soil contamination, municipal solid waste mishandling, and environmental impact assessments of certain localities. Cordoba, Al-Andalus also had the first waste containers and waste disposal facilities for litter collection.

Humanism

Many medieval Muslim thinkers pursued humanistic, rational and scientific discourses in their search for knowledge, meaning and values. A wide range of Islamic writings on love poetry, history and philosophical theology show that medieval Islamic thought was open to the humanistic ideas of individualism, occasional secularism, skepticism and liberalism.

Certain aspects of Renaissance humanism has its roots in the medieval Islamic world, including the "art of *dictation,* called in Latin, *ars dictaminis,*" and "the humanist attitude toward classical language", in this case classical Arabic.

Democratic Participation

In the early Islamic Caliphate, the head of state, the Caliph, had a position based on the notion of a successor to Muhammad's political authority, who, according to Sunnis, were ideally elected by the people or their representatives. After the Rashidun Caliphs, later Caliphates during the Islamic Golden Age had a lesser degree of democratic participation, but since "no one was superior to anyone else except on the basis of piety and virtue" in Islam, and following the example of Muhammad, later Islamic rulers often held public consultations with the people in their affairs.

Electing or Appointing a Caliph

Fred Donner, in his book *The Early Islamic Conquests* (1981), argues that the standard Arabian practice during the early Caliphates was for the prominent men of a kinship group, or tribe, to gather after a leader's death and elect a leader from amongst themselves, although there was no specified procedure for this shura, or consultative assembly. Candidates were usually from the same lineage as the deceased leader, but they were not necessarily his sons. Capable men who would lead well were preferred over an ineffectual direct heir, as there was no basis in the majority Sunni view that the head of state or governor should be chosen based on lineage alone. Al-Mawardi has written that the caliph should be Qurayshi. Abu Bakr Al-Baqillani has said that the leader of the Muslims simply should be from the majority. Abu Hanifa an-Nu'man also wrote that the leader must come from the majority.

Majlis ash-Shura

Traditional Sunni Islamic lawyers agree that *shura*, loosely translated as 'consultation of the people', is a function of the caliphate. The Majlis ash-Shura advise the caliph. The importance of this is premised by the following verses of the Qur'an:

> "...those who answer the call of their Lord and establish the prayer, and who conduct their affairs by Shura. [are loved by God]"

"...consult them (the people) in their affairs. Then when you have taken a decision (from them), put your trust in Allah"

The majlis is also the means to elect a new caliph. Al-Mawardi has written that members of the majlis should satisfy three conditions: they must be just, they must have enough knowledge to distinguish a good caliph from a bad one, and must have sufficient wisdom and judgment to select the best caliph. Al-Mawardi also said in emergencies when there is no caliphate and no majlis, the people themselves should create a majlis, select a list of candidates for caliph, then the majlis should select from the list of candidates. Some modern interpretations of the role of the Majlis ash-Shura include those by Islamist author Sayyid Qutb and by Taqiuddin al-Nabhani, the founder of a transnational political movement devoted to the revival of the Caliphate. In an analysis of the shura chapter of the Qur'an, Qutb argued Islam requires only that the ruler consult with at least some of the ruled (usually the elite), within the general context of God-made laws that the ruler must execute. Taqiuddin al-Nabhani, writes that Shura is important and part of the "the ruling structure" of the Islamic caliphate, "but not one of its pillars," and may be neglected without the Caliphate's rule becoming unIslamic. Non-Muslims may serve in the majlis, though they may not vote or serve as an official.

Religious Freedom

Democratic religious pluralism and freedom of religion existed in classical Islamic Sharia law, as the religious laws and courts of other religions, including Christianity, Judaism and Hinduism, were usually accommodated within the Islamic legal framework, as seen in the early Caliphate, Al-Andalus, Indian subcontinent, and the Ottoman Millet system. In medieval Islamic societies, the *qadi* (Islamic judges) usually could not interfere in the matters of non-Muslims unless the parties voluntarily choose to be judged according to Islamic law, thus the *dhimmi* communities living in Islamic states usually had their own laws independent from the Sharia law, such as the Jews who would have their own *Halakha* courts.

Dhimmis were allowed to operate their own courts following their own legal systems in cases that did not involve other religious groups, or capital offences or threats to public order. However, in the Ottoman Empire of the 18th and 19th centuries dhimmis frequently attended the Muslim courts. This was not only when their appearance was compulsory (for example in cases brought against them by Muslims) but also in order to record property and business transactions within their own communities. Cases were taken out against Muslims, against other dhimmis and even against members of the dhimmi's own family. Dhimmis often took cases relating to marriages, divorces and inheritance cases to the Muslim courts so that these cases would be decided under shari'a law. Oaths sworn by dhimmis in the Muslim courts were sometimes the same as the oaths taken by Muslims, sometimes tailored to the dhimmis' beliefs.

Non-Muslims were allowed to engage in religious practices that was usually forbidden by Islamic law. For example, non-Muslims were allowed to consume alcohol and pork, both of which were forbidden to Muslims. In some cases, even religious practices which Muslims found repugnant were also allowed. One example was the Zoroastrian practice of incestuous "self-marriage" where a man could marry his mother, sister or daughter. According to the famous Islamic legal scholar Ibn Qayyim (1292-1350), non-Muslims had the right to engage in such religious practices even if it offended Muslims, under the conditions that such cases not be presented to Islamic Sharia courts and that these religious minorities believed that the practice in question is permissible according to their religion. This ruling was based on the precedent that the prophet Muhammad did not forbid such self-marriages among Zoroastrians despite coming in contact with them and having knowledge of their practices. Religious minorities were also free to do whatever they wished in their own homes, provided they did not publicly engage in illicit sexual activity in ways that could threaten public morals.

Freedom of Expression

Another reason the Islamic world flourished during the Middle Ages was an early emphasis on freedom of speech. This was first declared in the Rashidun Caliphate by the second Caliph, Umar, in the 7th century:

> "Only decide on the basis of proof, be kind to the weak so that they can express themselves freely and without fear, deal on an equal footing with litigants by trying to reconcile them."

Another such example can be found in a letter written by the fourth Caliph, Ali ibn Abi Talib to his governor of Egypt, Malik al-Ashtar. The Caliph advices his governor on dealings with the poor masses thus;

> "Out of your hours of work, fix a time for the complainants and for those who want to approach you with their grievances. During this time you should do no other work but hear them and pay attention to their complaints and grievances. For this purpose you must arrange public audience for them during this audience, for the sake of Allah, treat them with kindness, courtesy and respect. Do not let your army and police be in the audience hall at such times so that those who have grievances against your regime may speak to you freely, unreservedly and without fear." Nahjul Balaagha letter 53

Citizens of the Rashidun Caliphate were also free to criticize the Rashidun Caliphs, as the rule of law was binding on the head of state just as much as it was for the citizens. For example, there was an incident when Umar heard loud sounds from a drunkard inside a house. After knocking on the door and no one answered, Umar climbed over the roof and into the courtyard, where he saw the owner and criticised him for letting a drunkard into his house. In turn, the owner of the house criticised Umar for breaking the law by entering his house without permission. After Umar forgave him, the owner criticised him again, asking him who gave him the right to "forgive what God has condemned as a crime?" There were also numerous other situations where citizens insulted Caliph Umar, but he tolerated the insults and simply provided them explanations. Similar situations also occurred during the time of Caliph Ali. For example, there was an occasion when he was giving a *Khutbah* speech and a Kharijite rudely interrupted him with insulting language. Ali's companions urged that the man be punished but Ali declined on the grounds that his "right to freedom of speech must not be imperilled."

During the Abbasid Caliphate, freedom of speech was also declared by al-Hashimi, a cousin of Caliph al-Ma'mun, in the following letter to a non-Muslim he was attempting to convert using reason:

> "Bring forward all the arguments you wish and say whatever you please and speak your mind freely. Now that you are safe and free to say whatever you please appoint some arbitrator who will impartially judge between us and lean only towards the truth and be free from the empery of passion, and that arbitrator shall be Reason, whereby God makes us responsible for our own rewards and punishments. Herein I have dealt justly with you and have given you full security and am ready to accept whatever decision Reason may give for me or against me. For "There is no compulsion in religion" (Qur'an 2:256) and I have only invited you to accept our faith willingly and of your own accord and have pointed

out the hideousness of your present belief. Peace be with you and the blessings of God!"

According to George Makdisi and Hugh Goddard, "the idea of academic freedom" in universities was "modelled on Islamic custom" as practiced in the medieval Madrasah system from the 9th century. Islamic influence was "certainly discernible in the foundation of the first delibrately-planned university" in Europe, the University of Naples Federico II founded by Frederick II, Holy Roman Emperor in 1224.

Human Rights

In the field of human rights, early Islamic jurists introduced a number of advanced legal concepts which anticipated similar modern concepts in the field. These included the notions of the charitable trust and the trusteeship of property; the notion of brotherhood and social solidarity; the notions of human dignity and the dignity of labour; the notion of an ideal law; the condemnation of antisocial behaviour; the presumption of innocence; the notion of "bidding unto good" (assistance to those in distress); and the notions of sharing, caring, universalism, fair industrial relations, fair contract, commercial integrity, freedom from usury, women's rights, privacy, abuse of rights, juristic personality, individual freedom, equality before the law, legal representation, non-retroactivity, supremacy of the law, judicial independence, judicial impartiality, limited sovereignty, tolerance, and democratic participation. Many of these concepts were adopted in medieval Europe through contacts with Islamic Spain and the Emirate of Sicily, and through the Crusades and the Latin translations of the 12th century.

The concept of inalienable rights was found in early Islamic law and jurisprudence, which denied a ruler "the right to take away from his subjects certain rights which inhere in his or her person as a human being." Islamic rulers could not take away certain rights from their subjects on the basis that "they become rights by reason of the fact that they are given to a subject by a law and from a source which no ruler can question or alter." There is evidence that John Locke's formulation of inalienable rights and conditional rulership, which were present in Islamic law centuries earlier, may have also been influenced by Islamic law, through his attendance of lectures given by Edward Pococke, a professor of Islamic studies.

Early Islamic law recognised two sets of human rights. In addition to the category of civil rights and political rights (covered in the Universal Declaration of Human Rights), Islamic law also recognised an additional category: social, economic and cultural rights. This latter category was not recognised in the Western legal tradition until the International Covenant on Economic, Social and Cultural Rights in 1966. The right of privacy, which was not recognised in Western legal traditions until modern times, was recognised in Islamic law since the beginning of Islam. In terms of women's rights, women generally had more legal rights under Islamic law than they did under Western legal systems until the 19th and 20th centuries. For example, "French married women, unlike their Muslim sisters, suffered from restrictions on their legal capacity which were removed only in 1965." Noah Feldman, a Harvard University law professor, notes:

> As for sexism, the common law long denied married women any property rights or indeed legal personality apart from their husbands. When the British applied their law to Muslims in place of Shariah, as they did in some colonies, the result was to strip married women of the property that Islamic law had always granted them – hardly progress toward equality of the sexes.

In the *North Carolina Law Review* journal, Professor John Makdisi of the University of North Carolina School of Law writes in "The Islamic Origins of the Common Law" article:

> he manner in which an act was qualified as morally good or bad in the spiritual domain of Islamic religion was quite different from the manner in which that same act was qualified as legally valid or invalid in the temporal domain of Islamic law. Islamic law was secular, not canonical... Thus, it was a system focused on ensuring that an individual received justice, not that one be a good person.

Count Leon Ostorog, a French jurist, wrote the following on classical Islamic law in 1927:

> Those Eastern thinkers of the ninth century laid down, on the basis of their theology, the principle of the Rights of Man, in those very terms, comprehending the rights of individual liberty, and of inviolability of person and property; described the supreme power in Islam, or Califate, as based on a contract, implying conditions of capacity and performance, and subject to cancellation if the conditions under the contract were not fulfilled; elaborated a Law of War of which the humane, chivalrous prescriptions would have put to the blush certain belligerents in the Great War; expounded a doctrine of toleration of non-Moslem creeds so liberal that our West had to wait a thousand years before seeing equivalent principles adopted.

Some scholars have suggested that the idea of "a charter defining the duties of a sovereign toward his subjects, as well as subjects toward the sovereign", which led to the "genesis of European legal structures" and the development of the *Magna Carta,* may have been "brought back by Crusaders who were influenced by what they had learned in the Levant about the governing system" established by Saladin. It has also been suggested that "much of the West's understanding of liberalism in law, economics and society has roots in medieval Islam."

Another influence of Islamic law on European law was the presumption of innocence, which was introduced to Europe by King Louis IX of France soon after he returned from Palestine during the Crusades. Prior to this, European legal procedure consisted of either trial by combat or trial by ordeal. In contrast, Islamic law was based on the presumption of innocence from its beginning, as declared by the Caliph Umar in the 7th century. Other freedoms and rights recognised in the Islamic legal system based on the Qur'an since the 7th century, but not recognised in the Western world until much later, include "the rights to know, to choose belief and behaviour, to read and write, the right to power, and even the right to choose government."

Rule of Law

Islamic jurists anticipated the concept of the rule of law, the equal subjection of all classes to the ordinary law of the land, where no person is above the law and where officials and private citizens are under a duty to obey the same law. A Qadi (Islamic judge) was also not allowed to discriminate on the grounds of religion, race, colour, kinship or prejudice. There were also a number of cases where Caliphs had to appear before judges as they prepared to take their verdict. The following hadith established the principle of rule of law in relation to nepotism and accountability:

Narrated 'Aisha: The people of Quraish worried about the lady from Bani Makhzum who had committed theft. They asked, "Who will intercede for her with Allah's Apostle?" Some said, "No one dare to do so except Usama bin Zaid the beloved one to Allah's Apostle." When Usama spoke about that to Allah's Apostle Allah's Apostle said: "Do you try to intercede for somebody in a case connected with Allah's Prescribed Punishments?" Then he got up and delivered a sermon saying, "What destroyed the nations preceding you, was that if a noble amongst them stole, they would forgive him, and if a poor person amongst them stole, they would inflict Allah's Legal punishment on him. By Allah, if Fatima, the daughter of Muhammad stole, I would cut off her hand."

Various Islamic lawyers do however place multiple conditions, and stipulations e.g. the poor cannot be penalised for stealing out of poverty, before executing such a law, making it very difficult to reach such a stage. It is well known during a time of drought in the Rashidun caliphate period, capital punishments were suspended until the effects of the drought passed.

According to Noah Feldman, a law professor at Harvard University, the legal scholars and jurists who once upheld the rule of law were replaced by a law governed by the state due to the codification of Sharia by the Ottoman Empire in the early 19th century:

How the scholars lost their exalted status as keepers of the law is a complex story, but it can be summed up in the adage that partial reforms are sometimes worse than none at all. In the early 19th century, the Ottoman empire responded to military setbacks with an internal reform movement. The most important reform was the attempt to codify Shariah. This Westernizing process, foreign to the Islamic legal tradition, sought to transform Shariah from a body of doctrines and principles to be discovered by the human efforts of the scholars into a set of rules that could be looked up in a book.

Once the law existed in codified form, however, the law itself was able to replace the scholars as the source of authority. Codification took from the scholars their all-important claim to have the final say over the content of the law and transferred that power to the state.

Accountability of Rulers

Sunni Islamic lawyers have commented on when it is permissible to disobey, impeach or remove rulers in the

Caliphate. This is usually when the rulers are not meeting public responsibilities obliged upon them under Islam. Al-Mawardi said that if the rulers meet their Islamic responsibilities to the public, the people must obey their laws, but if they become either unjust or severely ineffective then the Caliph or ruler must be impeached via the Majlis ash-Shura. Similarly Al-Baghdadi believed that if the rulers do not uphold justice, the ummah via the majlis should give warning to them, and if unheeded then the Caliph can be impeached. Al-Juwayni argued that Islam is the goal of the ummah, so any ruler that deviates from this goal must be impeached. Al-Ghazali believed that oppression by a caliph is enough for impeachment. Rather than just relying on impeachment, Ibn Hajar al-Asqalani obliged rebellion upon the people if the caliph began to act with no regard for Islamic law. Ibn Hajar al-Asqalani said that to ignore such a situation is *haraam,* and those who cannot revolt inside the caliphate should launch a struggle from outside. Al-Asqalani used two ayahs from the Qur'an to justify this:

> "...And they (the sinners on qiyama) will say, 'Our Lord! We obeyed our leaders and our chiefs, and they misled us from the right path. Our Lord! Give them (the leaders) double the punishment you give us and curse them with a very great curse'..."

Islamic lawyers commented that when the rulers refuse to step down via successful impeachment through the Majlis, becoming dictators through the support of a corrupt army, if the majority agree they have the option to launch a revolution against them. Many noted that this option is only exercised after factoring in the potential cost of life.

Right of Revolution

According to scholar Bernard Lewis, the Qur'an and Sunnah have several points to make on governance regarding the right of revolution in Islam:

The Quran, for example, makes it clear that there is a duty of obedience: "Obey God, obey the Prophet, obey those who hold authority over you." And this is elaborated in a number of sayings attributed to Muhammad. But there are also sayings that put strict limits on the duty of obedience. Two dicta attributed to the Prophet and universally accepted as authentic are indicative. One says, "there is no obedience in sin"; in other words, if the ruler orders something contrary to the divine law, not only is there no duty of obedience, but there is a duty of disobedience. This is more than the right of revolution that appears in Western political thought. It is a duty of revolution, or at least of disobedience and opposition to authority. The other pronouncement, "do not obey a creature against his creator," again clearly limits the authority of the ruler, whatever form of ruler that may be.

Medical Ethics

The ethical standards of Muslim physicians was first laid down in the 9th century by Ishaq bin Ali Rahawi, who wrote the *Adab al-Tabib* (*Conduct of a Physician*), the first treatist dedicated to medical ethics. He regarded physicians as "guardians of souls and bodies", and wrote twenty chapters on various topics related to medical ethics, including:

- What the physician must avoid and beware of
- The manners of visitors
- The care of remedies by the physician
- The dignity of the medical profession
- The examination of physicians
- The removal of corruption among physicians

Drugs

The earliest known prohibition of illegal drugs occurred under Islamic law, which prohibited the use of Hashish, a preparation of cannabis, as a recreational drug. Classical jurists in medieval Islamic jurisprudence, however, accepted the use of the Hashish drug for medicinal and therapeutic purposes, and agreed that its "medical use, even if it leads to mental derangement, remains exempt" from punishment. In the 14th century, the Islamic scholar Az-Zarkashi spoke of "the permissibility of its use for medical purposes if it is established that it is beneficial."

According to Mary Lynn Mathre, with "this legal distinction between the intoxicant and the medical uses of cannabis, medieval Muslim theologians were far ahead of present-day American law."

Medical Peer Review

The first documented description of a peer review process is found in the *Ethics of the Physician* by Ishaq bin Alī al-Rahwi (854–931) of al-Raha, Syria, where the notes of a practising Islamic physician were reviewed by peers and the physician could face a lawsuit from a maltreated patient if the reviews were negative.

Neuroethics

Most ancient and medieval societies believed that mental illness was caused by either demonic possession or as punishment from a god, which led to a negative attitude towards mental illness in Judeo-Christian and Greco-Roman societies. On the other hand, Islamic neuroethics and neurotheology held a more sympathetic attitude towards the mentally ill, as exemplified in Sura 4:5 of the Qur'an:

> "Do not give your property which God assigned you to manage to the insane: but feed and cloth the insane with this property and tell splendid words to him."

This Quranic verse summarized Islam's attitudes towards the mentally ill, who were considered unfit to manage property but must be treated humanely and be kept under care by a guardian, according to Islamic law. This positive neuroethical understanding of mental health consequently led to the establishment of the first psychiatric hospitals in the medieval Islamic world from the 8th century, and an early scientific understanding of neuroscience and psychology by medieval Muslim physicians and psychologists, who discovered that mental disorders are caused by dysfunctions in the brain.

Military Ethics

The early Islamic treatises on international law from the 9th century onwards covered the application of Islamic ethics, Islamic economic jurisprudence and Islamic military jurisprudence to international law, and were concerned with a number of modern international law topics, including the law of treaties; the treatment of diplomats, hostages, refugees and prisoners of war; the right of asylum; conduct on the battlefield; protection of women, children and non-combatant civilians; contracts across the lines of battle; the use of poisonous weapons; and devastation of enemy territory.

The Islamic legal principles of international law were mainly based on Qur'an and the Sunnah of Muhammad, who gave various injunctions to his forces and adopted practices toward the conduct of war. The most important of these were summarized by Muhammad's successor and close companion, Abu Bakr, in the form of ten rules for the Muslim army:

> Stop, O people, that I may give you ten rules for your guidance in the battlefield. Do not commit treachery or deviate from the right path. You must not mutilate dead bodies. Neither kill a child, nor a woman, nor an aged man. Bring no harm to the trees, nor burn them with

fire, especially those which are fruitful. Slay not any of the enemy's flock, save for your food. You are likely to pass by people who have devoted their lives to monastic services; leave them alone.

Prisoners of War

After Sultan al-Kamil defeated the Franks during the Crusades, Oliverus Scholasticus praised the Islamic laws of war, commenting on how al-Kamil supplied the defeated Frankish army with food:

> "Who could doubt that such goodness, friendship and charity come from God? Men whose parents, sons and daughters, brothers and sisters, had died in agony at our hands, whose lands we took, whom we drove naked from their homes, revived us with their own food when we were dying of hunger and showered us with kindness even when we were in their power."

Peace and Justice

As in other Abrahamic religions, peace is a basic concept of Islam. The Arabic term "Islam" itself is usually translated as "submission"; submission of desires to the will of God. It comes from the term *aslama,* which means "to surrender" or "resign oneself". The Arabic word *salaam* ("peace") has the same root as the word *Islam*. One Islamic interpretation is that individual personal peace is attained by utterly submitting to Allah. The greeting "Salaam alaykum", favoured by Muslims, has the literal meaning "Peace be with you". Muhammad is reported to have said once, "Mankind are the dependents, or family of God, and the most beloved of them to God are those who are the most excellent to His dependents." "Not one of you believes until he loves for his brother what he loves for himself." Great Muslim scholars of prophetic tradition such as Ibn Hajar al-Asqalani and Sharafuddin al Nawawi have said that the words 'his brother' mean any person irrespective of faith.

Welfare

The concepts of welfare and pension were introduced in early Islamic law as forms of *Zakat* (charity), one of the Five Pillars of Islam, since the time of the Abbasid caliph Al-Mansur in the 8th century. The taxes (including *Zakat* and *Jizya*) collected in the treasury of an Islamic government was used to provide income for the needy, including the poor, elderly, orphans, widows, and the disabled. According to the Islamic jurist Al-Ghazali (Algazel, 1058-1111), the government was also expected to store up food supplies in every region in case a disaster or famine occurs. The Caliphate was thus one of the earliest welfare states. From the 9th century, funds from the treasury were also used towards the *Waqf* (charitable trusts), often for the purpose of building of Madrassahs and Bimaristan hospitals.

●●

7

Muhammad and Islam

Muhammad ibn 'Abdullah also spelled Muhammed or Mohammed) is the founder of the religion of Islam and is regarded by Muslims as a messenger and prophet of God, the greatest law-bearer in a series of Islamic prophets and by most Muslims the last prophet as taught by the Qur'an 33:40–40. Muslims thus consider him the restorer of an uncorrupted original monotheistic faith (*islam*) of Adam, Noah, Abraham, Moses, Jesus and other prophets. He was also active as a diplomat, merchant, philosopher, orator, legislator, reformer, military general, and, according to Muslim belief, an agent of divine action.

Born in 570 in the Arabian city of Mecca, he was orphaned at an early age and brought up under the care of his uncle Abu Talib. He later worked mostly as a merchant, as well as a shepherd, and was first married by age 25. Discontented with life in Mecca, he retreated to a cave in the surrounding mountains for meditation and reflection. According to Islamic beliefs it was here, at age 40, in the month of Ramadan, where he received his first revelation from God. Three years after this event Muhammad started preaching these revelations publicly, proclaiming that "God is One", that complete "surrender" to Him (lit. *islam*) is the only way (*din*) acceptable to God, and that he himself was a prophet and messenger of God, in the same vein as other Islamic prophets.

Muhammad gained few followers early on, and was met with hostility from some Meccan tribes; he and his followers were treated harshly. To escape persecution first Muhammad sent some of his followers to Abyssinia before he and his remaining followers in Mecca migrated to Medina (then known as Yathrib) in the year 622. This event, the Hijra, marks the beginning of the Islamic calendar, which is also known as the Hijri Calendar. In Medina, Muhammad united the conflicting tribes, and after eight years of fighting with the Meccan tribes, his followers, who by then had grown to ten thousand, conquered Mecca. In 632, a few months after returning to Medina from his Farewell pilgrimage, Muhammad fell ill and died. By the time of his death, most of the Arabian Peninsula had converted to Islam; and he united the tribes of Arabia into a single Muslim religious polity.

The revelations (or *Ayat*, lit. "Signs of God")—which Muhammad reported receiving until his death—form the verses of the Qur'an, regarded by Muslims as the "Word of God" and around which the religion is based. Besides the Qur'an, Muhammad's life (*sira*) and traditions (*sunnah*) are also upheld by Muslims. They discuss Muhammad and other prophets of Islam with reverence, adding the phrase *peace be upon him* whenever their names are mentioned. While conceptions of Muhammad in medieval Christendom and premodern times were largely negative, appraisals in modern history have been far less so. Besides this, his life and deeds have been debated by followers and opponents over the centuries. Mohamed is revered as a respected true prophet and Manifestation of God in the Baha'i Faith but Judaism and Christianity reject his prophethood.

Names and Appellations in the Qur'an

The name *Muhammad* means "Praiseworthy" and occurs four times in the Qur'an. The Qur'an addresses Muhammad in the second person not by his name but by the appellations prophet, messenger, servant of God (*'abd*), announcer (*bashir*), warner (*nathir*), reminder (*mudhakkir*), witness (*shahid*), bearer of good tidings (*mubashshir*), one who calls [unto God] (*da'i*) and the light-giving lamp (*siraj munir*). Muhammad is sometimes addressed by designations deriving from his state at the time of the address: thus he is referred to as the enwrapped (*al-muzzammil*) in Qur'an 73:1 and the shrouded (*al-muddaththir*) in Qur'an 74:1. In the Qur'an, believers are not to distinguish between the messengers of God and are to believe in all of them (Surah 2:285). God has caused some messengers to excel above others 2:253 and in Surah 33:40 He singles out Muhammad as the "Seal of the Prophets". The Qur'an also refers to Muhammad as *Ahmad* "more praiseworthy".

Sources for Muhammad's Life

Being a highly influential historical figure, Muhammad's life, deeds, and thoughts have been debated by followers and opponents over the centuries, which makes a biography of him difficult to write.

The Qur'an

Muslims regard the Qur'an as the primary source of knowledge about the historical Muhammad. The Qur'an has a few allusions to Muhammad's life. The Qur'an responds "constantly and often candidly to Muhammad's changing historical circumstances and contains a wealth of hidden data."

Early Biographies

Next in importance are the historical works by writers of the third and fourth century of the Muslim era. These include the traditional Muslim biographies of Muhammad and quotes attributed to him (the *sira* and *hadith* literature), which provide further information on Muhammad's life.

The earliest surviving written *sira* is Ibn Ishaq's *Life of God's Messenger* written ca. 767 (150 AH). The work is lost, but was used verbatim at great length by Ibn Hisham and Al-Tabari.

Another early source is the history of Muhammad's campaigns by al-Waqidi (death 207 of Muslim era), and the work of his secretary Ibn Sa'd al-Baghdadi (death 230 of Muslim era).

Many scholars accept the accuracy of the earliest biographies, though their accuracy is unascertainable. Recent studies have led scholars to distinguish between the traditions touching legal matters and the purely historical ones. In the former sphere, traditions could have been subject to invention while in the latter sphere, aside from exceptional cases, the material may have been only subject to "tendential shaping".

In addition, the hadith collections are accounts of the verbal and physical traditions of Muhammad that date from several generations after his death. Hadith compilations are records of the traditions or sayings of Muhammad. They might be defined as the biography of Muhammad perpetuated by the long memory of his community for their exemplification and obedience.

Western academics view the hadith collections with caution as accurate historical sources. Scholars such as Madelung do not reject the narrations which have been compiled in later periods, but judge them in the context of history and on the basis of their compatibility with the events and figures.

Finally, there are oral traditions. Although usually discounted by historians, oral tradition plays a major role in the Islamic understanding of Muhammad.

Non-Arabic sources

The earliest Greek source for Muhammed is the 9th century writer Theophanes. The earliest Syriac source is the 7th century John bar Penkaye.

Pre-Islamic Arabia

The Arabian Peninsula was largely arid and volcanic, making agriculture difficult except near oases or springs. The landscape was thus dotted with towns and cities, two prominent ones being Mecca and Medina. Medina was a large flourishing agricultural settlement, while Mecca was an important financial center for many surrounding tribes. Communal life was essential for survival in the desert conditions, as people needed support against the harsh environment and lifestyle. Tribal grouping was encouraged by the need to act as a unit, this unity being based on the bond of kinship by blood. Indigenous Arabs were either nomadic or sedentary (or bedouins), the former constantly travelling from one place to another seeking water and pasture for their flocks, while the latter settled and focused on trade and agriculture. Nomadic survival was also dependent on raiding caravans or oases, the nomads not viewing this as a crime.

In pre-Islamic Arabia, gods or goddesses were viewed as protectors of individual tribes, their spirits being associated with sacred trees, stones, springs and wells. As well as being the site of an annual pilgrimage, the Kaaba shrine in Mecca housed 360 idol statues of tribal patron deities. Aside from these gods, the Arabs shared a common belief in a supreme deity called Allah (literally "the god"), who was remote from their everyday concerns and thus not the object of cult or ritual. Three goddesses were associated with Allah as his daughters: Allat, Manat and al-'Uzzá. Monotheistic communities existed in Arabia, including Christians and Jews. Hanifs – native pre-Islamic Arab monotheists – are also sometimes listed alongside Jews and Christians in pre-Islamic Arabia, although their historicity is disputed amongst scholars. According to Muslim tradition, Muhammad himself was a Hanif and one of the descendants of Ishmael, son of Abraham.

Life

Life in Mecca

Muhammad was born and lived in Mecca for the first 52 years of his life (570–622) which was divided into two phases, that is before and after declaring the prophecy.

Childhood and Early Life

Muhammad was born in the month of Rabi' al-awwal in 570. He belonged to the Banu Hashim, one of the prominent families of Mecca, although it seems not to have been prosperous during Muhammad's early lifetime. Tradition places the year of Muhammad's birth as corresponding with the Year of the Elephant, which is named after the failed destruction of Mecca that year by the Aksumite king Abraha who had in his army a number of elephants. Recent scholarship has suggested alternative dates for this event, such as 568 or 569.

Muhammad's father, Abdullah, died almost six months before he was born. According to the tradition, soon after Muhammad's birth he was sent to live with a Bedouin family in the desert, as the desert-life was considered healthier for infants. Muhammad stayed with his foster-mother, Halimah bint Abi Dhuayb, and her husband until he was two years old. Some western scholars of Islam have rejected the historicity of this tradition. At the age of six Muhammad lost his mother Amina to illness and he became fully orphaned. He was subsequently brought up for two years under the guardianship of his paternal grandfather Abd al-Muttalib, of the Banu Hashim clan of the Quraysh tribe. When Muhammad was eight, his grandfather also died. He now came under the care of his uncle Abu Talib, the new leader of Banu Hashim. According to Watt, because of the general disregard of the guardians in taking care of weak members of the tribes in Mecca in sixth century, "Muhammad's guardians saw that he did not starve to death, but it was hard for them to do more for him, especially as the fortunes of the clan of Hashim seem to have been declining at that time."

While still in his teens, Muhammad accompanied his uncle on trading journeys to Syria gaining experience in the commercial trade, the only career open to Muhammad as an orphan. According to tradition, when Muhammad was either nine or twelve while accompanying the Meccans' caravan to Syria, he met a Christian monk or hermit named Bahira who is said to have foreseen Muhammed's career as a prophet of God.

Little is known of Muhammad during his later youth, and from the fragmentary information that is available, it is hard to separate history from legend. It is known that he became a merchant and "was involved in trade between the Indian ocean and the Mediterranean Sea." Due to his upright character he acquired the nickname "al-Amin", meaning "faithful, trustworthy" and was sought out as an impartial arbitrator. His reputation attracted a proposal from Khadijah, a forty-year-old widow in 595. Muhammad consented to the marriage, which by all accounts was a happy one.

Wives and Children

Muhammad's life is traditionally defined into two periods: pre-hijra (emigration) in Mecca (from 570 to 622), and post-hijra in Medina (from 622 until 632). Muhammad is said to have had thirteen wives or concubines (there are differing accounts on the status of some of them as wife or concubine) All but two of his marriages were contracted after the migration to Medina.

At the age of 25, Muhammad married Khadijah bint Khuwaylid. The marriage lasted for 25 years and was a happy one. Muhammad relied upon Khadija in many ways and did not enter into marriage with another woman during this marriage. After the death of Khadija, it was suggested to

Muhammad by Khawla bint Hakim that he should marry Sawda bint Zama, a Muslim widow, or Aisha, daughter of Um Ruman and Abu Bakr of Mecca. Muhammad is said to have asked her to arrange for him to marry both. Traditional sources dictate that Aisha was six or seven years old when betrothed to Muhammad but the marriage was not consummated until she was nine or ten years old. Later, Muhammad married additional wives, nine of whom survived him. Aisha, who became known as Muhammad's favourite wife in Sunni tradition, survived him by many decades and was instrumental in helping to bring together the scattered sayings of Muhammad that would form the Hadith literature for the Sunni branch of Islam.

After migration to Medina, Muhammad (who was now in his fifties) married several women. These marriages were contracted mostly for political or humanitarian reasons, these wives being either widows of Muslims who had been killed in the battles and had been left without a protector, or belonging to important families or clans whom it was necessary to honor and strengthen alliances.

Muhammad did his own household chores and helped with housework, such as preparing food, sewing clothes and repairing shoes. Muhammad is also said to have had accustomed his wives to dialogue; he listened to their advice, and the wives debated and even argued with him.

Khadijah is said to have borne Muhammad four daughters (Ruqayyah bint Muhammad, Umm Kulthum bint Muhammad, Zainab bint Muhammad, Fatimah Zahra) and two sons (Abd-Allah ibn Muhammad and Qasim ibn Muhammad) who both died in childhood. All except two of his daughters, Fatimah and Zainab, died before him. Shi'a scholars contend that Fatimah was Muhammad's only daughter. Maria al-Qibtiyya bore him a son named Ibrahim ibn Muhammad, but the child died when he was two years old.

Muhammad's descendants through Fatimah are known as *sharifs, syeds* or *sayyids*. These are honorific titles in Arabic, *sharif* meaning 'noble' and *sayed* or *sayyid* meaning 'lord' or 'sir'. As Muhammad's only descendants, they are respected by both Sunni and Shi'a, though the Shi'as place much more emphasis and value on their distinction.

Beginnings of the Qur'an

At some point Muhammad adopted the practice of meditating alone for several weeks every year in a cave on Mount Hira near Mecca. Islamic tradition holds that during one of his visits to Mount Hira, the angel Gabriel appeared to him in the year 610 and commanded Muhammad to recite the following verses:

Proclaim! (or read!) in the name of thy Lord and Cherisher, Who created- Created man, out of a (mere) clot of congealed blood: Proclaim! And thy Lord is Most Bountiful,- He Who taught (the use of) the pen,- Taught man that which he knew not.(Qur'an 96:1-5)

According to some traditions, upon receiving his first revelations Muhammad was deeply distressed. When returned home, Muhammad was consoled and reassured by his wife, Khadijah and her Christian cousin, Waraqah ibn Nawfal. Shia tradition maintains that Muhammad was neither surprised nor frightened at the appearance of Gabriel but rather welcomed him as if he had been expecting him. The initial revelation was followed by a pause of three years during which Muhammad gave himself up further to prayers and spiritual practices. When the revelations resumed he was reassured and commanded to begin preaching: Your lord has not forsaken you nor does he hate (Qur'an 93:1-11).

According to Welch these revelations were accompanied by mysterious seizures, and the reports are unlikely to have been forged by later Muslims. Muhammad was confident that he could distinguish his own thoughts from these messages. According to the Qur'an, one of the main roles of Muhammad is to warn the unbelievers of their eschatological punishment (Qur'an 38:70, Qur'an 6:19). Sometimes the Qur'an does not explicitly refer to the Judgment day but provides examples from the history of some extinct communities and warns Muhammad's contemporaries of similar calamities (Qur'an 41:13–16). Muhammad is not only a warner to those who reject God's revelation, but also a bearer of good news for those who abandon evil, listen to the divine word and serve God. Muhammad's mission also involves preaching monotheism: The Qur'an demands Muhammad to proclaim and praise the name of his Lord and instructs him not to worship idols apart from God or associate other deities with God.

The key themes of the early Qur'anic verses included the responsibility of man towards his creator; the resurrection of dead, God's final judgment followed by vivid descriptions of the tortures in hell and pleasures in Paradise; and the signs of God in all aspects of life. Religious duties required of the believers at this time were few: belief in God, asking for forgiveness of sins, offering frequent prayers, assisting others particularly those in need, rejecting cheating and the love of wealth (considered to be significant in the commercial life of Mecca), being chaste and not to kill newborn girls.

Opposition

According to Muslim tradition, Muhammad's wife Khadija was the first to believe he was a prophet. She was soon followed by Muhammad's ten-year-old cousin Ali ibn Abi Talib, close friend Abu Bakr, and adopted son Zaid. Around 613, Muhammad began his public preaching (Qur'an 26:214). Most Meccans ignored him and mocked him, while a few others became his followers. There were three main groups of early converts to Islam: younger brothers and sons of great merchants; people who had fallen out of the first rank in their tribe or failed to attain it; and the weak, mostly unprotected foreigners.

According to Ibn Sad, the opposition in Mecca started when Muhammad delivered verses that condemned idol worship and the Meccan forefathers who engaged in polytheism. However, the Qur'anic exegesis maintains that it began as soon as Muhammad started public preaching. As the number of followers increased, he became a threat to the local tribes and the rulers of the city, whose wealth rested upon the Kaaba, the focal point of Meccan religious life, which Muhammad threatened to overthrow. Muhammad's denunciation of the Meccan traditional religion was especially offensive to his own tribe, the Quraysh, as they were the guardians of the Ka'aba. The powerful merchants tried to convince Muhammad to abandon his preaching by offering him admission into the inner circle of merchants, and establishing his position therein by an advantageous marriage. However, he refused.

Tradition records at great length the persecution and ill-treatment of Muhammad and his followers. Sumayyah bint Khabbab, a slave of Abu Jahl and a prominent Meccan leader, is famous as the first martyr of Islam, having been killed with a spear by her master when she refused to give up her faith. Bilal, another Muslim slave, was tortured by Umayyah ibn Khalaf who placed a heavy rock on his chest to force his conversion. Apart from insults, Muhammad was protected from physical harm as he belonged to the Banu Hashim clan.

In 615, some of Muhammad's followers emigrated to the Ethiopian Aksumite Empire and founded a small colony there under the protection of the Christian Ethiopian emperor Achama ibn Abjar.

An early hadith known as "The Story of the Cranes" was propagated by two Islamic scholars, Ibn Kathir al

Dimashqi and Ibn Hijir al Masri, where the former has strengthened it and the latter called it fabricated. The hadith describes Muhammad's involvement at the time of migration in an episode which historian William Muir called the "Satanic Verses." The account holds that Muhammad pronounced a verse acknowledging the existence of three Meccan goddesses considered to be the daughters of Allah, praising them, and appealing for their intercession. According to this account, Muhammad later retracted the verses at the behest of Gabriel. Islamic scholars have weakened the hadith and have denied the historicity of the incident as early as the tenth century. In any event, relations between the Muslims and their pagan fellow-tribesmen were already deteriorated and worsening.

In 617 the leaders of Makhzum and Banu Abd-Shams, two important Quraysh clans, declared a public boycott against Banu Hashim, their commercial rival, to pressurize it into withdrawing its protection of Muhammad. The boycott lasted three years but eventually collapsed as it failed in its objective.

Sunnah

The Sunnah represents the actions and sayings of Muhammad (preserved in reports known as Hadith), and covers a broad array of activities and beliefs ranging from religious rituals, personal hygiene, burial of the dead to the mystical questions involving the love between humans and God. The Sunnah is considered a model of emulation for pious Muslims and has to a great degree influenced the Muslim culture. The greeting that Muhammad taught Muslims to offer each other, "may peace be upon you" is used by Muslims throughout the world. Many details of major Islamic rituals such as daily prayers, the fasting and the annual pilgrimage are only found in the Sunnah and not the Qur'an.

The Sunnah also played a major role in the development of the Islamic sciences. It contributed much to the development of Islamic law, particularly from the end of the first Islamic century. Muslim mystics, known as sufis, who were seeking for the inner meaning of the Qur'an and the inner nature of Muhammad, viewed the prophet of Islam not only as a prophet but also as a perfect saint. Sufi orders trace their chain of spiritual descent back to Muhammad.

Isra and Mi'raj

Islamic tradition relates that in 620, Muhammad experienced the *Isra and Mi'raj*, a miraculous journey said to have occurred with the angel Gabriel in one night. In the first part of the journey, the *Isra*, he is said to have travelled from Mecca to "the farthest mosque" (in Arabic: *masjid al-aqsa*), which Muslims usually identify with the Al-Aqsa Mosque in Jerusalem. In the second part, the *Mi'raj*, Muhammad is said to have toured heaven and hell, and spoken with earlier prophets, such as Abraham, Moses, and Jesus. Ibn Ishâq, author of the first biography of Muhammad, presents this event as a spiritual experience whereas later historians like Al-Tabari and Ibn Kathir present it as a physical journey.

When he was transported to Heaven, he reported seeing an angel with *"70,000 heads, each head having 70,000 mouths, each mouth having 70,000 tongues, each tongue speaking 70,000 languages; and every one involved in singing God's (Allah's) praises."* After calculation this would mean the angel spoke 24 quintillion (2.401 x 10) languages for the praise of Allah.

Some western scholars of Islam hold that the oldest Muslim tradition identified the journey as one traveled through the heavens from the sacred enclosure at Mecca to the celestial *al-Baytu l-Masmur*; but later tradition identified Muhammad's journey from Mecca to Jerusalem.

Hijra

Migration to Medina

A delegation consisting of the representatives of the twelve important clans of Medina, invited Muhammad as a neutral outsider to Medina to serve as chief arbitrator for the entire community. There was fighting in Yathrib mainly involving its Arab and Jewish inhabitants for around a hundred years before 620. The recurring slaughters and disagreements over the resulting claims, especially after the Battle of Bu'ath in which all clans were involved, made it obvious to them that the tribal conceptions of blood-feud and an eye for an eye were no longer workable unless there was one man with authority to adjudicate in disputed cases. The delegation from Medina pledged themselves and their fellow-citizens to accept Muhammad into their community and physically protect him as one of themselves.

Muhammad instructed his followers to emigrate to Medina until virtually all his followers left Mecca. Being alarmed at the departure of Muslims, according to the tradition, the Meccans plotted to assassinate Muhammad. With the help of Ali, Muhammad fooled the Meccans who were watching him, and secretly slipped away from the town with Abu Bakr. By 622, Muhammad emigrated to Medina, a large agricultural oasis. Those who migrated from Mecca along with Muhammad became known as *muhajirun* (emigrants).

Establishment of a New Polity

Among the first things Muhammad did in order to settle down the longstanding grievances among the tribes of Medina was drafting a document known as the Constitution of Medina, "establishing a kind of alliance or federation" among the eight Medinan tribes and Muslim emigrants from Mecca, which specified the rights and duties of all citizens and the relationship of the different communities in Medina (including that of the Muslim community to other communities, specifically the Jews and other "Peoples of the Book"). The community defined in the Constitution of Medina, *Ummah,* had a religious outlook but was also shaped by practical considerations and substantially preserved the legal forms of the old Arab tribes. It effectively established the first Islamic state.

The first group of pagan converts to Islam in Medina were the clans who had not produced great leaders for themselves but had suffered from warlike leaders from other clans. This was followed by the general acceptance of Islam by the pagan population of Medina, apart from some exceptions. According to Ibn Ishaq, this was influenced by the conversion of Sa'd ibn Mu'adh (a prominent Medinan leader) to Islam. Those Medinans who converted to Islam and helped the Muslim emigrants find shelter became known as the *ansar* (supporters). Then Muhammad instituted brotherhood between the emigrants and the supporters and he chose Ali as his own brother.

Beginning of Armed Conflict

Following the emigration, the Meccans seized the properties of the Muslim emigrants in Mecca. Economically uprooted and with no available profession, the Muslim migrants turned to raiding Meccan caravans as an act of war, deliberately initiating armed conflict between the Muslims and Mecca. Muhammad delivered Qur'anic verses permitting the Muslims to fight the Meccans (see Qur'an 22:39–40). These attacks pressured Mecca by interfering with trade, and allowed the Muslims to acquire wealth, power and prestige while working towards their ultimate goal of inducing Mecca's submission to the new faith. In March of 624, Muhammad led some three hundred warriors in a raid on a Meccan merchant caravan. The Muslims set an ambush for them at Badr. Aware of the plan, the Meccan caravan eluded the Muslims. Meanwhile, a force from Mecca was sent to protect the caravan, continuing forward to confront the Muslims upon hearing that the caravan was safe. The Battle of Badr began in March of 624. Though outnumbered more than three to one, the Muslims won the battle, killing at least forty-five Meccans with only fourteen Muslims dead. They also succeeded in killing many Meccan leaders, including Abu Jahl. Seventy prisoners had been acquired, many of whom were soon ransomed in return for wealth or freed. Muhammad and his followers saw in the victory a confirmation of their faith. The Qur'anic verses of this period, unlike the Meccan ones, dealt with practical problems of government and issues like the distribution of spoils.

The victory strengthened Muhammad's position in Medina and dispelled earlier doubts among his followers. As a result the opposition to him became less vocal. Pagans who had not yet converted were very bitter about the advance of Islam. Two persons, Asma bint Marwan and Abu 'Afak had composed verses taunting and insulting the Muslims. They were killed by persons belonging to their own or related clans , but nothing was said and no blood-feud followed.

Muhammad expelled from Medina the Banu Qaynuqa, one of three main Jewish tribes. Following the Battle of Badr, Muhammad also made mutual-aid alliances with a number of Bedouin tribes to protect his community from attacks from the northern part of Hijaz.

Conflict with Mecca

The attack at Badr committed Muhammad to total war with Meccans, who were now anxious to avenge their defeat. To maintain their economic prosperity, the Meccans needed to restore their prestige, which had been lost at Badr. In the ensuing months, Muhammad led expeditions on tribes allied with Mecca and sent out a raid on a Meccan caravan. Abu Sufyan subsequently gathered an army of three thousand men and set out for an attack on Medina.

A scout alerted Muhammad of the Meccan army's presence and numbers a day later. The next morning, at the Muslim conference of war, there was dispute over how best to repel the Meccans. Muhammad and many senior figures suggested that it would be safer to fight within Medina and take advantage of its heavily fortified strongholds. Younger Muslims argued that the Meccans were destroying their crops, and that huddling in the strongholds would destroy Muslim prestige. Muhammad eventually conceded to the wishes of the latter, and readied the Muslim force for battle. Thus, Muhammad led his force outside to the mountain of Uhud (where the Meccans had camped) and fought the Battle of Uhud on March 23. Although the Muslim army had the best of the early encounters, indiscipline on the part of strategically placed archers led to a Muslim defeat, with 75 Muslims killed including Hamza, Muhammad's uncle and one of the best known martyrs in the Muslim tradition. The Meccans did not pursue the Muslims further, but marched back to Mecca declaring victory. They were not entirely successful, however, as they had failed to achieve their aim of completely destroying the Muslims. The Muslims buried the dead, and returned to Medina that evening. Questions accumulated as to the reasons for the loss, and Muhammad subsequently delivered Qur'anic verses which indicated that their defeat was partly a punishment for disobedience and partly a test for steadfastness.

Abu Sufyan now directed his efforts towards another attack on Medina. He attracted the support of nomadic tribes to the north and east of Medina, using propaganda about Muhammad's weakness, promises of booty, memories of the prestige of the Quraysh and use of bribes. Muhammad's policy was now to prevent alliances against him as much as he could. Whenever alliances of tribesmen against Medina were formed, he sent out an expedition to break them up. When Muhammad heard of men massing with hostile intentions against Medina, he reacted with severity. One example is the assassination of Ka'b ibn al-Ashraf, a chieftain of the Jewish tribe of Banu Nadir who had gone to Mecca and written poems that helped rouse the Meccans' grief, anger and desire for revenge after the Battle of Badr. Around a year later, Muhammad expelled the Banu Nadir from Medina. Muhammad's attempts to prevent formation of a confederation against him were unsuccessful, though he was able to increase his own forces and stop many potential tribes from joining his enemies.

Siege of Medina

With the help of the exiled Banu Nadir, the Quraysh military leader Abu Sufyan had mustered a force of 10,000 men. Muhammad prepared a force of about 3000 men and adopted a new form of defense unknown in Arabia at that time: the Muslims dug a trench wherever Medina lay open to cavalry attack. The idea is credited to a Persian convert to Islam, Salman the Persian. The siege of Medina began on March 31 627 and lasted for two weeks. Abu Sufyan's troops were unprepared for the fortifications they were confronted with, and after an ineffectual siege lasting several weeks, the coalition decided to go home. The Qur'an discusses this battle in verses Qur'an 33:9-33:27. During the battle, the Jewish tribe of Banu Qurayza, located at the south of Medina, had entered into negotiations with Meccan forces to revolt against Muhammad. Although they were swayed by suggestions that Muhammad was sure to be overwhelmed, they desired reassurance in case the confederacy was unable to destroy him. No agreement was reached after the prolonged negotiations, in part due to sabotage attempts by Muhammad's scouts. After the coalition's retreat, the Muslims accused the Banu Qurayza of treachery and besieged them in their forts for 25 days. The Banu Qurayza eventually surrendered and all the men, apart from a few who converted to Islam, were beheaded, while the women and children were enslaved. In the siege of Medina, the Meccans exerted their utmost strength towards the destruction of the Muslim community. Their failure resulted in a significant loss of prestige; their trade with Syria was gone. Following the Battle of the Trench,

Muhammad made two expeditions to the north which ended without any fighting. While returning from one of these, an accusation of adultery was made against Aisha, Muhammad's wife. Aisha was exonerated from the accusations when Muhammad announced that he had received a revelation confirming Aisha's innocence and directing that charges of adultery be supported by four eyewitnesses.

Truce of Hudaybiyyah

Although Muhammad had already delivered Qur'anic verses commanding the Hajj, the Muslims had not performed it due to the enmity of the Quraysh. In the month of Shawwal 628, Muhammad ordered his followers to obtain sacrificial animals and to make preparations for a pilgrimage (*umrah*) to Mecca, saying that God had promised him the fulfillment of this goal in a vision where he was shaving his head after the completion of the Hajj. Upon hearing of the approaching 1,400 Muslims, the Quraysh sent out a force of 200 cavalry to halt them. Muhammad evaded them by taking a more difficult route, thereby reaching al-Hudaybiyya, just outside of Mecca. According to Watt, although Muhammad's decision to make the pilgrimage was based on his dream, he was at the same time demonstrating to the pagan Meccans that Islam does not threaten the prestige of their sanctuary, and that Islam was an Arabian religion.

Negotiations commenced with emissaries going to and from Mecca. While these continued, rumors spread that one of the Muslim negotiators, Uthman bin al-Affan, had been killed by the Quraysh. Muhammad responded by calling upon the pilgrims to make a pledge not to flee (or to stick with Muhammad, whatever decision he made) if the situation descended into war with Mecca. This pledge became known as the "Pledge of Acceptance" or the "Pledge under the Tree." News of Uthman's safety, however, allowed for negotiations to continue, and a treaty scheduled to last ten years was eventually signed between the Muslims and Quraysh. The main points of the treaty included the cessation of hostilities; the deferral of Muhammad's pilgrimage to the following year; and an agreement to send back any Meccan who had gone to Medina without the permission of their protector.

Many Muslims were not satisfied with the terms of the treaty. However, the Qur'anic sura "Al-Fath" (The Victory) (Qur'an 48:1-29) assured the Muslims that the expedition from which they were now returning must be considered a victorious one. It was only later that Muhammad's followers would realise the benefit behind this treaty. According to Welch, these benefits included the inducing of the Meccans to recognise Muhammad as an equal; a cessation of military activity posing well for the future; and gaining the admiration of Meccans who were impressed by the incorporation of the pilgrimage rituals.

After signing the truce, Muhammad made an expedition against the Jewish oasis of Khaybar, known as the Battle of Khaybar. This was possibly due to it housing the Banu Nadir, who were inciting hostilities against Muhammad, or to regain some prestige to deflect from what appeared to some Muslims as the inconclusive result of the truce of Hudaybiyya. According to Muslim tradition, Muhammad also sent letters to many rulers of the world, asking them to convert to Islam. Hence he sent messengers (with letters) to Heraclius of the Byzantine Empire (the eastern Roman Empire), Khosrau of Persia, the chief of Yemen and to some others. In the years following the truce of Hudaybiyya, Muhammad sent his forces against the Arabs on Transjordanian Byzantine soil in the Battle of Mu'tah, in which the Muslims were defeated.

Final Years

Conquest of Mecca

The truce of Hudaybiyyah had been enforced for two years. The tribe of Banu Khuza'a had good relations with

Muhammad, whereas their enemies, the Banu Bakr, had an alliance with the Meccans. A clan of the Bakr made a night raid against the Khuza'a, killing a few of them. The Meccans helped the Banu Bakr with weapons and, according to some sources, a few Meccans also took part in the fighting. After this event, Muhammad sent a message to Mecca with three conditions, asking them to accept one of them. These were that either the Meccans paid blood money for those slain among the Khuza'ah tribe; or, that they should disavow themselves of the Banu Bakr; or, that they should declare the truce of Hudaybiyyah null.

The Meccans replied that they would accept only the last condition. However, soon they realized their mistake and sent Abu Sufyan to renew the Hudaybiyyah treaty, but now his request was declined by Muhammad.

Muhammad began to prepare for a campaign. In 630, Muhammad marched on Mecca with an enormous force, said to number more than ten thousand men. With minimal casualties, Muhammad took control of Mecca. He declared an amnesty for past offences, except for ten men and women who had mocked and ridiculed him in songs and verses. Some of these were later pardoned. Most Meccans converted to Islam and Muhammad subsequently destroyed all the statues of Arabian gods in and around the Kaaba. The Qur'an discusses the conquest of Mecca.

Conquest of Arabia

Soon after the conquest of Mecca, Muhammad was alarmed by a military threat from the confederate tribes of Hawazin who were collecting an army twice the size of Muhammad's. The Banu Hawazin were old enemies of the Meccans. They were joined by the Banu Thaqif (inhabiting the city of Ta'if) who adopted an anti-Meccan policy due to the decline of the prestige of Meccans. Muhammad defeated the Hawazin and Thaqif tribes in the Battle of Hunayn.

In the same year, Muhammad made the expedition of Tabuk against northern Arabia because of their previous defeat at the Battle of Mu'tah as well as reports of the hostile attitude adopted against Muslims. Although Muhammad did not make contact with hostile forces at Tabuk, he received the submission of some local chiefs of the region.

A year after the Battle of Tabuk, the Banu Thaqif sent emissaries to Medina to surrender to Muhammad and adopt Islam. Many bedouins submitted to Muhammad in order to be safe against his attacks and to benefit from the booties of the wars. However, the bedouins were alien to the system of Islam and wanted to maintain their independence, their established code of virtue and their ancestral traditions. Muhammad thus required of them a military and political agreement according to which they "acknowledge the suzerainty of Medina, to refrain from attack on the Muslims and their allies, and to pay the Zakat, the Muslim religious levy."

Last Years in Mecca

Muhammad's wife Khadijah and his uncle Abu Talib both died in 619, the year thus being known as the "year of sorrow." With the death of Abu Talib, the leadership of the Banu Hashim clan was passed to Abu Lahab, an inveterate enemy of Muhammad. Soon afterwards, Abu Lahab withdrew the clan's protection from Muhammad. This placed Muhammad in danger of death since the withdrawal of clan protection implied that the blood revenge for his killing would not be exacted. Muhammad then visited Ta'if, another important city in Arabia, and tried to find a protector for himself there, but his effort failed and further brought him into physical danger. Muhammad was forced to return to Mecca. A Meccan man named Mut'im b. Adi (and the protection of the tribe of Banu Nawfal) made it possible for him safely to re-enter his native city.

Many people were visiting Mecca on business or as pilgrims to the Kaaba. Muhammad took this opportunity to look for a new home for himself and his followers. After several unsuccessful negotiations, he found hope with some men from Yathrib (later called Medina). The Arab population of Yathrib were familiar with monotheism because a Jewish community existed there. Converts to Islam came from nearly all Arab tribes in Medina, such that by June of the subsequent year there were seventy-five Muslims coming to Mecca for pilgrimage and to meet Muhammad. Meeting him secretly by night, the group made what was known as the *"Second Pledge of al-`Aqaba"*, or the *"Pledge of War"* Following the pledges at Aqabah, Muhammad encouraged his followers to emigrate to Yathrib. As with the migration to Abyssinia, the Quraysh attempted to stop the emigration. However, almost all Muslims managed to leave.

Farewell Pilgrimage and Death

At the end of the tenth year after the migration to Medina, Muhammad carried through his first truly Islamic pilgrimage, thereby teaching his followers the rites of the annual Great Pilgrimage (Hajj).

After completing the pilgrimage, Muhammad delivered a famous speech known as The Farewell Sermon. In this sermon, Muhammad advised his followers not to follow certain pre-Islamic customs such as adding intercalary months to align the lunar calendar with the solar calendar. Muhammad abolished all old blood feuds and disputes based on the former tribal system and asked for all old pledges to be returned as implications of the creation of the new Islamic community. Commenting on the vulnerability of women in his society, Muhammed asked his male followers to "Be good to women; for they are powerless captives (awan) in your households. You took them in God's trust and legitimated your sexual relations with the Word of God, so come to your senses people, and hear my words ...". He also told them that they were entitled to discipline their wives but should do so with kindness. Muhammad also addressed the issue of inheritance by forbidding false claims of paternity or of a client relationship to the deceased and also forbidding his followers to leave their wealth to a testamentary heir. He also upheld the sacredness of four lunar months in each year. According to Sunni tafsir, the following Qur'anic verse was delivered in this incident: "Today I have perfected your religion, and completed my favours for you and chosen Islam as a religion for you."(Qur'an 5:3) According to Shia tafsir, it refers to appointment of Ali ibn Abi Talib at the pond of Khumm as Muhammad's successor, this occurring a few days later when Muslims were returning from Mecca to Medina.

A few months after the farewell pilgrimage, Muhammad fell ill and suffered for several days with head pain and weakness. He died on Monday, June 8, 632, in Medina, at the age of 63. With his head resting on Aisha's lap he murmured his final words soon after asking her to dispose of his last worldly goods, which were seven coins:

> Rather, God on High and paradise.
>
> —Muhammad

He is buried where he died, which was in Aisha's house and is now housed within the Mosque of the Prophet in the city of Medina. Next to Muhammad's tomb, there is another empty tomb that Muslims believe awaits Jesus.

Aftermath

Muhammad united the tribes of Arabia into a singular Arab Muslim religious polity in the last years of his life. With Muhammad's death, disagreement broke out over who would succeed him as leader of the Muslim community. Umar ibn al-Khattab, a prominent companion of Muhammad, nominated

Abu Bakr, Muhammad's friend and collaborator. Others added their support and Abu Bakr was made the first caliph. This choice was disputed by some of Muhammad's companions, who held that Ali ibn Abi Talib, his cousin and son-in-law, had been designated the successor by Muhammad at Ghadir Khumm. Abu Bakr's immediate task was to make an expedition against the Byzantine (or Eastern Roman Empire) forces because of the previous defeat, although he first had to put down a rebellion by Arab tribes in an episode referred to by later Muslim historians as the Ridda wars, or "Wars of Apostasy".

The pre-Islamic Middle East was dominated by the Byzantine and Sassanian empires. The Roman-Persian Wars between the two had devastated the inhabitants, making the empires unpopular amongst local tribes. Furthermore, most Christian Churches in the lands to be conquered by Muslims such as Nestorians, Monophysites, Jacobites and Copts were under pressure from the Christian Orthodoxy who deemed them heretics. Within only a decade, Muslims conquered Mesopotamia and Persia, Roman Syria and Roman Egypt. and established the Rashidun empire.

Early Reforms under Islam

According to William Montgomery Watt, for Muhammad, religion was not a private and individual matter but rather "the total response of his personality to the total situation in which he found himself. He was responding [not only]... to the religious and intellectual aspects of the situation but also to the economic, social, and political pressures to which contemporary Mecca was subject." Bernard Lewis says that there are two important political traditions in Islam – one that views Muhammad as a statesman in Medina, and another that views him as a rebel in Mecca. He sees Islam itself as a type of revolution that greatly changed the societies into which the new religion was brought.

Historians generally agree that Islamic social reforms in areas such as social security, family structure, slavery and the rights of women and children improved on the status quo of Arab society. For example, according to Lewis, Islam "from the first denounced aristocratic privilege, rejected hierarchy, and adopted a formula of the career open to the talents". Muhammad's message transformed the society and moral order of life in the Arabian Peninsula through reorientation of society as regards to identity, world view, and the hierarchy of values. Economic reforms addressed the plight of the poor, which was becoming an issue in pre-Islamic Mecca. The Qur'an requires payment of an alms tax (zakat) for the benefit of the poor, and as Muhammad's position grew in power he demanded that those tribes who wanted to ally with him implement the zakat in particular.

Slaves

The Qur'an considers emancipation of a slave to be a highly meritorious deed, or as a condition of repentance for many sins. Therefore Muhammad was the owner of slaves, whom he bought usually to free, including concubines (although this claim is disputed), a wetnurse, and one slave he bought, freed and adopted as his son (Zayd).

Legacy

Muslim Views

Following the attestation to the oneness of God, the belief in Muhammad's prophethood is the main aspect of the Islamic faith. Every Muslim proclaims in the *Shahadah* that "I testify that there is no God but Allah, and I testify that Muhammad is a messenger of Allah". The Shahadah is the basic creed or tenet of Islam. Ideally, it is the first words a newborn will hear, and children are taught as soon as they are able to understand it and it will be recited when they die. Muslims must repeat the shahadah in the call to prayer (*adhan*) and the prayer itself. Non-Muslims wishing to convert to Islam are required to recite the creed.

Muslims have traditionally expressed love and veneration for Muhammad. Stories of Muhammad's life, his intercession and of his miracles (particularly "Splitting of the moon") have permeated popular Muslim thought and poetry. The Qur'an refers to Muhammad as "a mercy (*rahmat*) to the worlds" (Qur'an 21:107). The association of rain with mercy in Oriental countries has led to imagining Muhammad as a rain cloud dispensing blessings and stretching over lands, reviving the dead hearts, just as rain revives the seemingly dead earth (see, for example, the Sindhi poem of Shah sAbd al-Latif). Muhammad's birthday is celebrated as a major feast throughout the Islamic world, excluding Wahhabi-dominated Saudi Arabia where these public celebrations are discouraged. Muslims experience Muhammad as a living reality, believing in his ongoing significance to human beings as well as animals and plants. When Muslims say or write the name of Muhammad or any other prophet in Islam, they usually follow it with *Peace be upon him* (Arabic: *sallAllahu `alayhi wa sallam*) like "Muhammad (Peace be upon him)".

According to the Qur'an, Muhammad is only the last of a series of Prophets sent by Allah for the benefit of mankind, and thus commands Muslims to make no distinction between them and to surrender to one God Allah. Qur'an 10:37–37 states that "...it (the Qur'an) is a confirmation of (revelations) that went before it, and a fuller explanation of the Book - wherein there is no doubt - from The Lord of the Worlds.". Similarly Qur'an 46:12–12 states "...And before this was the book of Moses, as a guide and a mercy. And this Book confirms (it)...", while Qur'an 2:136–136 commands the believers of Islam to "Say: we believe in God and that which is revealed unto us, and that which was revealed unto Abraham and Ishmael and Isaac and Jacob and the tribes, and that which Moses and Jesus received, and which the prophets received from their Lord. We make no distinction between any of them, and unto Him we have surrendered."

Historian Denis Gril believes that the Qur'an does not overtly describe Muhammad performing miracles, and the supreme miracle of Muhammad is finally identified with the Qur'an itself. However, Muslim tradition credits Muhammad with several supernatural events. For example, many Muslim commentators and some Western scholars have interpreted the Surah 54:1-2 as referring to Muhammad splitting the Moon in view of the Quraysh when they began persecuting his followers.

Other Views

European and Western Views

The learned circles of Middle Ages Europe - primarily Latin-literate scholars - had fairly extensive, concrete biographical knowledge about the life of Muhammad, though they interpreted that information through a Christian religious lens that viewed Muhammad as a charlatan driven by ambition and eagerness for power, and who seduced the Saracens into his submission under a religious guise. Popular European literature of the time lacked even this knowledge, and portrayed Muhammad as though he were worshipped by Muslims in the manner of an idol or a heathen god. Some medieval Christians believed he died in 666, alluding to the number of the beast, instead of his actual death date in 632; others changed his name from Muhammad to Mahound, the "devil incarnate". Bernard Lewis writes "The development of the concept of Mahound started with considering Muhammad as a kind of demon or false god worshipped with Apollyon and Termagant in an unholy trinity." A later medieval work, *Livre dou Tresor* represents Muhammad as a former monk and cardinal. Dante's *Divine Comedy* (Canto XXVIII), puts Muhammad, together with Ali, in Hell "among the sowers of discord and the schismatics, being lacerated by devils again and again."

After the reformation, Muhammad was no longer viewed by Christians as a god or idol, but as a cunning, ambitious, and self-seeking impostor. Guillaume Postel was among the first to present a more positive view of Muhammad. Boulainvilliers described Muhammad as a gifted political leader and a just lawmaker. Gottfried Leibniz praised Muhammad because "he did not deviate from the natural religion". Thomas Carlyle defines Muhammed as "A silent great soul, one of that who cannot but be earnest" . Edward Gibbon in his book *The History of the Decline and Fall of the Roman Empire* observes that "the good sense of Mohammad despised the pomp of royalty." Friedrich Martin von Bodenstedt (1851) described Muhammad as "an ominous destroyer and a prophet of murder." Later Western works, many of which, from the 18th century onward, distanced themselves from the polemical histories of earlier Christian authors. These more historically-oriented treatments, which generally reject the prophethood of Muhammad, are coloured by the Western philosophical and theological framework of their authors. Many of these studies reflect much historical research, and most pay more attention to human, social, economic, and political factors than to religious, theological, and spiritual matters..

It was not until the latter part of the 20th century that Western authors combined rigorous scholarship as understood in the modern West with empathy toward the subject at hand and, especially, awareness of the religious and spiritual realities involved in the study of the life of the founder of a major world religion. According to Watt and Richard Bell, recent writers have generally dismissed the idea that Muhammad deliberately deceived his followers, arguing that Muhammad "was absolutely sincere and acted in complete good faith". Watt says that sincerity does not directly imply correctness:

In contemporary terms, Muhammad might have mistaken his own subconscious for divine revelation. Watt and Lewis argue that viewing Muhammad as a self-seeking impostor makes it impossible to understand the development of Islam. Welch holds that Muhammad was able to be so influential and successful because of his firm belief in his vocation. Muhammad's readiness to endure hardship for his cause when there seemed to be no rational basis for hope shows his sincerity.

Other Religious Traditions

- Bahá'ís venerate Muhammad as one of a number of prophets or "Manifestations of God", but consider his teachings to have been superseded by those of Bahá'u'lláh, the founder of the Bahai faith.
- Muhammad is regarded as one of the Saints of Ecclesia Gnostica Catholica.
- The Church of Jesus Christ of Latter-day Saints does not regard Muhammad as a prophet, nor accept the Qur'an as a book of scripture. However, they do respect Muhammad as one who taught moral truths which can enlighten nations and bring a higher level of understanding to individuals.
- Guru Nanak, a founder of Sikhism, viewed Muhammad as an agent of the Hindu supreme being Brahma.

●●

8
Tawhid and Termagant

Tawhid is the concept of monotheism in Islam. It holds God (Allah) is one and unique (*ahad*).

The Qur'an asserts the existence of a single and absolute truth that transcends the world; a unique, independent and indivisible being, who is independent of the entire creation. The indivisibility of God implies the indivisibility of God's sovereignty which, in turn, leads to the concept of a just, moral and coherent universe, as opposed to an existential and moral chaos. Similarly, the Qur'an rejects the duality of God arguing that both good and evil generate from God's creative act and asserting that the evil forces have no power to create anything. Islamic theology rejects the doctrine of the Trinity where "the one God exists in three Persons and one substance, Father, Son, and Holy Spirit" as believed in mainstream Christianity and professed in the Nicene Creed. God in Islam is a universal god, rather than a local, tribal or parochial one—is an absolute, who integrates all affirmative values and brooks no evil.

Tawhid constitutes the foremost article of the Muslim profession. The first part of the Shahada is the declaration of belief in the oneness of God. To attribute divinity to a created entity is the only unpardonable sin mentioned in the Qur'an. Muslims believe that the entirety of the Islamic teaching rests on the principle of Tawhid. There is an uncompromising monotheism at the heart of the Islamic beliefs which distinguishes Islam from some other major religions.

Islamic intellectual history can be understood as a gradual unfolding of the manner in which successive generations of believers have understood the meaning and implications of professing God's Unity. Islamic scholars have different approaches toward understanding it. Islamic theology, jurisprudence, philosophy, Sufism, even to some degree the Islamic understanding of natural sciences, all seek to explain at some level the principle of tawhid.

Tawhid in the Qur'an

The Qur'an is the main information source for understanding the oneness of God in Islam. All Muslim authorities maintain that a true understanding of God is impossible unless he introduces himself due to the fact that God is beyond the range of human vision and senses. Therefore God tells people who he is by speaking through the prophet. According to this view the fundamental message of all of the prophets is "There is no god worthy of worship but Allah."

The Qur'an asserts the existence of a single, absolute truth that transcends the world; a unique being who is independent of the creation; a real being indivisible into hypostatic entities or incarnated manifestation. According to the Qur'an:

> "Say (O Muhammad): "He is Allâh, (the) One, The Self-Sufficient Master, He begets not, nor was He begotten; And there is none co-equal or comparable unto Him." (Sura 112:1-4)

> "Thy Lord is self-sufficient, full of Mercy: if it were His will, He could destroy you, and in your place appoint whom He will as your successors, even as He raised you up from the posterity of other people."(Sura 6:133)

According to Vincent J. Cornall, the Qur'an also provides a monist image of God by describing the reality as a unified whole, with God being a single concept that would describe or ascribe all existing things:"He is the First and the Last, the Evident and the Immanent: and He has full knowledge of all things."(Sura 57:3)" Some Muslims have however vigorously criticised interpretations that would lead to a monist view of God for what they see as blurring the distinction between the creator and the creature, and its incompatibility with the genuine and absolute monotheism of Islam.

The Qur'anic passages Sura 34:20-24, Sura 35:40 and Sura 46:4 provide a basic understanding of the serious nature and consequences of assigning partners or equals to God, a sin known in Islam as *Shirk*. God will forgive any sin except a person who dies while committing Shirk. The verse 34:20-24 rejects the idea of duality of God by arguing that both good and evil generate from God's creative act and that the evil forces have no creative power.

The Qur'an relates the story of Abraham in order to provide an example of an intellectual quest for understanding God as the Cause of Causes: Related in verses 6:75-79, Abraham moves progressively from worshipping the stars, the moon, and the sun to acknowledging God as the sole cause of the heavenly phenomena.

In order to explain the complexity of unity of God and of the divine nature, the Qur'an uses 99 terms referred to as "Excellent Names of Allah" (Sura 77:180). Aside from the supreme name "Allah" and the neologism *al-Rahman* (referring to the divine beneficence that creates and maintains the universe), other names may be shared by both God and human beings. According to the Islamic teachings, the latter is meant to serve as a reminder of God's immanence rather than being a sign of one's divinity or alternatively imposing a limitation on God's transcendent nature. Attribution of divinity to a created entity, *shirk,* is considered as a denial of the truth of God and thus a major sin.

Discerning Unity of God

Discerning unity of God in the multiplicity of created things has been one of the key problems of Islamic theology. Vincent J. Cornell, a scholar of Islamic studies quotes the following statement from Ali:

To know God is to know his oneness. To say that God is one has four meanings: two of them are false and two are correct. As for the two meaning that are false, one is that a person should say "God is one" and be thinking of number and counting. This is false because that which has no second cannot enter into the category of number. Do you not see that those who say that God is a third of a trinity fall into this infidelity? Another meaning is to say, "So-and-So is one of his people," namely, a species of this genus or a member of this species. This meaning is also false when applied to God, because it implies likening something to God, whereas God is above all likeness. As to the two meaning that are correct when applied to God, one is that it should be said that "God is one" in the sense that there is no likeness to him among things. Another is to say that "God is one" in the sense that there is no multiplicity or division conceivable in Him, neither outwardly, nor in the mind, nor in the imagination. God alone possesses such a unity.

Arguments for the Oneness of God

Theological Arguments

Theologians usually use reason and deduction to prove existence, unity and oneness of the God. They use teleological argument for the existence of God as a creator based on perceived evidence of order, purpose, design, or direction—or some combination of these—in nature. Teleology is the supposition that there is purpose or directive principle in the works and processes of nature. The arguments are thereby circular and thus invalid from a syllogistic point of view.

Another way which is used frequently by theologians is Reductio ad absurdum. They use it instead of positive arguments as a more efficient way to reject the idea of opponents. Quran has also used this way in several cases.

God as the Cause of Causes

Against the polytheism of pre-Islamic Arabia, the Qur'an argued that the knowledge of God as the creator of everything rules out the possibility of lesser gods since these beings must be themselves created. For the Qur'an, God is an immanent and transcendent deity who actively creates, maintains and destroys the universe. The reality of God as the ultimate cause of things is however veiled from human understanding because of the secondary causes and contingent realities of things in the world. Thus the belief in the oneness of God is equated in the Qur'an with the "belief in the unseen" (Sura 2:3).

The Qur'an summarizes its task in making this "unseen", to a greater or lesser degree "seen" so that the belief in the existence of God becomes a Master-Truth rather than an unreasonable belief. The Qur'an states that the God's signals are so near and yet so far, demanding its students to listen to what it has to say with humility (Sura 50:33, Sura 50:37). The Qur'an aims to draw attention to certain obvious facts, turning them into "reminders" of God instead of providing lengthy "theological" proofs for the existence and unity of God.

Ash'ari theologians rejected cause and effect in essence, but accepting it as something that facilitates humankind's investigation and comprehension of natural processes. These medieval scholars argued that the nature was composed of uniform atoms that were "re-created" at every instant by God. The laws of nature were only the customary sequence of apparent causes (customs of God), the ultimate cause of each accident being God himself.

God as the Necessary Existent

An ontological argument for the existence of God was first proposed by Avicenna (965-1037) in the *Metaphysics* section of *The Book of Healing* which is known as Contingency and necessity argument(*Imakan wa Wujub*).

Avicenna initiated a full-fledged inquiry into the question of being, in which he distinguished between essence (*Mahiat*) and existence (*Wujud*). He argued that the fact of existence can not be inferred from or accounted for by the essence of existing things and that form and matter by themselves cannot interact and originate the movement of the universe or the progressive actualization of existing things. Existence must, therefore, be due to an agent-cause that necessitates, imparts, gives, or adds existence to an essence. To do so, the cause must be an existing thing and coexist with its effect.

This was the first attempt at using the method of a priori proof, which utilizes intuition and reason alone. Avicenna's proof of God's existence is unique in that it can be classified as both a cosmological argument and an ontological argument. "It is ontological insofar as 'necessary existence' in intellect is the first basis for arguing for a Necessary Existent". The proof is also "cosmological insofar as most of it is taken up with arguing that contingent existents cannot stand alone and must end up in a Necessary Existent." Another argument Avicenna presented for God's existence was the problem of the mind-body dichotomy.

According to Avicenna, the universe consists of a chain of actual beings, each giving existence to the one below it and responsible for the existence of the rest of the chain below. Because an actual infinite is deemed impossible by Avicenna, this chain as a whole must terminate in a being that is wholly simple and one, whose essence is its very existence, and therefore is self-sufficient and not in need of something else to give it existence. Because its existence is not contingent on or necessitated by something else but is necessary and eternal in itself, it satisfies the condition of being the necessitating cause of the entire chain that constitutes the eternal world of contingent existing things. Thus his ontological system rests on the conception of God as the *Wajib al-Wujud* (necessary existent). There is a gradual multiplication of beings through a timeless emanation from God as a result of his self-knowledge.

Indivisibility of God's Sovereignty

The Qur'an argues that there can be no multiple sources of divine sovereignty since "behold, each god would have taken away what [each] had created, And some would have Lorded it over others!" The Qur'an argues that the stability and order prevailing throughout the universe shows that it was created and is being administered by only one God (Sura 28:70-72). Verses 27:60-64 for example read:

And who other than Him created the heavens and the earth and sent down for you water from the sky, whereby We cause to grow lush orchards - for it is not up to you to cause their trees to grow! Is there any other god besides God? Yet, these are the people who ascribe partners to Him!

And who other than Him made the earth a firm abode [for you], and set rivers traversing through it, and put firm mountains therein and sealed off one sea from the other? Is there any other god besides God? Indeed, most of them do not know!

And who other than Him responds to the distressed one when he calls Him and He relieves him of the distress and Who has made you [mankind] His viceregents on earth? Is there any other god besides God? - little do you reflect!

And who other than Him guides you in the darkness of the land and the sea? And who sends forth winds heralding

His mercy [rain]? Is there any other god besides God? Far exalted be He above what they associate with Him!

And who other than Him brings forth His creation and then re-creates it? And who gives you sustenance from the heaven and the earth? Is there any other god besides God? Say [O Muhammad!]: Bring your proof if you are right [in associating others with God]

The Qur'an in verse 21:22 states: "If there were numerous gods instead of one, [the heavens and the earth] would be in a sorry state". Later Muslim theologians elaborated on this verse saying that the existence of at least two gods would inevitably arise between them, at one time or another, a conflict of wills. Since two contrary wills could not possibly be realized at the same time, one of them must admit himself powerless in that particular instance. On the other hand, a powerless being can not by definition be a god. Therefore the possibility of having more than one god is ruled out.

Other Arguments

The Qur'an argues that human beings have an instinctive distaste for polytheism: At times of crisis, for example, even the idolaters forget the false deities and call upon the one true God for help. As soon as they are relieved from the danger, they however start associating other beings with God (Sura 29:65).

Next, the Qur'an argues that polytheism takes away from human dignity: God has honored human beings and given them charge of the physical world, and yet they disgrace their position in the world by worshipping what they carve out with their own hands.

Lastly, the Qur'an argues that monotheism is a not a later discovery made by the human race, but rather there is the combined evidence of the prophetic call for monotheism throughout human history starting from Adam. The Qur'an suggests several causes for deviation from monotheism to polytheism: Great temporal power, regarded by the holder and his subjects as 'absolute' — may lead the holder to think that he is God-like; such claims were commonly forced upon, and accepted by, those who were subject to the ruler. Also, certain natural phenomena (such as the sun, the moon and the stars) inspire feelings of awe, wonder or admiration that could lead some to regard these celestial bodies as deities. Another reason for deviation from monotheism is when one becomes a slave to his or her base desires and passions. In seeking to always satisfy the desires, he or she may commit a kind of polytheism.

Atheism

The Qur'anic verse 45:24 is sometimes cited as a Qur'anic argument against atheism. The verse reads: "And they say, 'This worldly life of ours is all there is — we die and we live, and nothing but time destroys us.' But they have no knowledge of it; they are only speculating."

Interpretations

Understanding of the meaning of Tawhid is one of the most controversial issues among Muslims. Islamic scholars have different approaches toward understanding it, comprising textualistic approach, theological approach, philosophical approach and Sufism and Irfani approach. These different approaches lead to different and in some cases opposite understanding of the issue.

Textualistic Approach

The Textualistists or literalists by reason of their conception of the divine Attributes, came to represent the divinity as a complex of names and qualifications alongside the divine essence itself. The attitude of the literalists is that

God possesses hands and face, as seated on a Throne, etc. This is due to the verses in the Quran which state such. For the Textualists, these are all real phenomena about God, which must be seen and understood as such.

Theological Viewpoints

Certain theologians use the term Tawhid in a much broader meaning to denote the totality of discussion of God, his existence and his various attributes. Others go yet further and use the term to ultimately represent the totality of the "principles of religion". In its current usage, the expressions "Tawhid" or "knowledge of Tawhid" are sometimes used as an equivalent for the whole Kalam, the Islamic theology.

Mu'tazili School

The Mu'tazilis liked to call themselves the *men of the tawhid* (ahl al-tawhid). In Maqalat al-Islamiyin, Abu al-Hasan al-Ash'ari describes the Mu'tazilite conception of the tawhid as follows:

God is unique, nothing is like him; he is neither body, nor individual, nor substance, nor accident. He is beyond time. He cannot dwell in a place or within a being; he is not the object of any creatural attribute or qualification. He is neither conditioned nor determined, neither engendered nor engendering. He is beyond the perception of the senses. The eyes cannot see him, observation cannot attain him, the imagination cannot comprehend him. He is a thing, but he is not like other things; he is omniscient, all-powerful, but his omniscience and his all-mightiness cannot be compared to anything created. He created the world without any pre-established archetype and without an auxiliary.

According to Henry Corbin, the result of this interpretation is the negation of the divine attributes, the affirmation of the created Quran, and the denial of all possibility of the vision of God in the world beyond. Mu'tazilis believed that God is deprived of all positive attributes, in the sense that all divine qualifications must be understood as being the essence itself. In contrast to Textualistic viewpoint, the Mu'tazilite attitude is known in the history of theology by the name of Agnosticism(ta'til), that is to say, it consists in depriving God of all operative action and ends finally in agnosticism. When, therefore, the Qur'an and certain hadith represent the divinity in anthropomorphic form, the Mu'tazilis saw it all as metaphor. The hand is the metaphorical designation of power; the face signifies the essence; the fact that God is seated on the Throne is a metaphorical image of the divine reign, and so on.

Ash'ari School

The solution proposed by Abu al-Hasan al-Ash'ari to solve the problems of tashbih and ta'til concedes that the divine Being possesses in a real sense the Attributes and Names mentioned in the Qur'an. Insofar as these Names and Attributes have a positive reality, they are distinct from the essence, but nevertheless they do not have either existence or reality apart from it. The inspiration of al-Ash'ari in this matter was on the one hand to distinguish essence and attribute as concepts, and on the other hand to see that the duality between essence and attribute should be situated not on the quantitative but on the qualitative level—something which Mu'tazilis thinking had failed to grasp. Al-Ash'ari is in agreement with the literalists regarding the reality of human characteristics assigned to God, but he warns against imparting any physical material sense to them when attributing them to God. In his view, the Muslim must believe that God really does possess hands, face and so on, but without 'asking how'. This is the famous bi-lakayfa, in which faith attests that it can dispense with reason. According to Henry Corbin, al-Ash'ari's great labour ended by leaving faith and reason face to face, unmediated.

Twelvers Theology

Twelvers theology is based on the Hadith which have been narrated from Muhammad, the last Prophet of Islam, the first, fifth, sixth, seventh and eighth Imams and compiled by Shia scholars such as Al-Shaykh al-Saduq in *al-Tawhid*. According to Shia theologians, the attributes and names of God have no independent and hypostatic existence apart from the being and essence of God. Any suggestion of these attributes and names being convinced of as separate is thought to entail polytheism. It would be even incorrect to say God knows by his knowledge which is in his essence but God knows by his knowledge which is his essence. Also God has no physical form and he is insensible.

Philosophical Viewpoints

Al-Farabi and especially Avicenna put forward new interpretation of Tawhid on the basis of the reason not Qur'an and Hadith. Before Avicenna the discussions among Muslim philosophers were about the unity of God as divine creator and his relationship with the world as creation. The earlier philosophers were affected by the Plotinus' ideas.

Whether this view can be reconciled with Islam, particularly given the question of what role is left for God's will, was to become a subject of considerable controversy within intellectual Islamic discourse.

Sufi and Irfani Viewpoint

In Islamic mysticism (Sufism and Irfan), Tawhid is not only the affirmation in speech of God's unity, but also as importantly a practical and existential realization of that unity. This is done by rejecting the concepts tied to the world of multiplicity, to isolate the eternal from the temporal in a practical way. The ideal is a radical purification from all worldliness.

For Muslim mystics (sufis), the affirmation in speech of God's unity is only the first step of Tawhid. Further steps involve a spiritual experience for the existential realization of that unity. Categorizations of different steps of Tawhid could be found in the works of Muslims Sufis like Junayd Baghdadi and al-Ghazali. It involves a practical rejection of the concepts tied to the world of multiplicity. Al-Junayd for example "distinguishes four steps, starting from the simple attestation of unicity which is sufficient for ordinary believers, and culminating in the highest rank reserved for the elite, when the creature totally ceases to exist before his Lord, thus achieving al-fana fi al-tawhid [annihilation in unity]."

Annihilation and Subsistence

According to the concept of Annihilation and Subsistence, "Man's existence, or ego, or self-hood...must be annihilated so that he can attain to his true self which is his existence and "subsistence" with God. All of man's character traits and habits, everything that pertains to his individual existence must become completely naughted and "obliterated" (mahw). Then God will give back to him his character traits and everything positive he ever possessed. But at this stage he will know consciously and actually - not just theoretically - and with a through spiritual realization, that everything he is derives absolutely from God. He is nothing but a ray of God's Attributes manifesting the Hidden Treasure."

Unity of Existence

The first detailed formulation of "Unity of Existence" (*wahdat al-wujud*) is closely associated to Ibn Arabi. Widely different interpretations of the meaning of the "Unity of Existence" have been proposed throughout the centuries by critics, defenders, and Western scholars. Ibn Arabi himself didn't use the term "Unity of Existence" and similar statements had been made by those before him. For example, according to al-Ghazali "There is nothing in wujud [existence] except

God...Wujud [Existence] only belongs to the Real One". Ghazali explains that the fruit of spiritual ascent of the Sufi is to "witness that there is no existence in the world save God and that 'All things are perishing except his face' (Qur'an 28:88)"

Many authors consider being or existence to be the proper designation for the reality of God. While all Muslims believe the reality of God to be one, critics hold that the term "existence" (wujud) is also used for the existence of things in this world and that the doctrine blurs the distinction between the existence of the creator and that of the creation. Defenders argued that Ibn Arabi and his followers are offering a "subtle metaphysics following the line of the Asharite formula: "The attributes are neither God nor other than God." God's "signs" (ayat) and "traces" (athar)—the creatures—are neither the same as God nor different from him, because God must be understood as both absent and present, both transcendent and immanent. Understood correctly, wahdat al-wujud elucidates the delicate balance that needs to be maintained between these two perspectives." Shah Wali Allah of Delhi argued that the Ibn Arabi's "unity of being" was experiential and based on a subjective experience of illumination or ecstasy, rather than an ontological reality.

Influences on the Muslim Culture

The Islamic doctrine of Tawhid puts forth a God whose rule, will or law are comprehensive and extend to all creatures and to all aspects of the human life. Early Muslims understood religion to thus cover the domains of state, law and society. It is believed that the entirety of the Islamic teaching rests on the principle of Tawhid. In the following, we provide a few examples of the influences of Tawhid on the Muslim culture:

Interpersonal Relationship

According to the Qur'an, one consequence of properly conceived relationship between God and Man as the served and servant, is the proper relationship among humans. In order to achieve the former, the Qur'an consistently "reminds" men of two points: 1. That God is one; everything except God (including the entirety of nature) is contingent upon God. 2. With all his might and glory, God is essentially the all-merciful God.

Satanic Logic

According to the Qur'an, Satan deviated from the oneness of God in the story of creation of man by permitting his own hierarchical value system to supersede God's will: God asked the angels to bow to Adam, who he had created from clay. Satan refused, saying that "I am better than him; you created me from fire and created him from clay". The Medieval Muslim scholar, al-Ghazali pointing out that the only legitimate "preference principle" in the sight of God is piety, writes: "every time a rich man believes that he is better than a poor one, or a white man believes that he is better than a black one, then he is being arrogant. He is adopting the same hierarchical principles adopted by Iblis [Satan] in his jahl [ignorance], and thus falling into shirk [opposite of Tawhid]."

Secularism and the Evolution of Public Policy

The modern secular state (a by-product of European positivism) resulted from the evolution of public policy in west. Islamic scholarship has not however gone through the same process for a variety of reasons: The doctrine of Tawhid implies that the cosmos is a unified harmonious whole, centered around the omnipotent and omnipresent God. As interpreted by Muslim scholars, national sovereignty thus exclusively belonged to God and no room was left for evolution of nation-state ideas. According to Ozay Mehmet, "Secularism, i.e. policies based on science and man-made rules rather than divine criteria, has been rejected as anti-Islamic. Traditionally, a Muslim is not a nationalist, or citizen of a nation-state; he has no political identity, only a religious membership in the Umma. For a traditional Muslim, Islam is the sole and sufficient identification tag and nationalism and nation-states are 'obstacles'"

Islamic art

The desire to preserve the unity and transcendence of God led to the prohibition of Muslims from creating representation or visual depictions of God, or of any Prophet including Muhammad. Many Arab Muslims later extended the ban to any representations in art of the human form. The key concern is that the use of statues or images may lead to idolatry. The dominant forms of expression in the Islamic art, thus, became calligraphy and arabesque.

TERMAGANT

In Medieval Europe, **Termagant** was the name given to a god that the Europeans believed Muslims worshipped. European literature from the Middle Ages often referred to Muslims as pagans, with sobriquets such as *the paynim foe.* These depictions naively represent Muslims worshipping Muhammad (Mahomet, Mahound) as a god and depict them worshipping various deities in the form of idols (cult images), ranging from Apollo to Lucifer, but their chief deity was typically named Termagant.

The origin of the name Termagant is unknown, and does not seem to derive from any actual aspect of Muslim belief or practice, however wildly distorted. W. W. Skeat in the 19th century, speculated that the name was originally "Trivagante", meaning 'thrice wandering', a reference to the moon, because of the Islamic use of crescent moon imagery. An Old English origin has also been suggested, from *tiw mihtig r* ("very mighty"), referring to the Germanic god Tiw. Another possibility is that it derives from a confusion between Muslims and the Zoroastrian Magi of ancient Iran: thus *tyr-magian,* or "Magian god".

Termagant in Literature

Whatever its origins, "Termagant" became established in the West as the name of the principal Muslim god, being regularly mentioned in metrical romances and *chansons de geste*. In the 15th-century Middle English romance *Syr Guy of Warwick,* a Sultan swears an oath:

So help me, Mahoune, of might,

And Termagant, my god so bright.

In the *Chanson de Roland,* the Muslims, having lost the battle of Roncesvalles, desecrate their "pagan idols" (lines 2589–90):

E Tervagan tolent sun escarbuncle, / E Mahumet enz en un fosset butent,

They strip the fire-red gem off Termagant / And throw Mohammed down into a ditch...

Tervagant is also a god/statue of the "king of Africa" in the Jean Bodel play in Old French (c.1200) *Le jeu de saint Nicolas.*

In the *Sowdone of Babylone,* the sultan makes a vow to Termagaunte rather than Mahound (Muhammad) (lines 135–40):

Of Babiloyne the riche Sowdon,

Moost myghty man he was of moolde;

He made a vowe to Termagaunte:

Whan Rome were distroied and hade myschaunce,

He woolde turne ayen erraunte

And distroye Charles, the Kinge of Fraunce.

In Geoffrey Chaucer's *Canterbury Tales,* the *Tale of Sir Thopas* (supposed to be told by Chaucer himself on the pilgrimage) is a parody of these chivalric romances. In the tale, a giant knight named "Sir Oliphaunt" is made to swear an oath by Termagant.

In Occitan literature the name Muhammed was corrupted as "Bafomet", forming the basis for the legendary Baphomet, at different times an idol, a "sabbatic goat", and key link in conspiracy theories. The troubadour Austorc d'Aorlhac refers to Bafomet and Termaganat (*Tervagan*) side-by-side in one *sirventes*, referring also to the latter's "companions".

Termagant also became a stock character in a number of medieval mystery plays. On the stage, Termagant was usually depicted as a turbanned creature who wore a long, Eastern style gown. As a stage-villain, he would rant at and threaten the lesser villains who were his servants and worshippers.

"Termagant" as a Shrewish Woman

Because of the theatrical tradition, by Shakespeare's day the term had come to refer to a bullying person. *Henry IV* contains a reference to "that hot termagant Scot". In *Hamlet*, the hero says of ham actors that "I would have such a fellow whipped for o'er-doing Termagant, it out-Herod's Herod". Herod, like Termagant, was also a character from medieval drama who was famous for ranting.

Mainly because of Termagant's depiction in long gowns, given that female roles were routinely played by male actors in Shakespearean times, English audiences got the mistaken notion that the character was female, or at least that he resembled a mannish woman. As a result, the name *termagant* came increasingly to be applied to a woman with a quarrelsome, scolding quality, and thus the name applies today to a quarrelsome, scolding woman. *Virago*, fishwife and *shrew* are also pejorative names for other types of unpleasant, aggressive woman. Nevertheless, the term is still sometimes used of men. The Australian politician Kim Beazley labelled a male opponent a termagant.

Other Termagants

- HMS *Termagant* is a longstanding ship's name in the British Royal Navy.
- In Washington Irving's "Rip Van Winkle", Dame Van Winkle is described by the narrator as being a "termagant wife".
- In Jack Vance's book *The Dragon Masters*, a sub-species of "dragon" is the man-sized termagant.
- In the microgame *Chitin: 1 The Harvest Wars*, published by Metagaming in the late 1970s, Termagant was a type of ground unit.
- In the fictional *Warhammer 40,000* universe, Termagaunts are a type of tyranid, creatures that resemble dinosaurs or insects.

Kaaba

The **Kaaba** is a cube-shaped building in Mecca, Saudi Arabia, and is the most sacred site in Islam. The building predates Islam, and, according to Islamic tradition, the first building at the site was built by Abraham. The building has a mosque built around it, the Masjid al-Haram. All Muslims around the world face the Kaaba during prayers, no matter where they are.

One of the Five Pillars of Islam requires every Muslim to perform the Hajj pilgrimage at least once in his or her lifetime if they are able to do so. Multiple parts of the Hajj require pilgrims to walk seven times around the Kaaba in a counter-clockwise direction (as viewed from above). This circumambulation, the Tawaf, is also performed by pilgrims during the Umrah (lesser pilgrimage). However, the most dramatic times are during the Hajj, when about three million (officially) pilgrims simultaneously gather to circle the building on the same day.

The Kaaba is a large masonry structure roughly the shape of a cube. It is made of granite from the hills near Mecca, and stands upon a 25 cm (10 in) marble base, which projects outwards about 35 cm (14 in). It is approximately 13.1 m (43 ft) high, with sides measuring 11.03 m (36.2 ft) by 12.86 m (42.2 ft). The four corners of the Kaaba roughly point toward the four cardinal directions of the compass. In the eastern corner of the Kaaba is the *Ruknu l-Aswad* "the Black Corner"" or *al-&ajaru l-Aswad* "the Black Stone". At the northern corner is the *Ruknu l-Îraqi* "the Iraqi corner". The western corner is the *Ruknu sh-Shami* "the Levantine corner" and the southern is *Ruknu l-Yamani* "the Yemeni corner".

The Kaaba is covered by a black silk and gold curtain known as the kiswah, which is replaced yearly. About two-thirds of the way up runs a band of gold-embroidered calligraphy with Qur'anic text, including the Islamic declaration of faith, the *Shahada.*

In modern times, entry to the Kaaba's interior is generally not permitted except for certain rare occasions and for a limited number of guests. The entrance is a door set 2 m (7 ft) above the ground on the north-eastern wall of the Kaaba, which acts as the façade. There is a wooden staircase on wheels, usually stored in the mosque between the arch-shaped gate of Banu Shaybah and the well of Zamzam. Inside the Kaaba, there is a marble and limestone floor. The interior walls are clad with marble halfway to the roof; tablets with Qur'anic inscriptions are inset in the marble. The top part of the walls are covered with a green cloth decorated with gold embroidered Qur'anic verses. Caretakers perfume the marble cladding with scented oil, the same oil used to anoint the Black Stone outside.

There is also a semi-circular wall opposite, but unconnected to, the north-west wall of the Kaaba known as the *hatim.* This is 90 cm (35 in) in height and 1.5 m (4.9 ft) in width, and is composed of white marble. At one time the space lying between the *hatim* and the Kaaba belonged to the Kaaba itself, and for this reason it is not entered during the *tawaf* (ritual circumambulation). Some believe that the graves of Abu Simbel, prophet Ishmael and his mother Hagar are located in this space.

Muslims throughout the world face the Kaaba during prayers, which occur five times a day. For most places around the world, coordinates for Mecca suffice. Worshippers in the Sacred Mosque pray in concentric circles around the Kaaba.

Black Stone

The Black Stone is a significant feature of the Kaaba, believed by Muslims to date back to the time of Adam and Eve. Located at the eastern corner of the Kaaba, it is about 30 cm (12 in) in diameter and surrounded by a silver frame. Although not strictly obligatory, pilgrims can kiss the Stone, as Muhammad is said to have done.

The following passage gives an insight to the significance of the Black Stone in Islam:

> Narrated 'Abis bin Rabia: Umar came near the Black Stone and kissed it and said, "No doubt, I know that you are a stone and can neither benefit anyone nor harm anyone. Had I not seen God's Apostle kissing you, I would not have kissed you."

Large crowds can make kissing the Stone impossible, so as pilgrims walk round the Kaaba they point to the Stone on each pass.

History

Islamic Tradition

According to the Qur'an, the Kaaba was re-built by Ibrahim (Abraham) and his son Ismasil (Ishmael). Islamic traditions assert that the Kaaba "reflects" a house in heaven called al-Baytu l-Masmur and that it was first built by the first man, Adam and is believed that it is the first building ever built on earth. Ibrahim and Ismail rebuilt the Kaaba on the old foundations.

Before Islam

As little is known of the history of the Kaaba, there are various opinions regarding its formation and significance.

The early Arabian population consisted primarily of warring nomadic tribes. When they did converge peacefully, it was usually under the protection of religious practices. Writing in the *Encyclopedia of Islam,* Wensinck identifies Mecca with a place called *Macoraba* mentioned by Ptolemy. His text is believed to date from the second century AD, before the rise of Islam, and described it as a foundation in southern Arabia, built around a sanctuary. The area probably did not start becoming an area of religious pilgrimage until around the year AD 500. It was around then that the Quraysh tribe (into which Muhammad was later born) took control of it, and made an agreement with the local Kinana Bedouins for control. The sanctuary itself, located in a barren valley surrounded by mountains, was probably built at the location of the water source today known as the Zamzam Well, an area of considerable religious significance.

In her book, *Islam: A Short History,* Karen Armstrong asserts that the Kaaba was dedicated to Hubal, a Nabatean deity, and contained 360 idols which either represented the days of the year, or were effigies of the Arabian pantheon. Once a year, tribes from all around the Arabian peninsula, be they Christian or pagan, would converge on Mecca to perform the *Hajj.*

Imoti contends that there were multiple such "Kaaba" sanctuaries in Arabia at one time, but this is the only one built of stone. The others also allegedly had counterparts to the Black Stone. There was a "red stone", the deity of the south Arabian city of Ghaiman, and the "white stone" in the Kaaba of al-Abalat (near the city of Tabala, south of Mecca). Grunebaum in *Classical Islam* points out that the experience of divinity of that time period was often associated with stone fetishes, mountains, special rock formations, or "trees of strange growth." The Kaaba was thought to be at the center of the world with the Gate of Heaven directly above it. The Kaaba marked the location where the sacred world intersected with the profane, and the embedded Black Stone was a further symbol of this as a meteorite that had fallen from the sky and linked heaven and earth. According to the *Boston Globe*, the Kaaba was a shrine for the Daughters of God (al-Lat, al-Uzza, and Manat) and Hubal.

According to Sarwar, about four hundred years before the birth of Muhammad, a man named "Amr bin Lahyo bin Harath bin Amr ul-Qais bin Thalaba bin Azd bin Khalan bin Babalyun bin Saba", who was descended from Qahtan and king of Hijaz (the northwestern section of Saudi Arabia, which encompassed the cities of Mecca and Medina), had placed a Hubal idol onto the roof of the Kaaba, and this idol was one of the chief deities of the ruling Quraysh tribe. The idol was made of red agate, and shaped like a human, but with the right hand broken off and replaced with a golden hand. When the idol was moved inside the Kaaba, it had seven arrows in front of it, which were used for divination.

To keep the peace among the perpetually warring tribes, Mecca was declared a sanctuary where no violence was allowed within 20 miles (32 km) of the Kaaba. This combat-free zone allowed Mecca to thrive not only as a place of pilgrimage, but also as a trading center.

Patricia Crone disagrees with most academic historians on most issues concerning the history of early Islam, including the history of the Kaaba. In *Makkan Trade and the Rise of Islam,* Crone writes that she believes that the identification of Macoraba with the Kaaba is false, and that Macoraba was a town in southern Arabia in what was then known as Arabia Felix.

Many Muslim and academic historians, stress the power and importance of the pre-Islamic Mecca. They depict it as a city grown rich on the proceeds of the spice trade. Crone believes that this is an exaggeration and that Makkan may only have been an outpost trading with nomads for leather, cloth, and camel butter. Crone argues that if Mecca had been a well-known center of trade, it would have been mentioned by later authors such as Procopius, Nonnosus, and the Syrian church chroniclers writing in Syriac. However, the town is absent from any geographies or histories written in the last three centuries before the rise of Islam.

According to The Encyclopædia Britannica, "before the rise of Islam it was revered as a sacred sanctuary and was a site of pilgrimage." According to the German historian Eduard Glaser, the name *"Kaaba"* may have been related to the southern Arabian or Ethiopian word *"mikrab"*, signifying a temple. Again, Crone disputes this etymology.

At the Time of Muhammad

At the time of Muhammad (CE 570–632), his tribe the Quraysh was in charge of the Kaaba, which was at that time a shrine containing hundreds of idols representing Arabian tribal gods and other religious figures, including Jesus and Mary. Muhammad earned the enmity of his tribe by claiming the shrine for the new religion of Islam that he preached. He wanted the Kaaba to be dedicated to the worship of the one God alone, and all the idols evicted. The Quraysh persecuted and harassed him continuously, and he and his followers eventually migrated to Medina in 622.

After this pivotal migration, or Hijra, the Muslim community became a political and military force. In 630, Muhammad and his followers returned to Mecca as conquerors, and he destroyed the 360 idols in and around the Kaaba. While destroying each idol, Muhammad recited Qu'ran 17:81 which says "Truth has arrived and falsehood has perished for falsehood is by its nature bound to perish."

The Kaaba was re-dedicated as an Islamic house of worship, and henceforth, the annual pilgrimage was to be a Muslim rite, the Hajj, which visits the Kaaba and other sacred sites around Mecca. Islamic histories also mention a reconstruction of the Kaaba around 600. A story found in Ibn Ishaq's *Sirat Rasul Allah*, one of the biographies of Muhammad (as reconstructed and translated by Guillaume), describes Muhammad settling a quarrel between Meccan clans as to which clan should set the Black Stone cornerstone in place. According to Ishaq's biography, Muhammad's solution was to have all the clan elders raise the cornerstone on a cloak, and then Muhammad set the stone into its final place with his own hands. Ibn Ishaq says that the timber for the reconstruction of the Kaaba came from a Greek ship that had been wrecked on the Red Sea coast at Shu'ayba, and the work was undertaken by a Coptic carpenter called Baqum.

It is also claimed by the Shisa that the Kaaba is the birth place of sAli ibn Abi Talib, the fourth caliph and cousin and son-in-law of the Islamic prophet Muhammad.

Since Muhammad's Time

The Kaaba has been repaired and reconstructed many times since Muhammad's day. Abd-Allah ibn al-Zubayr, an early Muslim who ruled Mecca for many years between the death of sAli and the consolidation of Ummayad power, is said to have demolished the old Kaaba and rebuilt it to include the *hatim*, a semi-circular wall now outside the Kaaba.

He did so on the basis of a tradition (found in several hadith collections) that the *hatim* was a remnant of the foundations of the Abrahamic Kaaba, and that Muhammad himself had wished to rebuild so as to include it.

This structure was destroyed (or partially destroyed) in 683, during the war between al-Zubayr and Umayyad forces commanded by Al-Hajjaj bin Yousef. Al-Hajjaj used stone-throwing catapults against the Meccans.

The Ummayads under sAbdu l-Malik ibn Marwan finally reunited all the former Islamic possessions and ended the long civil war. In 693 he had the remnants of al-Zubayr's Kaaba razed, and rebuilt on the foundations set by the Quraysh. The Kaaba returned to the cube shape it had taken during Muhammad's lifetime.

During the Hajj of 930, the Qarmatians attacked Mecca, defiled the Zamzam Well with the bodies of pilgrims and stole the Black Stone, removing it to the oasis region of Eastern Arabia known as al-Ahsaa, where it remained until the Abbasids ransomed it back in 952 CE.

Apart from repair work, the basic shape and structure of the Kaaba have not changed since then.

The Kaaba is depicted on the reverse of 500 Saudi Riyal, and the Iranian 2000 rials banknotes.

Cleaning

The building is opened twice a year for a ceremony known as "the cleaning of the Kaaba." This ceremony takes place roughly fifteen days before the start of the month of Ramadan and the same period of time before the start of the annual pilgrimage.

The keys to the Kaaba are held by the Bani Shaybat tribe. Members of the tribe greet visitors to the inside of the

Kaaba on the occasion of the cleaning ceremony. A small number of dignitaries and foreign diplomats are invited to participate in the ceremony. The governor of Mecca leads the honored guests who ritually clean the structure, using simple brooms. Washing of the Kaaba is done with a mixture of Zamzam and Persian rosewater.

Qibla and Prayer

The *Qibla* is the Muslim name for the direction faced during prayer While it may appear to some non-Muslims that Muslims worship the Kaaba, it is simply the focal point for prayer, similar to the direction of an altar in Christian churches. From 610 to 623, the direction of the Qibla had been toward the Noble Sanctuary (Temple Mount) in Jerusalem.

●●

9
Ismailism

Ismasilism is a branch of Shiaism. It is the second largest sect of Shiaism, after the mainstream Twelvers (*Ithnasashariyya*). The Ismasili get their name from their acceptance of Ismasil ibn Jasfar as the divinely appointed spiritual successor *(Imam)* to Jasfar as-Sadiq, wherein they differ from the Twelvers, who accept Musà al-Ka¿im, younger brother of Ismasil, as the true Imam.

Tracing its earliest theology to the lifetime of Muhammad, Ismasilism rose at one point to become the largest branch of Shi'ism, climaxing as a political power with the Fatimid Empire in the tenth through twelfth centuries. Ismailis believe in the oneness of God, as well as the closing of divine revelation with Muhammad, whom they see as the final prophet and messenger of God to all humanity. The Ismasili and the Twelvers both accept the same initial *A'immah* from the descendants of Muhammad through his daughter Fatimah az-Zahra and therefore share much of their early history. Both Shi'ite groups see the family of Muhammad *(Ahl al-Bayt)* as divinely chosen, infallible *(ismah)*, and guided by God to lead the Islamic community *(Ummah)*, a belief that distinguishes them from the majority Sunni branch of Islam.

After the death—or Occultation according to Seveners—of Muhammad ibn Ismail in the 8th century CE, the teachings of Ismailism further transformed into the belief system as it is known today, with an explicit concentration on the deeper, esoteric meaning *(batin)* of the Islamic religion. With the eventual development of Twelverism into the more literalistic *(zahir)* oriented Akhbari and later Usooli schools of thought, Shi'ism developed into two separate directions: the metaphorical Ismasili group focusing on the mystical path and nature of Allah, with the "Imam of the Time" representing the manifestation of truth and reality, with the more literalistic Twelver group focusing on divine law *(sharia)* and the deeds and sayings *(sunnah)* of Muhammad and the Twelve Imams who were guides and a light to God.

Though there are several paths *(tariqah)* within the Ismasilis, the term in today's vernacular generally refers to the Nizari path, which recognizes the Aga Khan as the 49th hereditary Imam and is the largest group among the Ismasilis. While some of the branches have extremely differing exterior practices, much of the spiritual theology has remained the same since the days of the faith's early Imams. In recent centuries Ismasilis have largely been an Indo-Iranian community, but Ismasili are found in India, Pakistan, Syria, Saudi Arabia, Yemen, China, Jordan, Uzbekistan, Tajikistan, Afghanistan, East Africa, Syria, and South Africa, and have in recent years emigrated to Europe, Australia, New Zealand, and North America.

History

Succession Crisis

Ismailism shares its beginnings with other early Shi'ah sects that emerged during the succession crisis that spread throughout the early Muslim community.

From the beginning, the Shi'ah asserted the right of 'Ali, Muhammad's cousin, to have both political and spiritual control over the community. This also included his two sons, who were the grandsons of Muhammad through his daughter Famimatu z-Zahrah.

The conflict remained relatively peaceful between the partisans of 'Ali and those who asserted a semi-democratic system of electing caliphs, until the third of the Rashidun caliphs, Uthman was killed, and 'Ali, with popular support, ascended to the caliphate.

Soon after his ascendancy, Aisha, the third of the Prophet's wives, claimed along with Uthman's tribe, the Ummayads, that Ali should take Qisas (blood for blood) from the people responsible for Uthman's martyrdom. 'Ali voted against it as he believed that situation at that time demanded a peaceful resolution of the matter. Both parties could rightfully defend their claims, but due to escalated misunderstandings, the Battle of the Camel was fought and both parties bore losses but soon reached an agreement.

Following this battle, Muawiya, the Umayyad governor of Syria, also staged a revolt under the same pretences. 'Ali led his forces against Muawiya until the side of Muawiya held copies of the Quran against their spears and demanded that the issue be decided by Islam's holy book. 'Ali accepted this, and an arbitration was done which ended in his favour.

A group among Ali's army believed subjecting his legitimate authority to arbitration was tantamount to apostasy, and abandoned his forces. This group was known as the Kharijites, and 'Ali wished to defeat their forces before they reached the cities where they would be able to blend in with the rest of the population. He was unable to do this, but nonetheless defeated their forces in the battles following afterward.

Regardless of these defeats, the Kharijites survived and became a violently problematic group in Islamic history. After plotting an assassination against 'Ali, Muawiya, and the arbitrator of their conflict, only 'Ali was successfully assassinated in 661 CE, and the Imamate passed on to his son Hasan and then later his son Husayn, or according to the

Nizari Ismasili, straight to Husayn. However, the political caliphate was soon taken over by Muawiya who was the only leader in the empire at that time with an army large enough to seize control.

Karbala and Afterward

The Battle of Karbala

After the passing away of Hasan, Husayn and his family were increasingly worried about the religious and political persecution that was becoming commonplace under the reign of Muawiya's son, Yazid. Amidst this turmoil in 680 CE, Husayn along with the women and children of his family, upon receiving invitational letters and gesture of support by Kufis, wished to go to Kufa and confront Yazid as an intercessor on part of the citizens of the empire. However, he was stopped by Yazid's army in Karbala, during the month of Muharram. His family was starved and deprived of water and supplies, until eventually the army came in on the tenth day and killed Husayn and his companions, and enslaved the rest of the women and family, taking them to Kufa.

This battle would become extremely important to the Shi'ah psyche. The Twelvers, as well as Mustaali Ismasili still mourn this event during a holiday known as Ashura. The Nizari Ismasili however do not mourn this event because of the belief that the light of the Imam never dies but rather passes on to the succeeding Imam, making mourning arbitrary.

The beginnings of Ismasili Daswah

After being set free by the caliph Yazid, Zainab, the daughter of Famimatu z-Zahra' and 'Ali and the sister of Hassan and Husayn, started to spread the word of Karbala to the Muslim world, making speeches regarding the event. This was the first organised Daswah of the Shi'ah community, which would later develop into an extremely spiritual institution for the Ismasilis.

After the poisoning of 'Ali al-Sajjad by Hisham ibn Abd al-Malik in 713 CE, Shiism's first succession crisis rose with Zayd ibn 'Ali's companions and the Zaydi Shi'ah that claim Zayd ibn 'Ali as the Imam, whilst the rest of the Shi'ah maintained Muhammad al-Baqir as the Imam. The Zaidis argued that any sayed, descendant of Muhammad through Hassan or Husayn, who rebelled against tyranny and the injustice of his age, can be the Imam. The Zaidis created the first Shi'ah states in Iran, Iraq and Yemen.

In contrast to his predecessors, Muhammad al-Baqir focused on academic Islamic scholarship in Medina, where he promulgated his teachings to many Muslims, both Shi'ah and non-Shi'ah, in an extremely organised form of Daswah. In fact, the earliest text of the Ismaili school of thought is said to be the "Umm al-kitab", a conversation between Muhammad al-Baqir and three of his disciples.

This tradition would pass on to his son, Ja'far al-Sadiq, who inherited the Imamate on his father's death in 743. Ja'far al-Sadiq excelled in the scholarship of the day and had many pupils, including three of the four founders of the Sunni madhabs.

However, following Jaffir's poisoning in 765, a fundamental split would occur in the community. Isma'il bin Jafar, who at one point seemed to be heir apparent, apparently predeceased his father in 755. While Twelvers either argue he was never heir apparent or that he truly predeceased his father hence Musa al-Kadhim was the true heir to the Imamate, Ismasilis argue that either the death was staged in order to draw harm away from al-Sadiq's successor or that his early death does not mean he was not an Imam, and rightfully the Imamate would pass to his son, Muhammad ibn Ismail.

Ascension of the Dais

For the Sevener Ismasili, the Imamate ended with Isma'il ibn Ja'far, whose son Muhammad ibn Ismail was the expected

Mahdi that Ja'far al-Sadiq had preached about. However, at this point the Ismasili Imams according to the Nizari and Mustaali found areas where they would be able to be safe from the recently founded Abbasid Empire which had defeated and seized control from the Umayyads in 750 AD.

At this point, much of the Ismaili community believed that Muhammad ibn Ismail had gone into the Occultation and that he would one day return. With the status and location of the Imams not known to the community, Ismailism began to propagate the faith through Dasiyyun from its base in Syria. This was the start of the spiritual beginnings of the Daswah that would later blossom on the Mustaali branch of the faith, as well as play important parts in the other three branches.

The Da'i was not a missionary in the typical sense, and he was responsible for both the conversion of his student as well as the mental and spiritual wellbeing. The Da'i was a guide and light to the Imam. The student and teacher relationship of the Da'i and his student was much like the one that would develop in Sufism. The student desired God, and the Da'i could bring him to God by making him recognize the stature and light of the Imam descended from the Imams, which in turn descended from God. The Da'i was the path, and the Face of God which was a Qur'anic term the Ismasili took to represent the Imam, was the destination.

Shams Tabrizi and Rumi is a famous example of the importance between the guide and the guided, and Rumi dedicated much of his literature to Shams Tabrizi and his discovery of the truth.

The Qarmatians

While many of the Ismasili were content with the Dai teachings, a group that mingled Persian nationalism and Zoroastrianism with Ismasili teachings surfaced known as the Qarmatians. With their headquarters in Bahrain, they accepted a young Persian former prisoner by the name of Abu'l-Fadl al-Isfahani, who claimed to be the descendant of the Persian kings as their Mahdi, and rampaged across the Middle-East in the tenth century, climaxing their violent campaign with the stealing of the Black Stone from the Kaaba in Mecca in 930 under Abu Tahir Al-Jannabi. Following the arrival of the Mahdi they changed their qiblah from the Kaaba to the Zoroastrian-influenced fire. After their return of the Black Stone in 951 and a defeat by the Abbasids in 976 they slowly dwindled and no longer have any adherents.

The Fatimid Empire

Rise of the Fatimid Empire

The political asceticism practiced by the Imams during the period after Muhammad ibn Ismail was to be short lived and finally concluded with the Imamate of Ubayd Allah al-Mahdi Billah, who was born in 873. After decades of Ismasilis believing that Muhammad ibn Ismail was in the Occultation and would return to bring an age of justice, al-Mahdi taught that the Imams had not been literally secluded, but rather had remained hidden to protect themselves and had been organizing the Da'i, and even acted as Da'i themselves. He taught that during the supposed Occultation of Muhammad ibn Ismail, many of Muhammad ibn Ismail's descendants lived as Imams secluded from the community, guiding them through the Da'i at times even taking the guise of Da'i.

After raising an army and successfully defeating the Alghabids in North Africa and a number of other victories, al-Mahdi Billah successfully established a Shi'ah political state ruled by the Imamate in 910 AD. This was the only time in history where the Shi'a Imamate and Caliphate were united after the first Imam, Ali ibn Abu Talib.

In parallel with the dynasty's claim of descent from 'Ali and Famimatu z-Zahrah, the empire was named "Fatimid."

However, this was not without controversy and with the extent that Ismasili doctrine had spread, the Abbasid caliphate assigned Sunni and Twelver scholars with the assignment to disprove the lineage of the new dynasty. This became known as the Baghdad Manifesto, and it traces the lineage of the Fatimid dynasty to a Jewish blacksmith. Its authenticity has been both questioned and supported by various Islamic scholars.

The Middle-East under Fatimid Rule

The Fatimid Empire expanded quickly under the subsequent Imams. Under the Fatimids, Egypt became the center of an empire that included at its peak North Africa, Sicily, Palestine, Syria, the Red Sea coast of Africa, Yemen and the Hejaz. Under the Fatimids, Egypt flourished and developed an extensive trade network in both the Mediterranean and the Indian Ocean, which eventually determined the economic course of Egypt during the High Middle Ages.

The Fatimids promoted two ideas that were radical for that time. The first was promotion by merit rather than genealogy. The second was religious toleration, under which both Jews and Coptic Christians flourished.

Also during this period the three contemporary branches of Ismailism formed. The first branch (Druze) occurred with the Imam Al-Hakim bi-Amr Allah. Born in 985, he ascended as ruler at the age of eleven. A religious group that was even forming in his lifetime broke off from mainstream Ismailism and refused to acknowledge his successor. Later to be known as the Druze, they believe Al-Hakim to be the manifestation of God and the prophecized Mahdi, who would one day return and bring justice to the world. The faith further split from Ismailism as it developed very unique doctrines which often classes it separately from both Ismailism and Islam.

The second split occurred following the death of Ma'ad al-Mustansir Billah in 1094. His rule was the longest of any caliph in both the Fatimid and other Islamic empires. Upon his passing away his sons, the older Nizar and the younger Al-Musta'li fought for political and spiritual control of the dynasty. Nizar was defeated and jailed, but according to Nizari tradition his son escaped to Alamut where the Iranian Ismasili had accepted his claim.

The Mustaali line split again between the Taiyabi and the Hafizi, the former claiming that the 21st Imam and son of Al-Amir went into occultation and appointed a Dasi al-Mumlaq to guide the community, in a similar manner as the Ismasili had lived after the death of Muhammad ibn Ismail. The latter claimed that the ruling Fatimid caliph was the Imam. However, in the Mustaali branch, the Dai came to have a similar but more important task. The term Dai al-Mutlaq literally means "the absolute or unrestricted missionary". This dai was the only source of the Imam's knowledge after the occultation of al-Qasim in Mustaali thought.

According to Tayyabi Mustali Isma'ili tradition, after the death of Imam al-Amir, his infant son, AtTaiyab abi-l-Qasim, about 2 years old, was protected by the most important woman in Musta'li history after Prophet's daughter Famimatu z-Zahrah. She was al-Malika al-Sayyida (Hurratul-Malika), which was a Queen in Yemen. She was promoted to the post of hujja long before by Imam Mustansir at the death of her husband and she now ran the dawat from Yemen in the name of Imaam Tayyib. She was instructed and prepared by Imam Mustansir and following Imams for the second period of Satr. It was going to be on her hands, that Imam Tayyib would go into seclusion, and she would institute the office of Dai al-Mutlaq. Syedna Zueb-bin-Musa was first to be instituted to this office and the line of Tayyib Dais that began in 1132 have passed from one Dai to another and is continuing till date.

The Mustaali split several times over disputes regarding who was the rightful *Dasi al-Mutlaq*, the leader of the community within The Occultation.

After 27 th dai Dawood bin qutub shah there is split ,follower of dawood called Dawoodi bohra and follower of Suleman called sulemani. Dawoodi bohra 's present 52nd Dai is Syedna mohd. Burhanuddin and following same tradition of fatimid era. The Sulaimani Bohra are mostly concentrated in Yemen and Saudi Arabia with some communities in the Indian Subcontinent. The Dawoodi Bohra and Alavi Bohra are mostly exclusive to the Indian Subcontinent. Other groups include Atba-i-Malak and Hebtiahs Bohra. Mustaali beliefs and practices, unlike those of the Nizari and Druze, are generally compatible with mainstream Islam, representing a continuation of Fatimid tradition and *fiqh'*.

Decline of the Empire

In the 1040s, the Zirids (governors of North Africa under the Fatimids) declared their independence from the Fatimids and their conversion to Sunni Islam, which led to the devastating Banu Hilal invasions. After about 1070, the Fatimid hold on the Levant coast and parts of Syria was challenged by first Turkish invasions, then the Crusades, so that Fatimid territory shrunk until it consisted only of Egypt.

After the decay of the Fatimid political system in the 1160s, the Zengid ruler Nur ad-Din had his general, Saladin, seize Egypt in 1169, forming the Sunni Ayyubid Dynasty. This signaled the end of the Hafizi Mustaali branch of Ismailism as well as the Fatimid Empire.

Table of Imams along with Caliphate

Table showing all ismaili imam along with earlier islam along with caliphate of time and present follower :

Alamut

Hassan-i-Sabbah

Very early in the empire's life, the Fatimids sought to spread the Ismasili faith which in turn would spread loyalties to the Imamate in Egypt. One of their earliest attempts would be taken by a Dai by the name of Hassan-i-Sabbah.

Hassan-i-Sabbah was born into a Twelver family living in the scholarly city of Qom in 1056 AD. His family later relocated to the city of Tehran which was an area with an extremely active Ismasili Daswah. He immersed himself in Ismasili thought, however he did not choose to convert until he was overcome with an almost fatal illness, where he finally feared dying without knowing the Imam of his time.

Afterwards, Hassan-i-Sabbah became one of the most influential Dais in Ismasili history, and would be important to the survival of the Nizari branch of Ismailism, which today is its largest branch.

Legend holds that he met with Imam Ma'ad al-Mustansir Billah and asked him who his successor would be, to which he responded, his eldest son Nizar.

Hassan-i-Sabbah would continue his Dai activities and they would climax with his taking of Alamut. Taking two years, he first converted most of the surrounding villages to Ismailism. Afterwards, he converted most of the staff to Ismailism and then took over the fortress, and presented the current leader with payment for the fortress. With no choice, the leader abdicated and Hassan-i-Sabbah turned Alamut into an outpost of Fatimid rule within Abbasid territory.

The Hashashin

Surrounded by the Abbasids and other hostile powers, and low in numbers, Hassan-i-Sabbah derived a way to attack the Ismasili enemies with a small loss and number. Using the method of assassination, from which the English word is derived from Hashashin, he ordered the killing of Sunni scholars and politicians that threatened the Ismasilis. Knives and daggers were used. Sometimes, in warning, a knife would be put into the pillow of the enemy and often they understood the message.

However, when an assassination was actually made the Hashashin would not be allowed to run away, but rather to strike further fear in the enemy by showing no emotion, they would stand there. This further increased the reputation of the Hashashin in the Sunni world.

Amin Maalouf, in his novel Samarkand, disputes the origin of the word assassin. According to him it is not derived from the name of the drug hashish which Westerners used to believe the sect took. Instead he proposes this story was fabricated by Orientalists to explain how faithfully the Ismasilis would carry out these suicide-assassinations without fearing death. Maalouf suggests that the term is derived from the word assaas (foundation), and Assassiyoon, meaning "those faithful to the foundation."

Threshold of the Imamate

After the imprisonment of Nizar by his younger brother Mustaal, it is claimed Nizar's son al-Hadi survived and fled to Alamut. He was offered a safe place in Alamut where Hassan-i-Sabbah welcomed him. However, it is believed this was not announced to the public and the lineage was hidden until a few Imams later.

It was announced with the advent of Imam Hassan II. In a show of his Imamate and to emphasize the interior meaning (the batin) over the exterior meaning (the zahir) he prayed with his back to Mecca, as did the rest of the congregation which prayed behind him, and ordered the community to break their Ramadan fasting with a feast at noon. He made a speech saying he was in communication with the Imam, which many of the Ismasilis understood to mean he was the Imam himself.

Afterwards his descendants would rule as the Imams at Alamut until its destruction by the Mongols.

Destruction by the Mongols

The stronghold at Alamut, though it had warded off the Sunni attempts to take it several times, including one by Saladin, would soon meet with destruction. By 1206, Genghis Khan had managed to unite many of the once antagonistic Mongol tribes into a ruthless, but nonetheless unified, force. Using many new and unique military techniques, Genghis Khan led his Mongol hordes across Central Asia into the Middle-East where they won a series of tactical military victories using a scorched-earth policy.

A grandson of Genghis Khan, Hulagu Khan, led the devastating attack on Alamut in 1256, only a short time before he would sack the Abbasid caliphate in Baghdad in 1258. As he would later do to the House of Wisdom in Baghdad, he destroyed Ismasili as well as Islamic religious texts. The Imamate that was located in Alamut along with its few followers were forced to flee and take refuge elsewhere.

Aftermath

After the fall of the Fatimid Empire and its bases in Iran and Syria, the three currently living branches of Ismasili generally developed geographically isolated from each other, with the exception of Syria (which has both Druze and Nizari) and Pakistan and rest of South Asia (which had both Mustaali and Nizari).

The Nizari kept large populations in Syria, Uzbekistan, Tajikistan, Afghanistan, Pakistan, India, and has smaller populations in China and Iran. This community is the only one with a living Imam, who is titled today as the Aga Khan.

The Druze mainly settled in Syria and Lebanon, and developed a community based upon the principles of reincarnation through their own descendants. Their leadership is based through community scholars, who are the only individuals allowed to read their holy texts. It is controversial whether this group falls under the classification of Ismasilism or Islam because of their unique beliefs.

Beliefs

View on the Qur'an

The Ismasilis believe the Qur'an has several layers of meaning, but they generally divide those types of meanings into two: the apparent (zahir) meaning and the hidden (batin) meaning. While a believer can understand the batin meaning to some extent, the ultimate interpretation lies in the office of the Imamate. The Imam's farmans (teachings) are binding upon the community. In this way, the Ismasili community can adapt to new times and new places. Oftentimes, the Imam of the Time is known as the "Bolta Quran" (the "speaking Qur'an"), meaning that he reinterprets the literary text in a way that can be understood for today's times.

The Ginans

The Ginans are Nizari Isma'ili religious texts. They are written in the form of poetry by Pirs to interpret the meanings of Qur'anic ayat into the languages of the Indian subcontinent, especially Gujarati and Urdu. In comparison to Ginans, Ismasilis of other origins, such as Persians, Arabs, and Central Asians have qasidas written by missionaries. See Works of Pir Sadardin

Reincarnation

Reincarnation exists in the Druze branch of Ismailism. The Druze believe that members of their community can only be reincarnated within the community. It is also known that Druze believe in five cosmic principles, represented by the five colored Druze star: intelligence/reason (green), soul (red), word (yellow), precedent (blue), and immanence (white). These virtues take the shape of five different spirits which, until recently, have been continuously reincarnated on Earth as prophets and philosophers including Adam, the ancient Greek mathematician and astronomer Pythagoras, and the ancient Pharaoh of Egypt Akhenaten, and many others. The Druze believe that, in every time period, these five principles were personified in five different people who came down together to Earth to teach humans the true path to God and nirvana, but that with them came five other individuals who would lead people away from the right path into "darkness".

Numerology

Ismasilis believe numbers have religious meanings. The number seven plays a general role in the theology of the Isma'iliyya, including mystical speculations that there are seven heavens, seven continents, seven orifices in the skull, seven days in a week, and so forth.

Imamate

In Nizari Ismailism, the Imam is seen through the Qur'anic phrase, "The Face of God." The Imam is truth and reality itself, and hence he is their path of salvation to God.

Sevener Ismasili doctrine holds that divine revelation had been given in six periods (daur) entrusted to six prophets, who they also call *Natiq* (Speaker), who were commissioned to preach a religion of law to their respective communities.

Whereas the Natiq was concerned with the rites and outward shape of religion, the inner meaning is entrusted to a *Wasi* (Representative). The Wasi would know the secret meaning of all rites and rules and would reveal them to a small circles of initiates.

The Natiq and the Wasi are in turn succeeded by a line of seven Imams, who would guard what they received. The seventh and last Imam in any period would in turn be the Natiq of the next period. The last Imam of the sixth period however would not bring about a new religion of law but supersede all previous religions, abrogate the law and introduce *din Adama al-awwal* ("the original religion of Adam") practised by Adam and the Angels in paradise before the fall, which would be without cult or law but consist merely in all creatures praising the creator and recognizing his unity. This final stage was called Qiyamah.

Pir and Dawah

Just as the Imam is seen by Ismailis as the Face of God, God's avatar within reality, the guide to the avatar is known as the Dai. During the period between the Imamates of Muhammad ibn Ismail and al-Madhi Billah, the relationship between the teacher and the student became a sacred one, and the Dai became a position much beyond a normal missionary. The Dai passed on the sacred and hidden knowledge of the Imam to the student who could then use that information to ascend to higher levels. First the student loved the Dai, and from the Dai he learned to love the Imam, who was but a manifestation of God. In Nizari Ismailism, the head Dai is called the Pir..

Zahir

In Ismailism, things have an exterior meaning, what is apparent. This is called zahir.

Batini

In Ismailism, things have an interior meaning that is reserved for a special few who are in tune with the Imam, or are the Imam himself. This is called batin.

Aql

As with other Shi'ah, Ismasilis believe that the understanding of God is derived from the first light in the universe, the light of Aql, which in Arabic roughly translates as reason. It is through this reason that all living and non-living entities know God, and all of humanity is dependent and united in this light. Contrastingly, in Twelver thought this includes the Prophets as well, especially Muhammad who is the greatest of all the incarnations of Aql.

Taqiyya

Ismasilis believe in the Shi'ite doctrine of taqiyya, which means to hide one's true religious beliefs. This doctrine, which is not found in Sunni theology, has been pivotal to the survival of Ismasili groups since they have been small minorities in many countries and empires hostile to them.

Seven Pillars

Walayah

A pillar which translates from Arabic as "guardianship." It denotes, "Love and devotion for God, the Prophets, the Imam, and the Dai." In Ismasili doctrine, God is the true desire of every soul, and he manifests himself in the forms of Prophets and Imams, and to be guided to his path, one requires a messenger or a guide: a Dai.

Taharah or Shahada

Taharah

A pillar which translates from Arabic as "purity." The Druze do not believe in this pillar and instead substitute shahada in its place.

Shahada

In place of Taharah, the Druze have the Shahada, or affirmation of faith.

Salah

A pillar which translates from Arabic as "prayer." Unlike Sunni and Twelver Muslims, Nizari Ismai'lis do not follow the mainstream Islamic practice in regards to the number of daily prayers. Nizari Ismai'lis believe that it is up to the Imam of the time to designate the style and form of prayer, and for this reason current Nizari prayer resembles a dua (supplication) and is recited three times a day. These three times have been related with the three prayer times mentioned in the Qur'an, i-e, Sunrise, before Sunset, and After Sunset. In this regard, Ismaili's believe, the Imam of the time has the right to amend the prayers according to the needs of the time. The Druze, who also choose not to follow Islamic shari'ah (legal code), attribute a solely metaphorical meaning to salah. In contrast, the Mustaali (Bohra) branch of Ismailism has kept five prayers and their style is generally closely related to Twelver groups.

Zakah

A pillar which translates as "charity." With the exception of the Druze sect, all Ismasilis form of zakat resembles mainstream Muslims. The Twelvers, pay khums which is 1/ 5 of one's unspent money at the end of the year. Ismasilies,also pay the tithe of 12.5% which is re used it furthering development projects in the eastern world, which benefit not only Ismailis but also the many other communities living in that area.

Sawm

A pillar which translates as "fasting." Mainstream Sunni and Shi'ite Muslims fast by abstaining from food, drink and sexual relations with one's spouse from dawn to sunset for 30 days during the holy month of Ramadan (9th month of the Islamic calendar). In contrast, the Nizari and Mustaali believe in a metaphorical as well as a literal meaning of fasting. The literal meaning is that one must fast as an obligation, such as during Ramadan, and the metaphorical meaning being that one is in attainment of the Divine Truth and must strive to avoid worldy activities which may detract from this goal. In particular, Ismasilis believe that the esoteric meaning of fasting involves a the "fasting of soul," whereby they attempt to purify the soul simply by avoiding sinful acts and doing good deeds, etc. In addition, the Nizari also fast on "Shukravari Beej" which falls on a Friday that coincides with the New Moon.

Hajj

A pillar which translates from Arabic as "pilgrimage", it is the pilgrimage to Mecca, Saudi Arabia. It is currently the largest annual pilgrimage in the world and is the fifth pillar of Islam, a religious duty that must be carried out at least once in one's lifetime by every able-bodied Muslim who can afford to do so. Ismaili sects do not ascribe to mainstream Islamic beliefs regarding the Hajj, considering it instead to metaphorically mean visiting the Imam himself, that being the greatest and most spiritual of all pilgrimages. However, as the Druze do not follow shariah, they do not believe in a literal pilgrimage to the Kaaba in Mecca like other Muslims do, while the Mustaali still hold on to the literal meaning as well.

Jihad

An Isiamic term, Jihad is a religious duty of Muslims. In Arabic, the word jihad is a noun meaning "struggle." Jihad appears frequently in the Qur'an and common usage as the idiomatic expression "striving in the way of God (al-jihad fi sabil Allah)". A person engaged in jihad is called a mujahid; the plural is mujahideen.

A minority among the Sunni scholars sometimes refer to this duty as the sixth pillar of Islam, though it occupies no such official status. In Twelver Shi'a Islam, however, Jihad is one of the 10 Practices of the Religion.

In western societies, the term jihad is often mistranslated as "holy war". Muslim authors tend to reject such an approach stressing also the non-militant connotations of the word. In technical literature regarding the concept of jihad the term "holy war" has often been used to describe it. However, scholars of Islamic studies often reject this association, stressing that the two terms are not synonymous.

Branches

Estimates on the total Ismai'li population range from 15–20 million. It is accepted that Ismai'lis constitute the second-largest Shi'a Muslim population. Within the Ismai'li sub-sect, the largest branch is Nizari with 18 Million. With its branches added together, the Mustaali are the second largest at 1-2 million, followed by the Druze at around 350,000 to 1 million.

Nizari

The largest part of the Ismasili community today accepts Prince Karim Aga Khan IV as their 49th Imam, who is descended from Muhammad through his daughter Famimah az-Zahra and 'Ali, Muhammad's cousin and son-in-law. The 46th Ismasili Imam, Aga Hassan 'Ali Shah, fled Iran in the 1840s after a failed coup against the Shah of the Qajar dynasty. Aga Hassan 'Ali Shah settled in Mumbai in 1848.

Like its predecessors, the present constitution is founded on each Ismasili's spiritual allegiance to the Imam of the Time (*Imam az-Zaman*), which is separate from the secular allegiance that all Ismasilis owe as citizens to their national entities. The present Imam and his predecessor emphasized Ismasilis' allegiance to their country as a fundamental obligation. These obligations discharged not by passive affirmation but through responsible engagement and active commitment to uphold national integrity and contribute to peaceful development.

In view of the importance that Islam places on maintaining a balance between the spiritual well-being of the individual and the quality of his life, the Imam's guidance deals with both aspects of the life of his followers. The Aga

Khan has encouraged Ismasilis settled in the industrialized world to contribute towards the progress of communities in the developing world through various development programmes. In recent years, Nizari Ismasilis, who have come to the US, Canada and Europe, many as refugees from Asia and Africa, have readily settled into the social, educational and economic fabric of urban and rural centres across the two continents. As in the developing world, the Nizari Ismasili community's settlement in the industrial world has involved the establishment of community institutions characterized by an ethos of self-reliance, an emphasis on education, and a spirit of philanthropy.

Mustaali

In time, the seat for one chain of the Dai was split between India and Yemen as the community split several times, each recognizing a different Dai. Today, the Dawoodi Bohras, which constitute the majority of the Mustaali Ismasili accept Mohammed Burhanuddin as the 52nd Dasi al-Mumlaq. The Dawoodi Bohras are based in India, along with the Alawi Bohra. The Sulaimani Bohra however still are in primarily Yemen and Saudi Arabia.

In recent years, there has been a rapprochement between the Sulaimani Mustaali and the Dawoodi Mustaali.

The Bohra are noted to be the more traditional of the three main groups of Ismasili, maintaining rituals such as prayer and fasting more consistently with the practices of other Shia sects. It is often said they resemble Sunni Islam even more than Twelvers do, though this would hold true for matters of the exterior (zahir) only, with little bearing on doctrinal differences.

Dawoodi Bohra

The Dawoodi Bohras are a very closely-knit community who seek advice from the Dai on spiritual and temporal matters.

Dawoodi Bohras is essentially and traditionally Fatimid and is headed by the Dai al-Mutlaq, who is appointed by his predecessor in office. The Dai al-Mutlaq appoints two others to the subsidiary ranks of mazun "licentiate" and Mukasir. These positions are followed by the rank of ra'sul hudood, bhaisaheb, miya-saheb, shaikh-saheb and mulla-saheb, which are held by several of Bohras. The 'Aamil or Saheb-e Raza who is granted the permission to perform the religious ceremonies of the believers by the Dai al-Mutlaq and also leads the local congregation in religious, social and community affairs, is sent to each town where a sizable population of believers exists. Such towns normally have a masjid (commonly known as mosque) and an adjoining jamaa'at-khaana (assembly hall) where socio-religious functions are held. The local organizations which manage these properties and administer the social and religious activities of the local Bohras report directly to the central administration of the Dai al-Mutlaq.

While the majority of Dawoodi Bohras have traditionally been traders, it is becoming increasingly common for them to become professionals. Some choose to become Doctors, consultants or analysts as well as a large contingent of medical professionals. Dawoodi Bohras are encouraged to educate themselves in both religious and secular knowledge, and as a result, the number of professionals in the community is rapidly increasing. Dawoodi Bohras believe that the education of women is equally important to that of men, and many Dawoodi Bohra women choose to enter the workforce. Al Jamea tus Saifiyah (The Arabic Academy) in Surat and Karachi is a sign to the educational importance in the Dawoodi community. The Academy has an advanced curriculum which encompasses religious and secular education for both men and women.

Today there are approximately one million Dawoodi Bohras. The majority of these reside in India and Pakistan, but there is also a significant diaspora resident in the Middle East, East Africa, Europe, North America and the Far East.

The ordinary Bohra is highly conscious of his identity and this is especially demonstrated at religious and traditional occasions by the appearance and attire of the participants. Dawoodi Bohra men wear a traditional white three piece outfit, plus a white and gold cap (called a *topi*), and women wear the *rida,* a distinctive form of the commonly known burqa which is distinguished from other forms of the veil due to it often being in color and decorated with patterns and lace.

Besides speaking the local languages, the Dawoodis have their own language called Lisanu l-Dawat "Tongue of the Dawat". This is written in Arabic script but is derived from Urdu, Gujarati and Arabic and Persian.

Sulaimani Bohra

Founded in 1592, they are mostly concentrated in Yemen, but are today also found in Pakistan and India. The denomination is named after its 27th Dai, (Sulayman ibn Hassan).

The total number of Sulaimanis currently are around 300,000, mainly living in the eastern district of Haraz in the North west of Yemen and in Najaran, Saudi Arabia. Beside the Banu Yam of Najaran, the Sulaimanis are in Haraz, among the inhabitants of the Jabal Magharibа and in Hawzan, Lahab and Attara, as well as in the district of Hamdan and in the vicinity of Yarim.

In India there are between 3000-5000 Sulaimanis living mainly in Baroda, Hyderabad, Mumbai and Surat. In Pakistan there is a well established Sulaimani community in Sind, some five to six thousand Sulaimanis live in rural areas of Sind, these Ismasili Sulaimani communities are in Sind from the time of Fatimid Ismasili Muizz li din Allah when he sent his Dais to Sind.

There are also some 900-1000 Sulaimanis mainly from Indian Sub-continent scattered around the World, in the Persian Gulf States, USA, Canada, Thailand, Australia, Japan and UK.

Alavi Bohra

While lesser known and smallest in number, Alavi Bohras accept as the 44th dasi al-mumlaq, Abu Haatim Taiyeb Ziyauddin Saheb. They are mostly concentrated in India.

The Alavi Bohra community has its headquarters at Baroda City, Gujarat, India. The 44th Dai al-Mutlaq, Taiyeb Ziyauddin Saheb, is the head of the community. The religious hierarchy of the Alavi Bohras is essentially and traditionally Fatimid and is headed by the Dai al-Mutlaq, who is appointed by his predecessor in office. The Dai al-Mutlaq appoints two others to the subsidiary ranks of mazun "licentiate" and Mukasir. These positions are followed by the rank of ra'sul hudood, bhaisaheb, miya-saheb, shaikh-saheb and mulla-saheb, which are held by several of Bohras. The 'Aamil or Saheb-e Raza who is granted the permission to perform the religious ceremonies of the believers by the Dai al-Mutlaq and also leads the local congregation in religious, social and community affairs, is sent to each town where a sizable population of believers exists. Such towns normally have a mosque and an adjoining jamaa'at-khaana (assembly hall) where socio-religious functions are held. The local organizations which manage these properties and administer the social and religious activities of the local Bohras report directly to the central administration of the Dai al-Mutlaq.

Hebtiahs Bohra

The Hebtiahs Bohra are a branch of Mustaali Ismaili Shi'a Islam that broke off from the mainstream Dawoodi Bohra after the death of the 39th Da'i al-Mutlaq in 1754.

Atba-i-Malak

The Abta-i Malak jamaat (community) are a branch of Mustaali Ismaili Shi'a Islam that broke off from the mainstream Dawoodi Bohra after the death of the 46th Da'i al-Mutlaq, under the leadership of Abdul Hussain Jivaji. They have further split into two more branches, the Atba-i-Malak Badra and Atba-i-Malak Vakil.

Druze

While on one view there is a historical nexus between the Druze and Ismasilis, any such links are purely historical and do not entail any modern similarities, given that one of the Druze's central tenets is trans-migration of the soul (reincarnation) as well as other contrasting beliefs with Ismasilism and Islam. Druze is an offshoot of Ismailism. Many historical links do trace back to Syria and particularly Masyaf.

Extinct Branches

Hafizi

This branch held that whoever the political ruler of the Fatimid Empire was, was also the Imam of the faith. This branch died with the Fatimid Empire.

Seveners

A branch of the Ismasili known as the *Sabasiyyin* "Seveners" hold that Ismasil's son, Muhammad, was the seventh and final Ismasili, who is said to be in the Occultation. However, most scholars believe this group is either extremely small or totally non-existent today.

Ainsarii

The Ainsarii were a sect of the Ismailis who survived the destruction of the stronghold of Alamut. An Ismaili sect of the Assassins, who continued to exist after the stronghold of that society was destroyed.

Inclusion in Amman Message and Islamic Ummah

Although Ismasilism is rejected by some Sunni and Shi'ite Muslim scholars as a heretical sect, the Amman Message, which was issued on November 9, 2004 (27th of Ramadan 1425 AH) by King Abdullah II bin Al-Hussein of Jordan, called for tolerance and unity in the Muslim world. Subsequently, a three-point dossier was issued by 200 Muslim academics from over 50 countries, focusing on issues of: defining who a Muslim is; and principles related to delivering religious edicts. As per the recognition via Islamic theology, Ismasilism was included as a legal Madh'hab. In the Amman Message Ismasilis are referred to as Jafari, a term that denotes both Ismasili and Twelvers due to their Imamate descending from Imam Jafar as-Sadiq.

●●

10

Reforms of Umar's Era

Umar was the second muslim Caliph and reigned during 634 to 644 CE. This article details the **reforms of Umar's era**. Umar undertook many administrative reforms and closely oversaw public policy, establishing an advanced administration for newly conquered lands, including several new ministries and bureaucracies, as well as ordering a census of all the Muslim territories. During his reign, the garrison cities of Basrah and al-Kufah were founded or expanded. In 638, he extended and renovated the Grand Mosque in Mecca and the Mosque of the Prophet in Medina. He also began the process of codifying Islamic law.

Reforms

Political

Umar was a political genius, he not only expanded his empire at an unprecedented rate but also buildup its political structure on firm and sound bases. Umar was very acute in the appointment of his provincial governors called Wali or amir. When ever a governor was appointed Umar man was sent with him that would read publicly his powers and jurisdictions. During the reign of Caliph Abu Bakr, the state was economically weak, while during Umar's reign because of increase in revenues and other sources of income, the state was on its way to economic prosperity.

Hence Umar felt it necessary that the officers be treated in strict way as to prevent the possible greed of money that may lead them to corruption. During his reign, at the time of appointment, every officer was required to make the oath:

1. That he would not ride a Turkic horse.
2. That he would not wear fine clothes.
3. That he would not eat sifted flour.
4. That he would not keep a porter at his door.
5. That he would always keep his door open to the public.

Caliph Umar himself followed the above postulates strictly. Umar also developed an intelligence department of secret services. This was one of the reason of Umar's iron fist rule on his empire. His agents were everywhere: in the army, in the bureaucracy and in the enemy land. For the officials of Umar it was said to be the most fearsome department. On discovery of any scandal on the part of any official, an investigation though a special department of accountability headed by Muhammad ibn Maslamah would be carried out and if the official would prove guilty he was immediately deposed from his office and his punishment was vary from publicly humiliating punishments to flogging. Before appointment, all financial assets and details of the political officer use to be recorded and were check each year. It was due to Umar's strong commitment to eradicate corruption and bribery. He is reported to have said to one of his Governor:

"I had send you as a governor, not as a merchant !"

Military

Caliph Umar organised the army as a State Department. This reform was introduced in 637 A.D. A beginning was made with the Quraish and the Ansars and the system was gradually extended to the whole of Arabia and to Muslims of conquered lands. A register of all adults who could be called to war was prepared, and a scale of salaries was fixed. All men registered were liable to military service. They were divided into two categories, namely:

1. Those who formed the regular standing army; and
2. Those that lived in their homes, but were liable to be called to the colors whenever needed.

The pay was paid in the beginning of the month of Muharram. The allowances were paid during the harvesting season. The armies of the Caliphs were mostly paid in cash salaries. In contrast to many post-Roman polities in Europe, grants of land, or of rights to collect taxes directly from the payers, were of only minor importance. A major consequence of this was that the army directly depended on the state for its subsistence which, in turn, meant that the military had to control the state apparatus. Promotions in the army were made on the strength of the length of service or exceptional merit. Officership was an appointment and not a rank. Officers were appointed to command for the battle or the campaign; and once the operation was concluded, they could well find themselves in the ranks again. Leave of absence was given to army men at regular intervals. The troops stationed at far off places were given leave after four months. Each army corps was accompanied by an officer of the treasury, an Accountant, aQadi, and a number of interpreters besides a number of Physicians and Surgeons. Expeditions were undertaken according to seasons. Expeditions in cold countries were undertaken during the summer, and in hot countries in winter. Umar established military cantonments on strategic positions through out empire to deal with any emergency efficiently and quickly. The garrison towns of Kufa, Busra and Fustat were founded by Umar. They were also provincial capital of their respective provinces.

Judicial

Umar's judicially reforms were revolutionary and very close to modern judicial doctrine. He stressed on independence of judiciary and declared it a sovereign state organ that could proceed with out any pressure of state. No was exempted from law not even Caliph himself. during early years of his rule he also acted as a chief justice of Madinah but later due to increasing burden of work he was left with no option but to assign his office to some other person, he accordingly appointed Abu Dardah, a well known Sahabi, though he didn't resigned completely from the office and Abu Dardah only acted as his secondary. Umar was the founder of Fiqh (*Islamic jurisprudence*). More than one thousand juristic pronouncements of Umar are on record and are followed by four Sunni schools of law in Islamic jurisprudence. In addition to this he also laid down the principle of Qiyas or logical deduction and also enunciated numerous rules about inference and generalization of laws which form the basis of Islamic jurisprudence. In his instructions to his judicial officers Umar is reported to have said:

> "When you do not find a judgment on an issue in the Quran or Hadith and you are in doubt about it, ponder over the question and ponder again. Then look for dicta on like and similar issues, and decide accordingly."

Umar was very keen in appointing qazis (*Islamic term for Chief Justice*). To all the major provincial cities, Umar would personally appointed judges. Umar entrusted the office of justice only to those selected persons who could fulfill his criteria for this office, some of which are as follow:

1. Must be well reputed for his morals, modesty, and interpersonal relations.
2. Must be intelligent, and astute in judicial decisions and enjoy his own personal view regarding all social issues that could enable them in the formulation of precedent or case law.
3. He must be highly qualified in fiqh

4. Must be socially a powerful and influential personality so that he might not come under pressure of any powerful perpetrator.

Appointment of judges in districts and small towns were made by his appointed provincial Wali (*Governors*).

Umar appointed judges with very high salaries and for lifelong tenure this as in modern times, was to make sure that judges could not be drawn to wards bribery and a non prejudice and unbiased verdicts could be reach. Umar also held that in the court the Judge should not be praised and that all acts should be judged according to the test of public interest. He also gave a general law that any act which did not harm any one and was otherwise not forbidden under law was permissible. He issued some special instructions and code of conducts to be followed in the courts according to which judges were instructed to deal with rich and poor alike in the court in one such letter to his judge in Iraq Umar has been quoted saying:

> "When prosecutor and defender appears in front of you then demand evenhanded evidence from them. Be so benevolent to the weak that it will bolster him and he could say every thing that is in his heart and do hearten the poor. Beware that if you will not be like this to poor and weak, they will put down their right and will go away and responsibility of this discrimination with him lays with one who didn't been gentle to him."

Social

One of Umar's most remarkable reform was establishment of Islamic calendar. Umar held the starting point of calendar to be the year of Hijra roughly corresponding the year 622, when Prophet Mohammad migrated to Madinah from Mecca. Umar prohibited the sale of wine and drunkers were punished with 80 lashes. Umar held that a slave woman who bore children to her master stood be set free. It was a practice among Arab poets to mention the name of some women in their poetry to make it attractive while other glorify their love affair with some girl mentioning her name in the poetic verses, it was a heinous practice and woman's modesty was directly targeted in it, Umar put a ban on this practice and declared it unlawful and a punishment was ruled out for the offenders. Similarly Umar also banned written satires and lampoons. Umar established a more exact system of calculation of the inheritance. Under Umar's rule, for first time in history, state intervention to control the price of merchandise was practiced. Umar established a stables for the lost camels. Umar started salary for Imams, Muadhans (*Callers to prayer*) teachers and public lectures. He also established an effective Postal service. Annually zakat was charged from Muslims, while from non-Muslim, jizya was charged, it was charged from non-Muslims adult males only and was usually 2 dirhams per head auunally, which was far too less than the tax charged by Eastern Roman empire and Sassanid Persian Empire, a reason that pleased the non-Muslim subjects. In addition to this non-Muslims were also exempted from military services. they were free to follow any religion they want. Umar's territorial domains including some of the world's most strategic places for trade caravans. Trade tax that Umar charged was far less than the tax charged by Roman and other empires. More over for the prosperous trade and trading incentives for merchants and for their comforts Umar established special chain of state-owned guest house and Guilds for certain trades. Umar held census in the empire and established an institution of *Diwa'an* (literary means register*), a department of registration which had names of all the population mentioned in it. The provincial and district headquarter had their own copies of diwa'an.* Name of every new born baby was entered in Diwa'an, parents were responsible to register their infants, the incentive was the handsome allowance that was started in 641, when Umar established Bayt al-mal or public treasury. It was a financial institution, responsible for the administration of allowance, taxes, Jizya and war spoil. Annual allowance was given to all Muslim population of the empire, men, women children and new born infants. The highest amount of allowance was set for the wives of Prophet Mohammad which was 12,000 dirhams. For adults the lowest allowance was 300 dirhams that was usually given to desert Bedouins. The allowance of infants was 100 dirhams. The registers where the names of the receivers of allowance were mentioned were usually in the regional Bayt al-mal, which were in major cities like Kufa, Busra, Damascus and Fustat etc or in the district headquarter where the amir resides or with respective tribal chiefs. Allowance in Madinah and near by villages was usually personally distributed by Umar.

Umar's purpose of giving allowance was soaring the economical condition of Muslims. Umar is reported to have express his views regarding the allowance in his famous saying:

> "The one who have wealth should invest it in profitable works, and if some one have fertile land he should cultivate it, because soon those rulers will come who will money only to those whom he wills to."

Umar is also quoted saying:

> """ Among Bedouin (*poor nomads*) who so ever will receive the allowance, he must purchase some goats when he receives allowance next year, he should sell those goats and along with the money of allowance should purchase cattle."

This was a remarkable exertion to improve the living standard of common man. Umar's these efforts however worked, and by the time of Umar's successor Caliph Uthman, Muslim population was prosper. Umar, a year later, when Muslim's allowance was startes, Umar also issued orders for the allowance for the poor and under privilege non-Muslims though out the empire.

The concepts of welfare and pension were introduced in early Islamic law as forms of *Zakat* (charity), one of the Five Pillars of Islam, under Umar in the 7th century. The taxes (including *Zakat* and *Jizya*) collected in the treasury of an Islamic government were used to provide income for the needy, including the poor, elderly, orphans, widows, and the disabled. According to the Islamic jurist Al-Ghazali (Algazel, 1058-1111), the government was also expected to stockpile food supplies in every region in case a disaster or famine occurred. The Caliphate can thus be considered the world's first major welfare state.

Religious

Umar was the first to realize the necessity of the proper sifting of the Hadith and thus founded the science of Hadith. Authentic Hadiths were compiled mostly related to religious, moral, social and community related affairs. These were copied and sent through out the empire to Judges, governors, teachers and scholars of all provinces for guidance. All these Hadiths had the status of law. Umar took special measures in keeping science of Hadith unadulterated. He accordingly forbade companions of Prophet Mohammad from reporting hadith in public. Later during caliph Uthman ibn Affan's reign this sanction was however withdrawal.

Prophet Mohammad initially prayed the tarawih, a special Muslim prayers during the holy month of Ramazan, in congregation but later discontinued this practice out of fear that Muslims would start to believe the prayers to be mandatory, rather than a sunnah. During his Caliphate Umar reinstated the practice of praying *tarawih* in congregation as there was no longer any fear of people taking it as something mandatory.

During Prophet Mohammad's and Abu Bakr's era divorce given at a time whether one or fifty were to be considered a single divorce that will followed by a Iddah of four months and ten days and during this period if the couple wanted to reconcile the first divorce will be void. during Umar's reign Muslims conquered Persian and Roman lands and thus came into contact with beautiful and charming Persian and Greek women. It had become a general practice that most of the Muslim soldiers would divorce their Arab wives and marry a Persian or Greek women. According to Islamic tradition, wife was financially responsibility of her husband during Iddah or reconciliation period and was to stay at her husband's home during iddah where now new Persian or Roman mistress of his husband reside as well, the Arab women use to be side lined and the four month iddah would become a period of intense mental stress and sorrow for her. This matter worried Umar who was apprehensive for its social results in future. This all peaked after 636 and Umar thus exercising the Islamic jurisprudence of ijtihad declared that from now to so on three Talaq (divorce) will be considered absolute and Nikah (*marriage*) will be dissolved letting the women free from any authority of his husband. This was done by Umar for public good specially for women for whom this was a sign of relief. One year later in 637 after the conquest of Byzantine capital city of eastern zone Antioch Umar declared that those Muslim who already have four wives cant divorce any of their wife to marry a Roman or Persian women.

Nikah Mut'a, a marriage with a pre-set time was a common practice among the pre-Islamic Arabs. Umar forbade it on the ground that it in many cases was usually immoral.

It was a common practice that a husband can not led the funeral prayer of his wife. Umar led one of his wife's funeral prayers. He also ruled that on the occasion of a funeral prayers four Takbirs should be offered.

God in Islam

In Islam, God, known in Arabic as Allah, is the all-powerful and all-knowing Creator, Sustainer, Ordainer, and Judge of the universe. Islam puts a heavy emphasis on the conceptualisation of God as strictly singular (*tawhid*). God is unique (*wahid*) and inherently one (*ahad*), all-merciful and omnipotent. According to tradition there are 99 Names of God (*al-asma al-husna* lit. meaning: "The best names") each of which evoke a distinct attribute of God. All these names refer to Allah, the supreme and all-comprehensive divine name. Among the 99 names of God, the most famous and most frequent of these names are "the Compassionate" (*al-rahman*) and "the Merciful" (*al-rahim*).

Creation and ordering of the universe is seen as an act of prime mercy for which all creatures sing God's glories and bear witness to God's unity and lordship. According to the Islamic teachings, God exists without a place. According to the Qur'an, "No vision can grasp Him, but His grasp is over all vision. God is above all comprehension, yet is acquainted with all things" (Qur'an 6:103)

God in Islam is not only majestic and sovereign, but also a personal God: according to the Qur'an, God is nearer to a person than his jugular vein. (Quran 50:16)God responds to those in need or distress whenever they call. Above all, God guides humanity to the right way, "the holy way."

Islam teaches that Allah is the same God worshipped by the members of other Abrahamic religions such as Christianity and Judaism. (29:46).

Oneness of God

Oneness of God or Tawhid is the act of believing and affirming that God (Arabic: Allah) is one and unique (*wahid*). The Qur'an asserts the existence of a single and absolute truth that transcends the world; a unique and indivisible being who is independent of the entire creation. According to the Qur'an:

> "Say: He is God, the One and Only; God, the Eternal, Absolute; He begetteth not, nor is He begotten; And there is none like unto Him." (Sura 112:1-4, *Yusuf Ali*)

Thy Lord is self-sufficient, full of Mercy: if it were God's will, God could destroy you, and in your place appoint whom God will as your successors, even as God raised you up from the posterity of other people." (Sura 6:133, *Yusuf Ali*)

According to Vincent J. Cornell, the Qur'an also provides a monist image of God by describing the reality as a unified whole, with God being a single concept that would describe or ascribe all existing things:"God is the First and the Last, the Outward and the Inward; God is the Knower of everything (Sura 57:3)" Some Muslims have however vigorously criticised interpretations that would lead to a monist view of God for what they see as blurring the distinction between the creator and the creature, and its incompatibility with the radical monotheism of Islam.

The indivisibility of God implies the indivisibility of God's sovereignty which in turn leads to the conception of universe as a just and coherent moral universe rather than an existential and moral chaos (as in polytheism). Similarly the Qur'an rejects the binary modes of thinking such as the idea of duality of God by arguing that both good and evil generate from God's creative act and that the evil forces have no power to create anything. God in Islam is a universal god rather than a local, tribal or parochial one; an absolute who integrates all affirmative values and brooks no evil.

Tawhid constitutes the foremost article of the Muslim profession. To attribute divinity to a created entity is the only unpardonable sin mentioned in the Qur'an. Muslims believe that the entirety of the Islamic teaching rests on the principle of Tawhid.

God's Attributes

The Qur'an refers to the attributes of God as God's "most beautiful names" (see 7:180, 17:110, 20:8, 59:24). According to Gerhard Böwering, "They are traditionally enumerated as 99 in number to which is added as the highest name (al-ism al-as"am), the supreme name of God, Allah. The locus classicus for listing the divine names in the literature of quraanic commentary is 17:110, "Call him Allah (the God), or call him Ar-Rahman (the Gracious); whichsoever you call upon, to him belong the most beautiful names," and also 59:22-24, which includes a cluster of more than a dozen divine epithets." The most commonly used names for god in Islam are:

- The Most High (al-Aziz)
- The Most Great (al-Mutakabbir)
- The Ever Forgiving (al-Ghaffar)
- The Ever Providing (al-Muhaymin)
- The Lord and Cherisher of the Worlds (Rabb al-Alameen)
- The Self Subsisting (al-Haqq)
- The Eternal Lord (al-Baqi)
- The Sustainer (al-Muqsith)
- The Peaceful (Alsalam)

Islamic theology makes a distinction between the attributes of God and the divine essence.

Furthermore, it is one of the fundamentals in Islam that God exists without a place and has no resemblance to his creations. For instance, God is not a body and there is nothing like him. In the Quran it says what mean "Nothing is like him in anyway,". Allah is not limited to Dimensions.

God's Omniscience

The Qur'an describes God as being fully aware of everything that happens in the universe, including private thoughts and feelings, and asserts that one can not hide anything from God:

> In whatever business thou mayest be, and whatever portion thou mayest be reciting from the Qur'an,- and whatever deed ye (mankind) may be doing,- We are witnesses thereof when ye are deeply engrossed therein. Nor is hidden from thy Lord (so much as) the weight of an atom on the earth or in heaven. And not the least and not the greatest of these things but are recorded in a clear record.
>
> —[10:61]

Cross-Religion Comparison

God in Islam vs God in pre-Islamic Arabian conceptions

In contrast with Pre-Islamic Arabian polytheism, God in Islam does not have associates and companions nor is there any kinship between God and jinn. Pre-Islamic pagan Arabs believed in a blind, powerful, inexorable and insensible fate over which man had no control. This was replaced with the Islamic notion of a powerful but provident and merciful God.

God in Islam vs God in Judaism

According to Francis Edwards Peters, "The Qur'an insists, Muslims believe, and historians affirm that Muhammad and his followers worship the same God as the Jews [see Qur'an 29:46]. The Quran's Allah is the same Creator God who covenanted with Abraham". Peters states that the Qur'an portrays Allah as both more powerful and more remote than Yahweh, and as a universal deity, unlike Yahweh who closely follows Israelites.

God in Islam vs God in Christianity

Islam vigorously rejects the Christian belief that God is three persons in one substance. In the Islamic conception of God, no intermediaries between God and creation exists and God's presence is believed to be everywhere, and yet he is not incarnated in anything.

The Christian West perceived Islam as a heathen religion during the first and second Crusade. Muhammad was viewed as a kind of demon or false god worshipped with Apollyon and Termangant in an unholy trinity. The traditional view of Christianity however was that Muhammad's God is the same as Jesus' God. Ludovico Marracci (1734), the confessor of Pope Innocent XI, states:

> That both Mohammed and those among his followers who are reckoned orthodox, had and continue to have just and true notions of God and his attributes, appears so plain from the Koran itself and all the Muslim laws, that it would be loss of time to refute those who suppose the God of Mohammed to be different from the true God.

Numerous passages in the Old testament refer to God's love. A central theme in the New Testament is God's love in sending of Jesus. In Islam, God's love is shown through his signs and the creation of the Earth where humans can live in moderate comfort.

> "O ye people! Adore your Guardian-Lord, who created you and those who came before you, that ye may have the chance to learn righteousness;

Who has made the Earth your couch, and the heavens your canopy; and sent down rain from the heavens; and brought forth therewith fruits for your sustenance; then set not up rivals unto God when ye know (the truth)." (Sura 2:21-22, *Yusuf Ali*)

The most common Muslim invocation of God is 'the Most-Gracious, the Most-Merciful'. Two other of the "beautiful names" of God are 'The Most Loving' (Al-Wadud) and 'The Bestower'(Al-Wahhab). In Islam, Watt says, God has provided the *opportunity* for each community to attain the great success (i.e. the life in Heaven) by sending messengers or prophets to them. Islam also has a doctrine of intercession of Muhammad on the Last Day that would be received favorably, though the sinners might be punished for their sins either in this life or for a limited time in hell.

●●

11
Druze Religious Community

The Druze are a religious community found primarily in Syria, Lebanon, Israel, and Jordan, whose traditional religion is said to have begun as an offshoot of Islam, but is unique in its incorporation of Gnosticism, Neoplatonism and other philosophies, similar to other followers of Ismaili Shi'a Islam.

Theologically, Druze consider themselves "an Islamic Unist, reformatory sect". The Druze call themselves *Ahl al-Tawhid* "People of Unitarianism or Monotheism" or *al-Muwahhidun* "Unitarians, Monotheists."

Location

The Druze people reside primarily in Syria, Lebanon, and Israel. The Israeli Druze are mostly in Galilee (81%) and around Haifa (19%). The Jordanian Druze can be found in Amman and Zarka; about 50% live in the town of Azraq, and a smaller number in Irbid and Aqaba. The Golan Heights, the mountainous region in north of Israel, is home to about 20,000 Druze.

The Institute of Druze Studies estimates that 40%–50% of Druze live in Syria, 30%–40% in Lebanon, 6%–7% in Israel, and 1%–2% in Jordan.

Large communities of expatriate Druze also live outside the Middle East in Australia, Canada, Europe, Latin America, the United States and West Africa. They use the Arabic language and follow a social pattern very similar to the other East Mediterraneans of the region.

There are thought to be as many as 1 million Druze worldwide, the vast majority in the Levant or East Mediterranean.

Origin of the Name

The most plausible theory of the origin of the name Druze is that it derived from the name of Anushtakin ad-Darazi, one of the early leaders of the faith. However, the Druze consider ad-Darazi a heretic who practiced *ghuluww* ("exaggeration"), which refers to the belief that God was incarnated in human beings, especially 'Ali and his descendants. Ad-Darazi was a da'i ("missionary") who first preached an unorthodox version of the faith to outsiders in 1016. He claimed to be the true leader of the faithful rather than Hamza ibn 'Ali (the appointed leader) and also that al-Hakim and his ancestors were incarnations of God.

Although he is considered a renegade by the Unitarian community, the name "Druze" is still used for identification and for historical reasons. Al-Hakim bi-Amr Allah executed ad-Darazi in 1018 for his teachings.

Some authorities see in the name "Druze" a descriptive epithet, derived from Arabic *derasa* ("those who read"), or *darrisa* (those in possession of Truth) or *dugs* ("the clever, initiated"). Others have speculated that the word comes from the Arabic-Persian word *Darazo* ("bliss") or from Shaykh Hussayn ad-Darazi, who was one of the early converts to the faith. In the early stages of the movement, the word "Druze" is rarely mentioned by historians, and in Druze religious texts only the word *Muwahhidun* ("Unitarian") appears. The only early Arab historian who mentions the Druze is the 11th century Christian scholar Yahyá ibn Sa'id al-Antaki, who clearly refers to the heretical group created by ad-Darazi rather than the followers of Hamza ibn 'Ali. As for Western sources, Benjamin of Tudela, the Jewish traveler who passed through Lebanon in or about 1165, was one of the first European writers to refer to the Druzes by name. The word *Dogziyin* ("Druzes") occurs in an early Hebrew edition of his travels, but it is clear that this is a scribal error. Be that as it may, he described the Druze as "mountain dwellers, monotheists, who believe in "soul eternity" and reincarnation."

Early History

The Druze faith began as a movement in Ismailism that was mainly influenced by Greek philosophy and gnosticism and opposed certain religious and philosophical ideologies that were present during that epoch.

The faith was founded by Hamza ibn 'Ali ibn Ahmad, a Persian Ismaili mystic and scholar. He came to Egypt in 1014 and assembled a group of scholars and leaders from across the Islamic world to form a new Unitarian movement. The order's meetings were held in the Raydan Mosque, near the Al-Hakim Mosque.

In 1017, Hamza officially revealed the Druze faith and began to preach his doctrine. Hamza gained the support of the Fatimid Caliph al-Hakim, who issued a decree promoting religious freedom prior to the declaration of the divine call.

Remove ye the causes of fear and estrangement from yourselves. Do away with the corruption of delusion and conformity. Be ye certain that the Prince of Believers hath given unto you free will, and hath spared you the trouble of disguising and concealing your true beliefs, so that when ye work ye may keep your deeds pure for God. He hath done thus so that when you relinquish your previous beliefs and doctrines ye shall not indeed lean on such causes of impediments and pretensions. By conveying to you the reality of his intention, the Prince of Believers hath spared you any excuse for doing so. He hath urged you to declare your belief openly. Ye are now safe from any hand which may bringeth harm unto you. Ye now may find rest in his assurance ye shall not be wronged. Let those who are present convey this message unto the absent so that it may be known by both the distinguished and the common people. It shall thus become a rule to mankind; and Divine Wisdom shall prevail for all the days to come.

Al-Hakim became a central figure in the Druze faith even though his own religious position was disputed among scholars. John Esposito states that al-Hakim believed that "he was not only the divinely appointed religio-political leader but also the cosmic intellect linking God with creation.", while others like Nissim Dana and Mordechai Nisan state that he is perceived as the manifestation and the reincarnation of God or presumably the image of God.

Some Druze and non-Druze scholars like Samy Swayd and Sami Makarem state that this confusion is due to confusion about the role of the early heretical preacher ad-Darazi, whose teachings the Druze rejected as heretical. These sources assert that al-Hakim refused ad-Darazi's claims of divinity, and ordered the elimination of his movement while supporting that of Hamza ibn Ali.

Al-Hakim disappeared one night while out on his evening ride - presumably assassinated, perhaps at the behest of his formidable elder sister Sitt al-Mulk. The Druze believe he went into Occultation with Hamza ibn Ali and three other prominent preachers, leaving the care of the "Unitarian missionary movement" to a new leader, Baha'u d-Din.

Persecution during the Fatimid Times

Al-Hakim was replaced by his underage son, 'Ali az-Zahir. The sect founded by Hamzah ibn 'Ali, which was prominent in the Levant, North Africa, Egypt, Arabia, Iraq, Persia, Yemen, and other parts of the Near East, acknowledged az-Zahir as the Caliph but followed Hamzah as its Imam. The young Caliph's regent, Sitt al-Mulk, ordered the army to destroy the movement in 1021. At the same time, Baha' ad-Din as-Samuki assumed leadership of the Druze.

The killing ranged from Antioch to Alexandria, where tens of thousands of Druze were slaughtered by the Fatimid army. The largest massacre was at Antioch, where 5000 Druze religious leaders were killed, followed by that of Aleppo. The massacres are well described in the remaining scriptures written by as-Samuki, which recorded how the Fatimid army brutally put to death infants, women, and men.

The Closing of the Faith

Az-Zahir finally agreed to leave the Druze alone in 1026 - notably, three years after Sitt al-Mulk's death - and as-Samuki sent feelers and missionaries deeper into the Levant.

After two decades of building strong new communities in the Levant, as-Samuki declared that the sect would no longer accept new pledges in 1043, and since that time proselytization has been prohibited.

During the Crusades

It was during the period of Crusader rule in Syria (1099–1291) that the Druze first emerged into the full light of history in the Gharb region of the Chouf Mountains. As powerful warriors serving the Muslim rulers of Damascus against the foreign invaders, the Druze were given the task of keeping watch over the Crusaders in the seaport of Beirut, with the aim of preventing them from making any encroachments inland. Subsequently, the Druze chiefs of the Gharb placed their considerable military experience at the disposal of the Mamluk rulers of Egypt (1250–1516); first, to assist them in putting an end to what remained of Crusader rule in coastal Syria, and later to help them safeguard the Syrian coast against Crusader retaliation by sea.

In the early period of the Crusader era, the Druze feudal power was in the hands of two families, the Tanukhs and the Arslans. From their fortresses in the Gharb district (modern Aley Province) of southern Mount Lebanon, the Tanukhs led their incursions into the Phoenician coast and finally succeeded in holding Beirut and the marine plain against the Franks. Because of their fierce battles with the crusaders, the Druzes earned the respect of the Sunni Muslim Caliphs and thus gained important political powers. After the middle of the twelfth century, the Ma'an family superseded the Tanukhs in Druze leadership. The origin of the family goes back to a Prince Ma'an who made his appearance in the Lebanon in the days of the 'Abbasid Caliph al-Mustarshid (1118 AD-1135 AD). The Ma'ans chose for their abode the Chouf district in the southern part of Western Lebanon, overlooking the maritime plain between Beirut and Sidon, and made their headquarters in Baaqlin, which is still a leading Druze village. They were invested with feudal authority by Sultan Nur-al-Din and furnished respectable contingents to the Muslim ranks in their struggle against the Crusaders.

Persecution during the Mamluk and Ottoman Period

Having cleared Syria of the Franks, the Mamluk Sultans of Egypt turned their attention to the schismatic Muslims of Syria. In 1305, after the issuing of a fatwa by the Hanbali Sunni scholar Ibn Taymiyyah calling for jihad against the Druze, Alawites, Ismaili, and twelver Shiites, al-Malik al-Nasir inflicted a disastrous defeat on the Druze at Keserwan and forced outward compliance on their part to orthodox Sunni Islam. Later, under the Ottoman Turks, they were severely attacked at Ayn-Sawfar in 1585 after the Ottomans claimed that they assaulted their caravans near Tripoli.

Consequently, the sixteenth and seventeenth centuries were to witness a succession of armed Druze rebellions against the Ottomans, countered by repeated Ottoman punitive expeditions against the Chouf, in which the Druze population of the area was severely depleted and many villages destroyed. These military measures, severe as they were, did not succeed in reducing the local Druze to the required degree of subordination. This led the Ottoman government to agree to an arrangement whereby the different nahiyes (districts) of the Chouf would be granted in *iltizam* ("fiscal concession") to one of the region's amirs, or leading chiefs, leaving the maintenance of law and order and the collection of its taxes in the area in the hands of the appointed amir. This arrangement was to provide the cornerstone for the privileged status which ultimately came to be enjoyed by the whole of Mount Lebanon in Ottoman Syria, Druze and Christian areas alike.

Ma'an Dynasty

With the advent of the Ottoman Turks and the conquest of Syria by Sultan Selim I in 1516, the Ma'ans were acknowledged by the new rulers as the feudal lords of southern Lebanon. Druze villages spread and prospered in that region, which under Ma'an leadership so flourished that it acquired the generic term of *Jabal Bayt-Ma'an* (the mountain of the Ma'an family) or *Jabal al-Druze*. The latter title has since been usurped by the Hawran region, which since the middle of the nineteenth century has proven a haven of refuge to Druze emigrants from Lebanon and has become the headquarters of Druze power.

Under Fakhreddin II, the Druze dominion increased until it included almost all Syria, extending from the edge of the Antioch plain in the north to Safad in the south, with a part of the Syrian desert dominated by Fakhreddin's castle at Tadmur (Palmyra), the ancient capital of Zenobia. The ruins of this castle still stand on a steep hill overlooking the town. Fakhr-al-Din became too strong for his Turkish sovereign in Constantinople. He went so far in 1608 as to sign a commercial treaty with Duke Ferdinand I of Tuscany containing secret military clauses. The Sultan then sent a force against him, and he was compelled to flee the land and seek refuge in the courts of Tuscany and Naples in 1614.

In 1618 political changes in the Ottoman sultanate had resulted in the removal of many enemies of Fakhr-al-Din from power, signaling the prince's triumphant return to Lebanon soon afterwards.

In 1632 Ahmad Koujak was named Lord of Damascus. Koujak was a rival of Fakhr-al-Din and a friend of the sultan Murad IV, who ordered Koujak and the sultanat navy to attack Lebanon and depose Fakhr-El-Din.

This time the prince decided to remain in Lebanon and resist the offensive, but the death of his son Ali in Wadi el-Taym was the beginning of his defeat. He later took refuge in Jezzine's grotto, closely followed by Koujak who eventually caught up with him and his family.

Fakhr-al-Din finally traveled to Turkey, appearing before the sultan, defending himself so skillfully that the sultan gave him permission to return to Lebanon.

Later, however, the sultan changed his orders and had Fakhr-al-Din and his family killed on 13 April 1635 in Istanbul, the capital city of the Ottoman Empire, bringing an end to an era in the history of Lebanon, a country which would not regain its current boundaries, which Fakhr-al-Din once ruled, until Lebanon was proclaimed a republic in 1920.

Fakhr-al-Din was the first ruler in modern Lebanon to open the doors of his country to foreign Western influences. Under his auspices the French established a khan (hostel) in Sidon, the Florentines a consulate, and Christian missionaries were admitted into the country. Beirut and Sidon, which Fakhr-al-Din beautified, still bear traces of his benign rule.

Shihab Dynasty

As early as the days of Saladin, and while the Ma'ans were still in complete control over southern Lebanon, the Shihab tribe, originally Hijaz Arabs but later settled in Hawran, advanced from Hawran, in 1172, and settled in Wadi-al-Taym at the foot of Mt. Hermon. They soon made an alliance with the Ma'ans and were acknowledged as the Druze chiefs in *Wadi-al-Taym*. At the end of the seventeenth century (1697) the Shihabs succeeded the Ma'ans in the feudal leadership of Druze southern Lebanon, although they professed Sunni Islam. Secretly, they showed sympathy with Druzism, the religion of the majority of their subjects.

The Shihab leadership continued until the middle of the 19th century and culminated in the illustrious governorship of Amir Bashir Shihab II (1788–1840) who, after Fakhr-al-Din, was the most powerful feudal lord Lebanon produced. Though governor of the Druze Mountain Bashir was a crypto-Christian, and it was he whose aid Napoleon solicited in 1799 during his campaign against Syria.

Having consolidated his conquests in Syria (1831–1838), Ibrahim Pasha, son of the viceroy of Egypt, Muhammad Ali Pasha, made the fatal mistake of trying to disarm the Christians and Druzes of the Lebanon and to draft the latter into his army. This was contrary to the principles of the life of independence which these mountaineers had always lived, and resulted in a general uprising against Egyptian rule. The uprising was encouraged, for political reasons, by the British. The Druzes of Wadi-al-Taym and Sawran, under the leadership of Shibli al-Aryan, distinguished themselves in their stubborn resistance at their inaccessible headquarters, *al-Laja*, lying southeast of Damascus.

Qaysites and the Yemenites

The conquest of Syria by the Muslim Arabs in the middle of the seventh century introduced into the land two political factions later called the Qaysites and the Yemenites. The Qaysite party represented the $ijaz and Bedouin Arabs who were regarded as inferior by the Yemenites who were earlier and more cultured emigrants into Syria from southern Arabia. Druzes and Christians grouped in political rather than religious parties so the party lines in Lebanon obliterated racial and religious lines and the people grouped themselves regardless of their religious affiliations, into one or the other of these two parties. The sanguinary feuds between these two factions depleted, in course of time, the manhood of the Lebanon and ended in the decisive battle of Ain Dara in 1711, which resulted in the utter defeat of the Yemenite party. Many Yemenite Druzes thereupon immigrated to the Hawran region and thus laid the foundation of Druze power there.

Civil War of 1860

The Druzes and their Christian Maronite neighbors, who had thus far lived as religious communities on friendly terms, entered a period of social disturbance in the year 1840, which culminated in the civil war of 1860. For this disturbance the Ottoman Sultan was, in a great measure, responsible. The Sultan, realizing that the only way to bring the semi-independent people of Lebanon under his direct control was to sow the seeds of discord among the people themselves, inaugurated in the mountain a policy long tried and found successful in the Ottoman provinces, the policy of "divide and rule".

Also, after the Shehab dynasty converted to Christianity, the Druze community and feudal leaders came under attack from the regime with the collaboration of the Catholic Church, and the Druze lost most of their political and feudal powers. Also, the Druze formed a strong ally with Britain and allowed Protestant missionaries to enter Mount Lebanon, creating tension between them and the Catholic Maronites, who were supported by the French.

The Maronite-Druze conflict in 1840-60 was an outgrowth of the Maronite Christian independence movement directed against the Druze and Ottoman-Turks. The civil war was not therefore a religious war, except in Damascus where it spread and where the population was anti-Christian. The movement culminated with the 1859-60 massacre and defeat of the Christians by the Druzes, who were aided by the Turks. The civil war of 1860 cost the Christians some ten thousand lives in Damascus, Zahle, Deir al-Qamar, Hasbaya and other towns of Lebanon.

The European powers then determined to intervene and authorized the landing in Beirut of a body of French troops under General Beaufort d'Hautpoul, whose inscription can still be seen on the historic rock at the mouth of Nahr al-Kalb. French intervention on behalf of the Maronites did not help the Maronite national movement since France was restricted in 1860 by Britain which did not want the Ottoman Empire dismembered. But European intervention pressured the Turks to treat the Maronites more justly. Following the recommendations of the powers, the Ottoman Porte granted Lebanon local autonomy, guaranteed by the powers, under a Christian governor. This autonomy was maintained until World War I.

In Lebanon, Syria, and Israel, the Druze have official recognition as a separate religious community with its own religious court system. Their symbol is an array of five colors: green, red, yellow, blue, and white. Each color pertains to a symbol defining its principles: green for *Aql* "the Universal Mind", red for *Nafs* "the Universal Soul", yellow for *Kalima* "the Truth/Word", blue for *Sabq* "the Potentiality/Cause", and white for *Tali* "the Actuality/Effect". These principles are why the number five has special considerations among the religious community; it is usually represented symbolically by a five-pointed star.

In Syria

In Syria, most Druze live in the Jebel al-Druze, a rugged and mountainous region in the southwest of the country, which is more than 90 percent Druze inhabited; some 120 villages are exclusively so.

The Druze always played a far more important role in Syrian politics than its comparatively small population would suggest. With a community of little more than 100,000 in 1949, or roughly three percent of the Syrian population, the Druze of Syria's southeastern mountains constituted a potent force in Syrian politics and played a leading role in the nationalist struggle against the French. Under the military leadership of Sultan Pasha al-Atrash, the Druze provided much of the military force behind the Syrian Revolution of 1925-1927. In 1945, Amir Hasan al-Atrash, the paramount political leader of the Jebel al-Druze, led the Druze military units in a successful revolt against the French, making the Jebel al-Druze the first and only region in Syria to liberate itself from French rule without British assistance. No Syrians played a more heroic role in the struggle against colonialism or shed more blood for independence than the Druze. At independence the Druze, made confident by their successes, expected that Damascus would reward them for their many sacrifices on the battlefield. They demanded to keep their autonomous administration and many political privileges accorded them by the French and sought generous economic assistance from the newly independent government.

Well-led by the Atrash household and jealous of their reputation as Arab nationalists and proud warriors, the Druze leaders refused to be beaten into submission by Damascus or cowed by threats. When a local paper in 1945 reported that President Shukri al-Quwatli (1943–1949) had called the Druzes a "dangerous minority", Sultan Pasha al-Atrash flew into a rage and demanded a public retraction. If it were not forthcoming, he announced, the Druzes would indeed become "dangerous" and a force of 4,000 Druze warriors would "occupy the city of Damascus." Quwwatli could not dismiss Sultan Pasha's threat. The military balance of power in Syria was tilted in favour of the Druzes, at least until the military build up during the 1948 War in Palestine. One advisor to the Syrian Defense Department warned in 1946 that the Syrian army was "useless", and that the Druzes could "take Damascus and capture the present leaders in a breeze."

During the four years of Adib Shishakli's rule in Syria (December 1949 to February 1954) (in August 25, 1952: Adib al-Shishakli created the Arab Liberation Movement (ALM), a progressive party with pan-Arabist and socialist views .), the Druze community was subjected to a heavy attack by the Syrian regime. Shishakli believed that among his many opponents in Syria, the Druzes were the most potentially dangerous, and he was determined to crush them. He frequently proclaimed: "My enemies are like a serpent: the head is the Jebel al-Druze, the stomach Hims, and the tail Aleppo. If I crush the head the serpent will die." Shishakli dispatched 10,000 regular troops to occupy the Jebel al-Druze. Several towns were bombarded with heavy weapons, killing scores of civilians and destroying many houses. According to Druze accounts, Shishakli encouraged neighboring bedouin tribes to plunder the defenseless population and allowed his own troops to run amok.

Shishakli launched a brutal campaign to defame the Druzes for their religion and politics. He accused the entire community of treason, at times claiming they were agents of the British and Hashimites, at others that they were fighting for Israel against the Arabs. He even produced a cache of Israeli weapons allegedly discovered in the Jabal. Even more painful for the Druze community was his publication of "falsified Druze religious texts" and false testimonials ascribed to leading Druze sheikhs designed to stir up sectarian hatred. This propaganda was also broadcast in the Arab world, mainly Egypt. Shishakli was assassinated in Brazil on September 27, 1964 by a Druze seeking revenge for Shishakli's bombardment of the Jebel al-Druze.

He forcibly integrated minorities into the national Syrian social structure, his "Syrianization" of Alawite and **Druze** territories had to be accomplished in part using violence, he declared: "My enemies are like serpent. The head is the Jabal Druze, If I crush the head the serpent will die" (Seale 1963:132). To this end, al-Shishakli encouraged the stigmatization of minorities.He saw minority demands as tantamount to treason. His increasingly **chauvinistic notions of Arab nationalism** were predicated on the denial that "minorities" existed in Syria.

After the Shishakli's military campaign, the Druze community lost a lot of its political influence, but many Druze military officers played an important role when it comes to the Baathist regime currently ruling Syria.

In Syria, Today

The main Druze leader of Lebanon spoke out against what he termed the oppression , the Druze leader spoke to the BBC. about "these kinds of regimes" (Syria), terrorist regimes . The Syrian regime does not permit its Druze citizens to visit their relatives and friends.

In Lebanon

The Druze community played an important role in the formation of the modern state of Lebanon, and even though they are a minority they played an important role in the Lebanese political scene. Before and during the Lebanese Civil War (1975–1990), the Druze were in favour of Pan-Arabism and Palestinian resistance represented by the PLO. Most of the community supported the Progressive Socialist Party formed by the Lebanese leader Kamal Jumblatt and they fought alongside other leftist and Palestinian parties against the Lebanese Front that was mainly constituted of Christians. After the assassination of Kamal Jumblatt on March 16, 1977, his son Walid Jumblatt took the leadership of the party and played an important role in preserving his father's legacy and sustained the existence of the Druze community during the sectarian bloodshed that lasted until 1990.

In August 2001, Patriarch Nasrallah Boutros Sfeir toured the predominantly Druze Chouf region of Mount Lebanon and visited Mukhtara, the ancestral stronghold of Druze leader Walid Jumblatt. The tumultuous reception that Sfeir received not only signified a historic reconciliation between Maronites and Druze, who fought a bloody war in 1983-1984, but underscored the fact that the banner of Lebanese sovereignty had broad multi-confessional appeal and was a cornerstone for the Cedar Revolution. The second largest political party supported by Druze is the Lebanese Democratic Party led by Prince Talal Arslan the son of one of the independence leaders Prince Magid Arslan. Also political parties such as the Syrian Social Nationalist Party, Lebanese Unification Movement and Lebanese Communist Party have a considerable amount of supporters in the community.

In Israel

In Israel, the majority of the approximately 120,000 Druze consider themselves a distinct religious group. Since 1957, the Israeli government has also designated the Druze a distinct ethnic community, at the request of the community's leaders.

A minority of the Druze in the Golan region, controlled by Israel since the Six-Day War of 1967 and officially annexed by Israel in 1981, but not internationally recognised, have a separate legal status from those in the Galilee region, and are considered permanent residents under the Golan Heights Law of 1981. Few of them have accepted full Israeli citizenship, and the majority are citizens of Syria. Druze in the Golan are not drafted into the Israeli army (although a minority serve voluntarily) and many travel to Syria regularly to visit family or receive university degrees in Damascus. A year after Israel annexed the Golan, on April 14, 1982, the Druze communities around Mt. Hermon launched a six-month non-violent general strike in protest of Israel's annexation of the Golan.

The rest of the Druze population are citizens of Israel. Druze citizens are prominent in the Israel Defense Forces and in politics. A considerable number of Israeli Druze soldiers have fallen in Israel's wars since the 1948 Arab-Israeli War. The bond between Jewish and Druze soldiers is commonly known by the term "a covenant of blood", although in recent years the phrase has been criticised as the Israeli government has been accused for failing to open up employment opportunities to Druze youth outside of the army.

The Druze in Israel, their culture is Arab and their language Arabic but they opted against mainstream Arab nationalism in 1948 and have since served (first as volunteers, later within the draft system) in the Israel Defense Forces and the Border Police. They are located in the north of the country, mainly on hilltops; historically as a defense against attack and persecution. , which they were subject to historically from the Arab-Muslims . The Druze, who mostly do not identify with the cause of Arab nationalism. In the years preceding the founding of the State of Israel, Arab nationalists persecuted the **Druze**.

In 1996, Azzam, a Druze Israeli businessman, was accused by Egypt of spying for Israel and was imprisoned for eight years, an accusation denied by the Israeli government.

Until his death in 1993, the Druze community in Israel was led by Shaykh Amin Tarif, a charismatic figure regarded by many within the Druze community internationally as the preeminent religious leader of his time.

In January 2004, the spiritual leader of the Druze community in Israel, Shaykh Mowafak Tarif, signed a declaration calling on all non-Jews in Israel to observe the Seven Noahide Laws as laid down in the Bible and expounded upon in Jewish tradition. The mayor of the Galilean city of Shefa-'Amr also signed the document. The declaration includes the commitment to make a "...better humane world based on the Seven Noahide Commandments and the values they represent commanded by the Creator to all mankind through Moses on Mount Sinai."

Support for the spread of the Seven Noahide Commandments by the Druze leaders reflects the biblical narrative itself. The Druze community reveres the non-Jewish father-in-law of Moses, Jethro, whom some Muslims identify with Shuaayb. According to the biblical narrative, Jethro joined and assisted the Jewish people in the desert during the Exodus, accepted monotheism, but ultimately rejoined his own people. The tomb of Jethro near Tiberias is the most important religious site for the Druze community. It has been claimed that the Druze are actually descendants of Jethro.

Five Druze lawmakers currently have been elected to serve in the 18th Knesset, a disproportionately large number considering their population.

Beliefs of the Druze

The Druze are considered to be a social group as well as a religion, but not a distinct ethnic group. Also complicating their identity is the custom of Taqiya—concealing or disguising their beliefs when necessary—that they adopted from Shia Islam and the esoteric nature of the faith, in which many teachings are kept secretive. Druze in different states can have radically different lifestyles. Some claim to be Muslim, some do not. The Druze faith is said to abide by Islamic principles, but they tend to be separatist in their treatment of Druze-hood, and their religion differs from mainstream Islam on a number of fundamental points.

Druze does not allow conversion to the religion. Marriage between Druze and non-Druze is strongly discouraged for religious, political and historical reasons.

God in the Druze Faith

The Druze conception of the deity is declared by them to be one of strict and uncompromising unity. The main Druze doctrine states that God is both transcendent and immanent, in which He is above all attributes but at the same time He is present.

In their desire to maintain a rigid confession of unity, they stripped from God all or most divine attributes *(tanzih)* which-in the eyes of mainstream Islam-may have lead to polytheism *(shirk)*. In God, there are no attributes distinct from his essence. He is wise, mighty, and just, not by wisdom, might, and justice, but by his own essence. God is "the Whole of Existence", rather than "above existence" or on His throne, which would make Him "limited." There is neither "how", "when", nor "where" about him; he is incomprehensible.

In this dogma, they are similar to the semi-philosophical, semi-religious body which flourished under Al-Ma'mun and was known by the name of Mu'tazila and the equally interesting fraternal order of the Brethren of Purity *(Ikhwan al-Safa)*.

But unlike the *Mu'tazilla*, and similar to some branches of Sufism, the Druze believe in the concept of *Tajalli* (meaning "theophany"). *Tajalli*, which is more often misunderstood by scholars and writers and is usually confused with the concept of incarnation,

> ...is the core spiritual beliefs in the Druze and some other intellectual and spiritual traditions.... In a mystical sense, it refers to the light of God experienced by certain

> mystics who have reached a high level of purity in their spiritual journey. Thus, God is perceived as the Lahut [the divine] who manifests His Light in the Station (Maqaam) of the Nasut [material realm] without the Nasut becoming Lahut. This is like one's image in the mirror: one is in the mirror but does not become the mirror. The Druze manuscripts are emphatic and warn against the belief that the Nasut is God.... Neglecting this warning, individual seekers, scholars, and other spectators have considered al-Hakim and other figures divine.
>
> ...In the Druze scriptural view, Tajalli 'takes a central stage.' One author comments that Tajalli occurs when the seeker's humanity is annihilated so that divine attributes and light are experienced by the person."

The concept of God incarnating either as or in a human seems "to contradict with what the Druze scriptural view has to teach about the Oneness of God, while tajalli is at the center of the Druze and some other, often mystical, traditions."

Scriptures

Esotericism

The Druze believe that many teachings given by Prophets, religious leaders, and Holy Books, had esoteric meanings preserved for those of intellect, in which some teachings are mere symbols and allegoristic in nature and for that they divide the understanding of holy books and teachings into three layers. These layers according to the Druze are:

- The obvious or exoteric *(Zahir)*, accessible to anyone who can read or hear;
- The hidden or esoteric *(Batin)*, accessible to those who are willing to search and learn through the concept of *(exegesis)*; and

- The hidden of the hidden, a concept known as Anagoge, inaccessible to all but a few really enlightened individuals who truly understand the nature of the universe.

Unlike some Islamic esoteric movements known as the *batinids* at that time, the Druzes don't believe that the esoteric meaning abrogates or necessarily abolishes the exoteric one. For example, Hamza bin Ali, refutes such claims by stating that, if the esoteric interpretation of Taharah (purity), is the purity of the heart and soul, it doesn't mean that a person can discard his physical purity, as Salah (prayer) is useless if a person is untruthful in his speech and for that the esoteric and exoteric meanings complement each other.

Precepts of the Druze Faith

The Druze follow seven precepts that are considered the core of the faith, and are perceived by them as the essence of the pillars of Islam. The Seven Druze precepts are:

1. Veracity in speech and the truthfulness of the tongue.
2. Protection and mutual aid to the brethren in faith.
3. Renunciation of all forms of former worship *(specifically, invalid creeds)* and false belief.
4. Repudiation of the devil *(Iblis)*, and all forces of evil (translated from Arabic *Toghyan* meaning *"despotism"*).
5. Confession of God's unity.
6. Acquiescence in God's acts no matter what they be.
7. Absolute submission and resignation to God's divine will in both secret and public.

Uqqal and Juhhal

The Druze are divided into two groups. The largely secular majority, called *al-Juhhal* ("the Ignorant") are not granted access to the Druze holy literature or allowed to attend the initiated *Uqqal*'s religious meetings. They are around 80% of the Druze population and are not obliged to follow the ascetic traditions of the *Uqqal*.

The initiated religious group, which includes both men and women (about 20% of the population), is called *al-Uqqal*, ("the Knowledgeable Initiates"). They have a special mode of dress designed to comply with Quranic traditions. Women can opt to wear *al-mandil*, a loose white veil, especially in the presence of other people. They wear *al-mandil* on their heads to cover their hair and wrap it around their mouths and sometimes over their noses as well. They wear black shirts and long skirts covering their legs to their ankles. Male *uqqal* grow mustaches, and wear dark Levantine/Turkish traditional dresses, called the *shirwal*, with white turbans that vary according to the *Uqqal*'s hierarchy.

Al-uqqal have equal rights to *al-Juhhal*, but establish a hierarchy of respect based on religious service.The most influential 5% of *Al-uqqal* become *Ajawid*, recognised religious leaders, and from this group the spiritual leaders of the Druze are assigned. While the *Shaykh al-Aql*, which is an official position in Syria, Lebanon, and Israel, is elected by the local community and serves as the head of the Druze religious council, judges from the Druze religious courts are usually elected for this position. Unlike the spiritual leaders, the *Shaykh al-Aql's* authority is local to the country he is elected in, though in some instances spiritual leaders are elected to this position.

The Druze believe in the unity of God, and are often known as the "People of Monotheism" or simply "Monotheists". Their theology has a Neo-Platonic view about how God interacts with the world through emanations and is similar to some gnostic and other esoteric sects. Druze philosophy also shows Sufi influences.

Druze principles focus on honesty, loyalty, filial piety, altruism, patriotic sacrifice, and monotheism. They reject tobacco smoking, alcohol, consumption of pork and marriage to non-Druze. Also, in contrast to most Islamic sects, the Druze reject polygamy, believe in reincarnation, and are not obliged to observe most of the religious rituals. The Druze believe that rituals are symbolic and have an individualistic effect on the person, for which reason Druze are free to perform them or not. The community does celebrate Eid al-Adha, however, considered their most significant holiday.

Origins of the Druze People

Ethnic Origins

The Druze faith extended to many areas in the Middle East , but most of the surviving modern Druze can trace their origin to the *Wadi al-Taym* in South Lebanon, which is named after an Arab tribe *Taym-Allah (formerly Taym-Allat)* which, according to the greatest Persian historian, al-Tabari, first came from Arabia into the valley of the Euphrates where they were Christianized prior to their migration into the Lebanon. Many of the Druze feudal families whose genealogies have been preserved by the two modern Syrian chroniclers Haydar al-Shihabi and al-Shidyaq seem also to point in the direction of this origin. Arabian tribes emigrated via the Persian Gulf and stopped in Iraq on the route that was later to lead them to Syria. The first feudal Druze family, the Tanukh family, which made for itself a name in fighting the Crusaders, was, according to Haydar al-Shihabi, an Arab tribe from Mesopotamia where it occupied the position of a ruling family and was apparently Christianized.

The Tanukhs must have left Arabia as early as the second or third century A.D. The Ma'an tribe, which superseded the Tanukhs and produced the greatest Druze hero in history, Fakhr-al-Din, had the same traditional origin.

The *Talhuq* family and *'Abd-al-Malik,* who supplied the later Druze leadership, have the same record as the Tanukhs. The *Imad family* is named for *al-Imadiyyah,* near Mosul in northern Iraq, and, like the Jumblatts, is thought to be of Kurdish origin. The Arsalan family claims descent from the Hirah Arab kings, but the name *Arsalan* (Persian and Turkish for lion) suggests Persian influence if not origin.

The most accepted theory is that the Druzes are a mixture of stocks in which the Arab largely predominates while being grafted onto an original mountain population of Aramaic blood.

Nevertheless, many scholars formed their own hypotheses: for example, Lamartine (1835) discovered in the modern Druzes the remnants of the Samaritans; Earl of Carnarvon (1860), those of the Cuthites whom Esarhaddon transplanted into Palestine; Professor Felix von Luschan (1911), according to his conclusions from anthropometric measurements, makes the Druze, Maronites, and Alawites of Syria, together with the Armenians, Bektashis, 'Ali-Ilahis, and Yezidis of Asia Minor and Persia, the modern representatives of the ancient Hittites.

During the 18th century, there were two branches of Druze living in Lebanon: the Yemeni Druze, headed by the Hamdan and Al-Atrash families; and the Kaysi Druze, headed by the Jumblat and Arsalan families.

The Hamdan family was banished from Mount Lebanon following the battle of Ain Dara in 1711. This battle was fought between two Druze factions: the Yemeni and the Kaysi. Following their dramatic defeat, the Yemeni faction migrated to Syria in the Jebel-Druze region and its capital, Soueida. However, it has been argued that these two factions were of political nature rather than ethnic, and had both Christian and Druze supporters.

Genetics

In a 2005 study of ASPM gene variants, Mekel-Bobrov et al. found that the Israeli Druze people of the Carmel region have among the highest rate of the newly-evolved ASPM haplogroup D, at 52.2% occurrence of the approximately 6,000-year-old allele. While it is not yet known exactly what selective advantage is provided by this gene variant, the haplogroup D allele is thought to be positively selected in populations and to confer some substantial advantage that has caused its frequency to rapidly increase.

According to DNA testing, Druze are remarkable for the high frequency (35%) of males who carry the Y-chromosomal haplogroup L, which is otherwise uncommon in the Mideast (Shen et al. 2004). This haplogroup originates from prehistoric South Asia.

Cruciani in 2007 found E1b1b1a2 (E-V13) [one from Sub Clades of E1b1b1a1 (E-V12)] in high levels (>10% of the male population) in Turkish Cypriot and Druze Arab lineages.

Also, a new study concluded that the Druze harbor a remarkable diversity of mitochondrial DNA lineages that appear to have separated from each other thousands of years ago. But instead of dispersing throughout the world after their separation, the full range of lineages can still be found within the Druze population.

The researchers noted that the Druze villages contained a striking range of high frequency and high diversity of the X haplogroup, suggesting that this population provides a glimpse into the past genetic landscape of the Near East at a time when the X haplogroup was more prevalent.

These findings are consistent with the Druze oral tradition, that claims that the adherents of the faith came from diverse ancestral lineages stretching back tens of thousands of years.

Index